Designing an All-Inclusive Democracy

DAX. — La Statue de Borda

This first statue of M. chevalier Jean-Charles de Borda was inaugurated in Dax by the President of the Republic at the end of the 19th century. It was replaced by a stone monument in 1950, and supplemented by a bust in the Naval School at Brest in 2002.

The above photograph was supplied by 'La Société de Borda, Dax, France', with whose kind permission it is now re-printed.

Peter Emerson (Editor)

Designing an All-Inclusive Democracy

Consensual Voting Procedures
For Use in Parliaments,
Councils and Committees

The Modified Borda Count
The Quota Borda System and
The Matrix Vote

With 106 Tables

 Springer

Peter Emerson
The de Borda Institute
36 Ballysillan Road
Belfast BT14 7QQ
Northern Ireland
pemerson@deborda.org

Library of Congress Control Number: 2007924243

ISBN 978-3-540-33163-6 Springer Berlin Heidelberg New York

This work is subject to copyright. All rights are reserved, whether the whole or part of the material is concerned, specifically the rights of translation, reprinting, reuse of illustrations, recitation, broadcasting, reproduction on microfilm or in any other way, and storage in data banks. Duplication of this publication or parts thereof is permitted only under the provisions of the German Copyright Law of September 9, 1965, in its current version, and permission for use must always be obtained from Springer. Violations are liable to prosecution under the German Copyright Law.

Springer is a part of Springer Science+Business Media

springer.com

© Springer-Verlag Berlin Heidelberg 2007

The use of general descriptive names, registered names, trademarks, etc. in this publication does not imply, even in the absence of a specific statement, that such names are exempt from the relevant protective laws and regulations and therefore free for general use.

Production: LE-TeX Jelonek, Schmidt & Vöckler GbR, Leipzig
Cover-design: WMX Design GmbH, Heidelberg

SPIN 11730934   43/3100YL - 5 4 3 2 1 0   Printed on acid-free paper

To the victims of majoritarianism, everywhere,
and especially to those who died in such conflicts in
Northern Ireland, 1969-94,
Rwanda, 1994,
and
the former Yugoslavia, 1991-99.

Foreword

Peter Emerson is vividly aware of two principles which most people grasp hazily at best, and often not at all. The first is that the basis of democracy is *not* that the wishes of the majority should always prevail: it is, rather, that that option should be chosen which best accords with everyone's wishes.

From where does the idea of the majority gain its power? From one simple type of case, and from that only: one in which there is a choice between just two options, and we know only which option each, among those who are to decide, prefers to the other. In this case we do not know, and perhaps have no means of finding out, the *strength* of these preferences. The only fair thing that can be done is, in such a case, to count up, for each option, how many prefer it: that option which the majority prefers must be chosen.

It is *only* in a case of this kind that a majority ought to be considered decisive. Suppose that we *do* know the strength of preferences. And suppose that, out of 35 people, 19 very slightly prefer option *A* to option *B*, while the remaining 16 very strongly prefer *B* to *A*. Then *B* is probably the fairer choice, even though a majority prefers *A*.

The other principle Peter Emerson strongly maintains against prevailing prejudices is that, when a choice is to be made, it is best made between several different options than between just two. We have a tradition of holding votes between just two options: a motion is presented, and those in favour vote Aye, and those opposed vote No.

Under a system of the kind Emerson wishes to promote, there would be several different options. Often they may be able to be ordered in a sequence. At each end of this would be the extreme options, with various compromises in between. It will often, though not always, happen that one of the courses of action intermediate between the extremes will command the most general support, although neither it nor any other of the several options would gain a majority of 1st preferences. We not only need a system under which all reasonable options are presented simultaneously for decision, but also one that will enable that option which best satisfies the divergent preferences to be selected.

We recently had a ludicrous example of the effect of Yes/No voting. The House of Commons debated how best to reform the selection of members of the House of Lords.[1] There were several proposals how to do this. Obviously, Peter Emerson's principle should have been followed, so that all these proposals were presented *together*, and the most generally popular chosen. It makes one wonder whether MPs are rational

---

1 Emerson has published a detailed analysis of what Lord Meghnad Desai called the "daftest" system of umpteen majority votes in *Representation*, Vol 41, No 4, 2005, p 276. Ed.

beings that each proposal was put up one by one, the MPs voting for or against each one. Each member then voted for a proposal only if it was the one he most favoured, and against if not; naturally each proposal was rejected. There could not have been a more ridiculous example of the folly of the traditional principle that each vote should be between just two options.

If people have a number of options between which to choose, they can hardly be asked to vote otherwise than by writing down against the options as listed on their ballot papers numbers to indicate their order of preference. How the winning option is to be decided from the ballot papers so filled in is open to a wide range of possibilities, the most interesting of them illustrated and discussed by Emerson in this book.

One famous criterion for deciding the winner was proposed by the Marquis de Condorcet in 1785. From the ballot papers we can work out what would happen if the voters had to choose between any two of the options, for we can tell how many would have preferred the one and how many the other. If there is one option, say C, that would have had a majority in its favour in every contest in which it was put up against one of the other options, then C ought, according to Condorcet, to be chosen as the winner. (In fact, in the literature on voting, such an option is called the 'Condorcet winner'.)

This is a much fairer method than that under which the winner is the option with the greatest number of 1st preferences. The Condorcet winner may even be the option with the smallest number of 1st preferences. Suppose there are two extreme proposals A and H, and a compromise proposal D. Because support for A and H is strong, fewer voters rank D as their 1st preference than so rank either A or H. Yet most supporters of A will prefer D to H, and most supporters of H will prefer D to A. This may have the effect that a majority of voters prefers D to A, while a different majority prefers D to H; D thus satisfies Condorcet's condition, and, as giving more general satisfaction than either A or H ought, as a good compromise, to be the winner.

Condorcet's criterion may be fairer than any other based on majorities or pluralities, but it still relies on *majorities*: the winner is to be that option, if there is one (there need not be), which is preferred by some majority to each of the other options. If any option has an absolute majority over all the other options, it will of course satisfy Condorcet's criterion. For this reason it does not accord with Peter Emerson's first principle.

Now his two principles are interlinked in an interesting way. Let us go back to our example in which, out of 35 people, 19 very slightly preferred option A to option B, while the remaining 16 very strongly preferred B to A. Suppose, now, that A and B were not the only options between which they had to choose, but that there were five others, C, D, E, F and G. The voters are asked to rank all the options in order of preference. The 19-strong majority all rank A 1st and B 2nd. The 16-strong minority all rank B 1st and A 7th-cum-last. These preference orderings give positive evidence of the strengths of preferences. Clearly the members of the majority have only comparatively slight preferences for A over B, while the members of the minority all have a very strong preference for *B* over *A*. Here the number of options intervening on a voter's preference scale between one option and another serves as an indicator of his preference for one over the other. It may not be a perfect indicator; but it obviously is pretty good evidence.

Readers will find more than one voting system described in this book that relies on this idea. It leads to the fairest outcomes. This brings us to a third principle that animates Peter Emerson's work; it is perhaps the most important of the three. People tend to think of voting systems as an unimportant and boringly technical subject. It is indeed a technical subject. If we are to compare different systems, we must analyse their effects. But it is an extremely important subject: the voting system we adopt shows what our democratic ideals are and realises them in practice. Our voting system embodies our conception of what we think democracy consists of; it shows what principles we believe it should embody. This is the third principle underlying Emerson's work. If we hope that our democracy should fulfil our ideals for it, it is worth the slog of studying the technical aspects of voting theory to make sure that those ideals are realised.

I believe in all three of the principles I have expounded as guiding Peter Emerson's work, and applaud his whole-heartedness in advocating them. I hope many people will read this book. I feel sure that most who do will be persuaded by it. I hope they will be fired to press for the adoption of its proposals.

Professor Sir Michael Dummett
New College, Oxford
3.10.2006

Acknowledgements

It is quite hard to be a dissident. It was, of course, much more difficult for the Russian in Soviet times. It was extremely tough, too, for those who faced religious persecution in times not all in the past.

That is not to say that in today's plural, democratic West, some of those who question certain ideas are not estranged. Admittedly, many of our practices are questionable and questioned. Others, however, are not. And one of the latter relates to our ubiquitous habit of using the simple majority vote, a crude instrument to put it mildly. It is divisive. It is hopelessly inaccurate. And it can be a cause of war.

Therefore I dissent. I both criticise current practice and advocate an alternative. Via open meetings and public demonstrations, my colleagues and I have often shown that a better methodology can help those who, in a majoritarian milieu, tend to argue with words or worse. Northern Ireland, after all, is one of the world's best social choice laboratories. And all of our consensus experiments have been successful. One, indeed, was prescient, when in Oct. 1991, we suggested an alternative to the referendum scheduled for Bosnia.

For some reason, however, there are those in the media and academia who do not wish even to discuss social choice theory. To a certain extent, therefore, the life of one who dissents against majoritarianism can be frustrating and even lonely.

No-one, however, can work in isolation. To those who have kept me going for the last 20 years or so, I am most grateful. And to those who helped with this book, again, my sincere thanks. It started eight years ago, at a seminar on the matrix vote held in Queen's University, Belfast, to which both Elizabeth Meehan and Phil Kearney lent their support. In fact, it goes back even earlier, to some of the first consensus gatherings, like the 1993 power-sharing conference, which Christine Bell chaired.

The first draft of this book, written in 1998, is now in my archive. A second version rests alongside. And even this third version has had a long gestation period, not only because of helpful criticism from the other contributors - Hannu Nurmi and Maurice Salles - but also from those who are not appearing in this volume, such as Arend Lijphart. My thanks are due to them all, while the responsibility for any remaining errors, numerical or literary, is mine alone.

My thanks are also due to those who have taken a more back-stage role: to all the committee members and patrons of the de Borda Institute, who continue to offer their help in numerous ways; to my proof-reader, Alan Quilley, whose red pen, it seems, never runs out of ink; to Noel Murphy, who gave me so much assistance with the type-setting; to Paddy McEvoy, who helped with the title; and crucially, to Barbara Fess and her team in Springer-Verlag, for their kind advice and inexhaustible patience.

Peter Emerson
Belfast, 19.11.2006.

Abbreviations

AGM	annual general meeting
AMS	additional member system
AOB	any other business
AV	alternative vote
BC	Borda count
CDU	Christian Democratic Union (Germany)
CMM	coordinated management of meaning
CSU	Christian Social Union (Germany)
DRC	Democratic Republic of the Congo
DUP	Democratic Unionist Party (NI)
EU	European Union
FDP	Free Democratic Party (Germany)
FPP	first-past-the-post
G8	G7, the 'Group of 7', plus Russia; the 7 consists of Canada, France, Germany, Italy, Japan, UK and US.
GM	Genetically modified
GP	Green Party
IDEA	Institute for Democracy and Electoral Assistance
IMF	International Monetary Fund
IRV	instant runoff voting
KPD	Communist Party of Germany
MBC	modified Borda count
MLA	Member of the Legislative Assembly (NI)
MMP	multi-member proportional
MP	Member of Parliament
NGO	non-governmental organisation
NI	Northern Ireland
NIHRC	NI human rights commission
NURC	National Unity and Reconciliation Commission (Rwanda)
ODIHR	Office for Democratic Institutions and Human Rights
OSCE	Organisation for Security and Co-operation in Europe
OUP	Oxford University Press
PM	Prime Minister
PR	proportional representation
pref	preference
QBS	quota Borda system
SDLP	Social Democratic and Labour Party (NI)
SF	*Sinn Féin* (NI)
SPD	Social Democratic Party (Germany)
STV	single transferable vote
TD	*Teachtaí Dála* (Member of *Dáil Éireann,* the Irish parliament)
UK	United Kingdom
UN	United Nations
USA	United States of America
UUP	Ulster Unionist Party (NI)
WWII	World War II

Contents

	Foreword by Professor Sir Michael Dummett	vii
	Acknowledgements	xi
	Abbreviations	xiii
	Introduction	1

PART I DESIGNING AN ALL-INCLUSIVE DEMOCRACY — 13

Chapter 1   Collective Decision-making
            THE MODIFIED BORDA COUNT (MBC) — 15

Chapter 2   A Pluralist Parliament for a Plural Society
            THE QUOTA BORDA SYSTEM (QBS) — 39

Chapter 3   Electing a Power-sharing Executive
            THE MATRIX VOTE — 61

Chapter 4   The Art or Science of Manipulation — 86

PART II A CRITIQUE — 97

Chapter 5   The Theory of Voting and the Borda Systems — 99
            Maurice Salles

Chapter 6   Assessing Borda's Rule and Its Modifications — 109
            Hannu Nurmi

Chapter 7   Human Rights and Voting Procedures in Plural Societies — 120
            Christine Bell

Chapter 8   Inclusive Decision-making in Mediation and Politics — 124
            Phil Kearney and Aileen Tierney

PART III - CONCLUSION — 133

Chapter 9   The *Realpolitik* of Consensus Voting — 135
            Peter Emerson with Assistance from Elizabeth Meehan

PART IV – APPENDICES — 147

Appendix I	A Comparison of Different Voting Procedures	149
Appendix II	The Average Preference Rating and the Consensus Coefficient	160
Appendix III	Partial Voting	162
Appendix IV	Further Analysis of the Matrix Vote	164
	Glossary	165
	List of Tables	173
	Biographical Notes	175
	Bibliography	177
	Index	181

Introduction

MAJORITARIANISM – A CAUSE OF WAR

Many national constitutions give politicians an unnecessarily large amount of power, albeit within the parameters of what is called democracy. Little wonder, then, that the faith which society has in these political structures is frail, and many people bemoan our 'ya-boo' politics, its adversarial nature, and the seemingly endless squabbles of personality rather than principle. Worst of all is the fact that such arguments and the subsequent majority votes are often a cause of violence if not, indeed, of war!

This book describes a non-adversarial democratic structure, one which should be applicable to *every* level of collective decision-making. What follows, therefore, may be used in national governments, community groups, international assemblies, trade unions, the local sports club, and even in the home. Democracy, after all, is for everybody. In this book, however, we will concentrate on examples as if talking about politics at the national level, for if a win-win structure can work here, it can probably work anywhere.

For far too long, the world has seen societies torn apart, as numerous complex questions of sovereignty and ideology are reduced to dichotomies. "Are you British or Irish?" they ask, "Communist or Capitalist?" "Democrat or Republican?" "Hutu or Tutsi?" In conflict resolution work, however, mediators rely on *open* questions. They first ask the various parties to the dispute what options are possible. Then, with lots of amendments and adjustments in a process called shuttle diplomacy, they determine the various parties' preferences. And finally, they identify that option which has the best average preference.

Now democracy, as we said a moment ago, is for *all* the people. It is not just for a (white, male, Protestant, Serb, Armenian, Hutu, Greek Cypriot, Moslem, Jewish, Shia) majority. It is literally for everybody. The democratic process, therefore, should allow for an accommodation, a meeting of minds, a confluence of ideas; indeed, at its best, it should be a means by which can be identified the collective wisdom. This can never be achieved by a *closed* vote. It can be facilitated, however, in open discussion, with, if required, an open, i.e., multi-option, vote.

Democratic Principles

The first task, therefore, is to decide upon what principles a democracy should be based, not least because current practice is full of anomalies.

* In debate, the democratic process often involves some give-and-take. On other occasions there is none, namely, when people take a majority vote!

* "Politics," they say, "is the art of compromise." In majority voting, however, as often as not, it is *A* or *B*, yes-or-no, and there is no compromise at all!

* "The consent of the people," they add. But a majority vote cannot measure consent; in fact, it measures the very opposite, the degree of *dissent* - so many 'for' and so many 'against'.

* "Democracy by the people and for the people," they continue. So parliaments represent *all* the people. Governments, however, represent only the bigger 'half' of them. (There are, of course, the exceptions: power-sharing in some post-conflict zones, and the all-party coalition in Switzerland.)

* In offices and factories, computers are everywhere. In some parliaments, alas, MPs still use the most primitive measure of collective opinion ever invented - the 2,500 year-old majority vote - either by hand or occasionally, in an odd mixture of a most ancient vinegar in a very new bottle, electronically.

* "The will of the people," they also cry. But in many elected chambers, they use the party whip, so the vote cannot identify the will of parliament, nor even the will of a majority in parliament; rather, it identifies the will of only the cabinet! Furthermore, in lands where the premier alone chooses the government, the will of the cabinet may be little more than the will of that one prime minister.

* No matter how complex the problem, decision-making is invariably reduced to a binary process involving one (or, if need be, several) for-or-against majority vote(s). So nearly every political question is reduced to a choice (or a series of choices) of only two options, *A* or *B*, *C* or *D*. The question is always *closed*. But there are, in fact, very few questions which can be termed 'black or white'; there is always the grey. If, then, the question has been asked as a *closed* question, it has probably been asked incorrectly![1]

* Thus the majority vote is often a means of manipulation - after all, the answer is usually the question.

* This all suggests that maybe majority voting is not very democratic at all. *Inter alia*, the democratic process should be the means by which every individual votes for that which he/she thinks is best for society as a whole. Unfortunately, in many instances, people vote for that which they feel will most benefit themselves.

* The situation is made even worse, of course, if and when - as in our final anomaly - the system allows the leader alone to decide when she or he - Thatcher, Mugabe, Blair, etc. - resigns. In contrast to some political parties, most democratic organisations have AGMs and annual elections.

---

1 There is perhaps one closed question - "On which side of the road shall we drive?" - yet the only country to hold a referendum on this topic - Sweden in 1955 - actually used a 3-option question: 'left', 'right' and 'blank'. To illustrate the point that not all debates should be reduced to dichotomies, compare if you will the following alternatives: "Capital punishment, yes or no?" or "How shall we deal with the convicted murderer?" Secondly, would it not be better to replace the question "NI - in a United Kingdom or a united Ireland?" by a short list of about 4 or 5 options established in a due democratic manner, as in a public enquiry?

Initially, then, we must define the term 'democracy'. A minimal interpretation might describe it as a means by which power is transferred without bloodshed. In this regard, if that is what it achieves, any voting procedure is to be welcomed. That is not to say, however, that the simple majority vote in parliament and the first-past-the-post, FPP, electoral system should be regarded as the apogee of human co-operation. Let us seek a more sophisticated *modus operandi*.

Democracy should be a means by which is identified "the will of the people". In a society of millions, one way this can be done is by electing a representative parliament, and then by identifying "the will of that parliament", as per the following steps:

i) the people devise a democratic structure, a written constitution perhaps, which sets down the rules for a decision-making process and an electoral system;

ii) the people elect the parliament, and parliament elects its executive;

iii) and then on each and every matter of non-urgent policy, parliament identifies its collective will, whereupon the executive executes that policy.

There are other variations, of course, not least the presidential style of governance. In which instance, society may opt to elect directly not only its parliament but also its executive. Secondly, on especially sensitive matters like, for example, questions of national sovereignty, it may be better to let the people identify their collective will directly, i.e., in a national poll; indeed, these and other matters should perhaps be subject to a citizens' initiative.

Suffice to say that in these pages, we seek only to lay down the basic guidelines and, for that purpose, we will stick to the indirect model as in the above steps. They involve three voting procedures:

1. a decision-making process, so that on any non-immediate matter of dispute, the electorate or their representatives may come to a collective decision;

2. a fair electoral system by which the electorate may choose its representatives,

3. and another by which parliament may elect a proportional, balanced government.

The Collective Will - Democracy Defined

If parliament has been elected under a fair electoral system, the collective will of the people should approximate to the collective will of parliament. And the collective will of parliament (and, therefore, of the people) can be defined as:

+ either the unanimous viewpoint, if such exists, and there are, of course, some matters which are not controversial; or, on matters initially problematic, the successful distillation of a constructive debate, the members' collective wisdom;

+ on subjects of dispute, albeit after a long and difficult discussion, a mutual agreement, their common consensus; or

+ on *very* contentious issues, their best possible compromise.

Democracy, I repeat, is for everybody. The democratic process, therefore, should not be a means by which some come to gain dominance over others (as in a majoritarian structure), but rather a process in which all (or nearly all) come to an accommodation.

And because democracy is for everybody, we must break away from the habit of thinking in terms of supposedly mutually exclusive, dichotomous alternatives. The planet will not survive unless we maintain a high level of bio-diversity; and human society will not properly prosper, intellectually, unless it can develop a system of governance which sustains human diversity.

Democracy must be plural. So any voting procedure must surely offer the voter a choice of more than two options![2] After all, a decision taken by a for-or-against vote cannot be a *collective* agreement; that is obvious. The outcome may *confirm* the will of the majority but, unless the vote is (almost) unanimous, it cannot confirm the will of all. Little wonder, then, that in many conflict zones, society has rejected majority rule[3] and has tried to replace it with a form of power-sharing.

'Peace-ful' Politics ... in Decision-making

The democratic process is said to be an integral part of any peace process. The systems of voting, therefore, should themselves be 'peace-ful'. Instead of arguing and then voting (for-or-)*against* each other in what is inevitably a win-or-lose process, the people or their representatives should discuss problems *with* each other, and then vote *with* each other, voting only 'for' the various options in their order of preference, in a win-win voting procedure.

The outcome is the option which gains the best average preference rating. An average, after all, involves not just a majority but, literally, everybody. The outcome, then, in let us say a 6-option ballot, may be the 1st preference of only a few, but the 2nd or 3rd preference of nearly everybody. This is the underlying rationale of a win-win voting procedure, the modified Borda count, (MBC).

Before the advent of the computer, counting such a multi-option preference vote was problematic. Today, of course, it is all too easy. Therefore the de Borda Institute commissioned *Decision-maker*, a computer program which analyses any voters' profile according to an MBC and, for comparative purposes, most of the other decision-making voting procedures discussed in this book. The CD-Rom is in the inside cover.

---

2   As already noted, in many instances, a majority vote *identifies*, not the will of those who vote, but only the will of he/she who wrote the question. This is invariably true in any party political structure where the members of parliament are under a party whip... as is the case in most European countries.

     It is also true to say that in a large number of referendums, the answer is again the question. The vote may *confirm* the will of the people, if, that is, the question or its negation is indeed the will. But a single two-option majority vote cannot facilitate the *identification* of the collective will of a few, let alone of millions. Farquharson and Emerson (2002).

3   For some strange reason, however, they have not rejected the majority vote.

'Peace-ful' Politics ... in Elections

In a related manner, win-win electoral systems also differ from the more adversarial procedures.[4] In democratic theory, and especially in post-conflict societies, elected representatives should represent, as best they may, *all* of their constituents. Accordingly, in the election itself, voters should have the opportunity of expressing their opinions on some if not all of the candidates. Again, therefore, a preferential system of voting is required, with the added proviso of a quota to make it proportional.

To a certain extent, most forms of proportional representation (PR) fall into the win-win category, not least because there are two or more winners. To be really 'peace-ful', however, a preference form of PR is required, for this allows the voters, if they so wish, to vote *with* their neighbours, even with those of a different religion and/or ethnicity. The act of voting, if you like, can be an act of reconciliation, and the Catholic/Protestant of Northern Ireland, the Catholic/Orthodox/Moslem of Bosnia, and the Druze/Maronite/Orthodox/Shia/Sunni of Lebanon, may vote, not only for "one of their own" but also, if they want to, for one or more of their erstwhile foes.[5]

Ideally, then, we need a preferential and proportional electoral system which not only allows, but actually *encourages* the voter to regard the democratic process, not so much as a contest between various groups of individuals, but more as an exercise in co-operation. The appropriate mechanism is the quota Borda system, QBS, which is based on an MBC.

'Peace-ful' Politics ... in Governance

The same spirit of compromise should apply to the workings of parliament. Accordingly, on all non-urgent matters of contention, rather than allow the debate to deteriorate from a multi-option discussion into a divisive, dichotomous diatribe, every MP should endeavour to find the most widely acceptable policy, not least because such a tactic and such a policy are probably in the best collective interests of his/her constituents. If it is done correctly, consensus voting can facilitate the identification of the best possible compromise, in the very best sense of that word.

---

4   The worst of the win-or-lose electoral systems is first-past-the-post (FPP), as used in Britain and much of the former British Empire. But many PR (proportional representation) -list systems, both single preference PR-list and the relatively high threshold PR-STV, (single transferable vote), often tend to be adversarial as well.

5   NI uses PR-STV. This *allows* the voter to give a 2nd and any subsequent preferences to other candidates of other parties. In practice, however, voters may (and often do) cast all their preferences for the candidates of a single party.

   The main system in Bosnia is a form of PR-open list which allows the voter only a single preference.

   In Lebanon, the voter is asked to vote for those of every confessional group in his/her constituency. In one constituency in Beirut, for example, the electorate votes in 17 separate FPP contests for 17 representatives - some Christian and some Moslem. In theory, then, the people may argue about politics, by all means... but not about religion! Khazen (1998). See also p 60.

Whenever parliament is making a collective judgement, therefore, it should seek to attain either a verbal or a 'votal' consensus. Accordingly, on these non-urgent matters of contention, policy decisions should be based on a multi-option vote. Similarly, when it comes to the election (rather than, as is normally the case, the *selection*) of a government - a team of ministers of various talents - it is again necessary to identify "the will of parliament". Rather than allow one individual - the premier - to wield absolute power in the appointment of all the members of the cabinet, the government should be chosen, collectively, by parliament.

The appropriate electoral system must allow each MP, not only to identify, in his/her order of preference, which members he/she wishes to serve in cabinet, but also to state in which ministerial post he/she wishes these nominees to serve. We therefore need a *tabular* form of preferential PR; and the outcome should be a cabinet in which each minister does the job for which, in the consensus of parliament, they are most suited. The appropriate voting system is called a QBS matrix vote.

THE OUTLINE OF THE BOOK

When our forebears first decided to renounce violence and go democratic, they did not first have a fight about it; democracy emerged, and it is still evolving. In like manner, I do not expect the reforms described in this book to be introduced by a majority vote. Consensus voting will be enacted in consensus.

In Part I, we will look at the voting procedures necessary for a proper democratic structure. The first theme, decision-making, is in Chapter 1 and on the CD-ROM. Then, in one of the examples, a hypothetical parliament uses a consensual decision-making process, the modified Borda count, MBC, to come to a collective opinion on the size of its future power-sharing executive. In Chapter 2, we describe an inclusive electoral system, the quota Borda system, QBS, by which the people can elect their parliament. Next, Chapter 3 examines the matrix vote: the means whereby a parliament can elect a balanced and proportional government, even though each member of the cabinet has a different function and maybe too a different status. And finally, Chapter 4 looks at whether or not these three voting procedures can be easily manipulated.

Part II is a critique in which a number of experts analyse the proposed voting systems. Firstly, in Chapter 5, Maurice Salles discusses voting theory, the science which is seldom referred to when politicians discuss decision-making. As noted above and in the foreword, multi-option discussions often descend into binary arguments, and when there are only two options on the agenda, the voting procedure has to be a majority vote. There are, however, many voting procedures which can be used in a multi-option ballot and, because of various forms of PR, even more electoral systems. In addition, there is one two-dimensional voting procedure, the matrix vote. Social choice theory applies to them all.

Chapter 6, from Hannu Nurmi, examines the mathematical properties of the three procedures. Nothing, of course, is perfect, and there are no formulae which can guarantee a) that voters will prefer to vote "sincerely" (as opposed to tactically), and

b) that the outcome is indeed the voters' collective will. It is also true to say, however, that some voting systems are definitely better than others in that they are a more accurate measure of the common consensus.

A holistic approach would suggest that, if indeed these inclusive voting procedures are more democratic in mathematical theory, then so too should they be more democratic in practice. In international agreements such as the UN Charter, democratic rights have not been enunciated in any great detail. It is nevertheless obvious, especially in any post-conflict society, that the chosen system of governance must be all-inclusive. In Chapter 7, Christine Bell determines whether or not the three Borda methodologies satisfy this requirement.

If they do, as Aileen Tierney and Phil Kearney suggest, these voting systems could also be used in mediation work. In most domestic and some industrial disputes, the numbers of people directly involved may be small, and it may not be necessary to resort to a voting procedure. In political disputes, however, involving as they do societies measured in thousands if not millions, mediation is best effected via a combined verbal *and* votal procedure.

Finally, in Part III, Chapter 9, Elizabeth Meehan assists the author in considering the practicalities of these voting systems, both in any national fora and in international gatherings. Academics may often propose good ideas, but whether these are then put to good use depends on a number of factors.

Historical Perspective - the Modified Borda Count

The original Borda count, though not then so named, was proposed in the year 1435 by one Nicholas Cusanus, a writer and theologian who later became a cardinal.[6] He suggested this voting procedure should be used when electing the Holy Roman Emperor but alas his suggestion was refused.

In 1784, Jean Charles de Borda - and hence the name of the voting procedure, the Borda count - advocated this points system for *l'Académie des Sciences,* again as an electoral system. It worked well, but sixteen years later, a new member came along who did not like this 'consensus nonsense'. *Non,* he said, for he preferred the simple, straight forward, majority vote, and it was with just such a vote that he was declared to be first Consul and then Emperor. He was, of course, Napoleon Bonaparte.[7]

Le chevalier Jean-Charles de Borda was born in the small town of Dax, in France. And the good folk of Dax decided they should honour their most famous son, even if he was not particularly famous anywhere else. Accordingly, they decided to erect a statue in his honour in the town square. Sadly, however, no-one had a picture of the

---

6   Sigmund. As Prof. Nurmi points out, however, it may even date from the 12th century; (p 111).

7   Black, 1958, p 180.

said son. Never mind, they decided, with a surname containing the little 'de', the guy was obviously a bit of an aristocrat; so they sculptured a bronze statue of a suitably well dressed feller in thoughtful mode, and thus 'he' stood... until he was knocked off during the war but, now replaced, a different 'he' stands again.

The Rev. Dodgson (alias Lewis Carroll) was the next to invent a Borda count, again not using that name because, by all accounts, he seems to have come to favour such a rankings system without ever having heard of M. de Borda.

The present author also came to this conclusion quite independently. He was living in Belfast at the time, and partially because he is the child of an Irish Protestant father and an English Catholic mother - illegitimate in any majoritarian democracy - he soon tired of the simple *closed* question. "Are you Protestant or Catholic?" Neither. "Are you British or Irish?" Both.

In 1977, he proposed a multi-option voting procedure in a letter to the local press.[8] Later on, thinking that the best way to promote such obvious common sense was to demonstrate the methodology, he organised a conference in 1986 for the New Ireland Group. This public meeting involved the participation of members of both *Sinn Féin* (SF) and the Official (now Ulster) Unionist Party (UUP) etc., a rare event in those troubled days! No wonder over 200 people packed the hall. They sat in a circle, they debated, they voted by preferences... and it worked: they found a consensus.

Only later, in 1991, having written a second book on the subject and having by this time organised a fourth 'experiment'[9] - with the voting procedures now computerised - he was advised to do some research. For apart from (simple, weighted, qualified and consociational forms of) majority voting, there are of course lots of other ways of making decisions.[10] Sadly, most decision-makers have not studied the subject at all![11] Secondly, many political scientists seldom conduct experiments. The author, however, has carried out a number of tests in both Northern Ireland and Eastern Europe and, after many discussions and much thought as a result of these, he then devised the MBC or preferendum as it was then called; this was first outlined in 1994.[12]

---

8 The *Irish News*, 3rd May 1977; and this was followed by a more detailed description in Emerson (1978).

9 One of those present at this conference, held six months *before* the outbreak of war in Bosnia, was from Sarajevo. When the participants, who again included members of the UUP and SF, had found their votal consensus, Mr. Petar Radji-Histić said an MBC "would be very useful in my country". Sadly, on EU insistence, they used a two-option referendum... and it started the war. See p 142.

10 A comparison of some of the more well known voting procedures is on pp 29-31 and in Appendix I.

11 "... the theory of voting... appears to be wholly unknown to anyone concerned with its practical applications." Dummett, 1984, p 5.

12 Emerson (1994).

Historical Perspective - The Quota Borda System and Matrix Vote

The first hint of a QBS election system would appear to have come from the same Rev. Dodgson,[13] but the main work in this field has been done by Professor Sir Michael Dummett.[14]

The matrix vote, however, was invented just the once - by the author in 1978. In 1986, in the public meeting mentioned above, a matrix vote exercise was conducted in which a role play of a procedure for electing the various committee chairpersons of Belfast City Council was enacted. Again, the experiment worked.

I described the procedures for a BC matrix vote in one book, and for an MBC version in a later volume.[15] Finally, when the Belfast Peace Talks were under way, a seminar was held on this very topic.

Mathematics and Computers

In the old days, people used to make, as it were, point decisions - and that was a sort of majority vote. As society progressed, our forebears chose to use linear voting procedures - preferential voting - two of which are the MBC and the QBS. And a third logical development is to employ a voting mechanism which is tabular, a matrix vote.

Having first identified the criteria upon which voting procedures should be based, we may ask the mathematician to sort out the rules for the count, and the computer programmer to put it all on a CD-ROM. In effect, therefore, as far as the user is concerned, nothing need ever be too complicated.

And there is nothing complicated in this book anyway, except perhaps for the essay by Maurice Salles in Chapter 5. The main mathematical operations required are addition and just the odd instance of multiplication and division, but there is little in the main text which is beyond the 10-times table.

If anything is a little complicated, I have put it into a separate Appendix, which the reader may avoid if he/she so wishes. But I would like to emphasise the fact that nothing in Part I is too difficult. Furthermore, while the maths of a matrix vote might appear to be a little daunting, it is all much more open and far less complicated than all the plots and plans which pass for politics at present.

Notes on Notation

+ Options, policies and ministries are lettered *A, B, C, D, E* and *F*.
+ Candidates and MPs of alternate gender - from Ms. *J* to Mr. *U* - are named Messrs. *J, K ... U*, while society as a whole consists of just 12 persons: Messrs. *j, k ... u*. In addition, a Mr. *i* appears in Chapter 5.

---

13 McLean and Urken, p 316.   14 Dummett (1997).   15 Emerson (1991 and 1994).

\+ And there are four political parties - *W, X, Y* and *Z*.

There are, then, just 12 persons in society, and 12 MPs in parliament; the breakdown is as follows:

	People		MPs			
Messrs.	*j, k, l* and *m*	support, and	*J, K, L* and *M*	are in,	party	*W*,
	n, o and *p*	support, and	*N, O* and *P*	are in,	party	*X*,
	q and *r*	support, and	*Q* and *R*	are in,	party	*Y*,
and	*s* and *t*	support, and	*S* and *T*	are in,	party	*Z*,
while	*u*	supports, and	*U*	is an independent.		

If and when parliament tends to split into two opposing factions, it is assumed that parties *W* and *Y* are potential allies, along with the independent *U*, while the opposing bloc consists of parties *X* and *Z*. Whether you, the reader, imagine these blocs to be 'left-wing' and 'right-wing', hawk and dove,[16] hard and soft,[17] 'realo and fundi',[18] Catholic and Protestant, Muslim and Hindu, Serb and Croat, Kikuyu and Luo,[19] or whatever, is up to you.

Suffice to say that the very idea of an all-inclusive democratic structure is to enable society to break away from these simplistic and often artificial divisions in society. Nevertheless, we must always remember that there are many, on both sides of every divide, who have a vested interest in division. The modified Borda count, (MBC), the quota Borda system, (QBS), and the matrix vote are all designed to cope with just such a situation while at the same time allowing and even encouraging society to develop a more peaceful plural polity.

Majoritarianism – Indeed, a Cause of War

There are many lessons of history to be learnt here. Hitler, after all, came to power through a parliamentary process and via a majority vote.[20] At about the same time,

---

16 The two tags used to describe the more or less bellicose, not least during the Cold War.

17 These two adjectives were used by the two opposing sides of the Russian Social Democratic Workers' Party which then split. That was in 1903. Lenin won the vote by "the accidental arithmetic of a single ballot" and called his 'half' the Bolsheviks (the majority people) while the losers became the Mensheviks (members of the minority). *Stalin*, Isaac Deutscher, Pelican, 1966, p 71.

18 These two adjectives described the so-called realists and fundamentalists in the German Green Party when it too split into two.

19 Two of the larger tribes in Kenya, which have sometimes been at odds, most recently in the Nov. 2005 constitutional referendum.

20 On 23rd Mar, 1933, Hitler got the 2/3rds majority required to change the German constitution: the so-called Enabling Act. The KPD (communists) and some of the SPD (socialists) were banned from the Reichstag, and only the remaining members of the SPD had the courage to speak and vote against. *Germany, 1918-1990, The Divided Nation*, Mary Fulbrook, Fontana, p 68.

Italy became fascist in two majority vote referendums.[21] And Stalin got rid of his various politbureau opponents, each of them in turn - Trotsky, Zinoviev and Kamenev, and finally Bukharin - by 'persuading' an ever-changing politbureau majority to turn against their erstwhile colleagues.

In more recent conflicts, too, majority voting, or the prospect thereof, has often been part of the problem. Without doubt, majority rule was a cause of the troubles in Northern Ireland. In Sri Lanka, "majoritarian democracy... was a major cause of ethnic conflict."[22] While in the Balkans, "all the wars in the former Yugoslavia started with a referendum".[23]

The genocide in Rwanda was also based on the *closed* question - "Are you Hutu or Tutsi?" Furthermore, those unspeakable acts of violence were 'justified' by a ghastly corruption of what was, in fact, a belief in majoritarianism.[24]

And so it goes on. The lessons remain unlearnt. The referendum clause in the July 2002 Machakos Protocol, set to end the war in South Sudan, is similar to the equivalent part of the 1999 Rambouillet Agreement. The latter clause was a cause of war in Kosova, and when the offensive wording was eventually removed via the good offices of Viktor Chernomyrdin, the then Russian Foreign Minister, the war ceased - QED.[25] By a related logic, it may well be that the very peace agreement for South Sudan, in particular the referendum clause of the above Machakos Protocol, was actually a cause of war in Darfur.

A consensual democracy would never allow one group in society, no matter how big its 'majority', to thus gain a monopoly. What follows in this text are voting procedures which almost guarantee that all may participate and that, *ipso facto*, none may ever dominate.

Additional Complications

For our little forays into the world of mathematics, let me add a few symbols:

n = the number of options on the ballot paper,

m = a number less than n which refers to the number of options a voter has voted for if he/she has submitted not a full but just a partial vote,

V = the valid vote, the total number who voted minus the invalid vote,

---

21 Emerson, 2002, p 106.

22 *Sri Lanka*, Rudhika Coomaraswamy, in *Can Democracy be Defined?* Sunil Bastian and Robin Luckham (eds.), Zed Books, 2003, p 146.

23 Sarajevo's now legendary newspaper, *Oslobodjenje*, 7.2.1999.

24 When initiating the genocide, the *Interahamwe* used the war-cry: "*Rubanda Nyamwinshi*", "the majority people". *The Rwanda Crisis*, Gérard Prunier, Hurst & Co, 1997, p 183.

25 Emerson (2000).

P_A = average preference rating of option A; if all concerned submit full ballots, an average preference rating is defined as the total of all the preferences cast in its favour divided by V, the valid vote; so if 50% of the voters give option A their 2nd preference and 50% give it their 4th, option A will have an average preference rating of 3.

S_A = the BC/MBC score, i.e., the points total, of option A.

C_A = the consensus coefficient of option A. It is defined as A's MBC score, S_A, divided by the maximum possible score, which is V times n. S_A/V.n

$>$ = more popular than; so $D > B$ means that D is more popular than B. And if 6 voters prefer D against 4 who prefer B, we may say, $D > B = 6:4$

Life gets a little more complicated in Chapter 5:

$x \succeq y$ x is at least as good as y,

$x \succ y$ x is preferred to y,

$x \sim y$ there is an indifference between x and y,

$x \succeq_i y$ Mr. i considers that x is at least as good as y,

$x \succeq_s y$ "society" considers that x is at least as good as y,

$A \subseteq B$ A is a subset of B (not excluding equality), and

$\# X$ the number of elements in X (X being finite).

A function $f: A \rightarrow B$ is a rule that assigns to each element $x \in A$ one and only one element $f(x) \in B$. (The sign $\in$ means 'which is a member of'.) Such a function once we have a domain A and a range B can also be denoted by $f: x \mapsto f(x)$

$a \Leftrightarrow b$ 'a if and only if b', or 'a is equivalent to b'.

Terminology

When the text refers to a 1st or subsequent preference, I use this ordinal connotation. In other contexts, as in the first stage or firstly, the word is spelt out in full.

Secondly, certain words like 'sum', 'score' and 'total' might be synonymous in the dictionary, but in this text:

* apropos the matrix vote, the word 'sum' refers to the points a candidate gets for a certain ministerial post;
* the word 'score' applies to the MBC, QBS and the matrix vote, and is applicable to all the points an option or candidate may receive; and
* the word 'total' concerns all other additions.

Finally, there are quite a few numbers in this book. Sometimes, i), I write the number out in full, one; ii), I frequently use the number itself, 2; and occasionally, iii), as when 3 people cast three 3rd preferences, I use all three formats.

PART I

DESIGNING AN ALL-INCLUSIVE DEMOCRACY

Chapter 1

Collective Decision-making
The Modified Borda Count, MBC[1]

PURPOSE

Those who believe in democracy usually regard the collective decision of many as more likely to be wiser, or at least less dangerous, than the individual decision of just one person. Some would go further and suggest our collective human wisdom is actually getting close to "the truth".[2]

There is a need, therefore, for a decision-making procedure by which can be identified our common consensus, if and when such exists. This should be possible by measuring the opinion of each individual - and an accurate opinion is best measured by a multi-option preference vote - and then by distilling this information into one collective will.

So, in practical terms, what should happen in a parliament? Well, having first identified in debate what options are possible, all MPs should state their opinions - i.e., their preferences - on the options which have been short-listed, and the collective will can then be identified as the option with the best average preference rating.

The democratic process should be the means by which all may contribute, in which all may participate. A democracy is not only *for* everybody; a democracy *needs* everybody. And a plural democracy must allow for a meeting of minds. Accordingly, the purpose of this Chapter is to devise a procedure, by which it is possible to identify the common ground: this is either everyone's best possible compromise, or their consensus, or at best, their collective wisdom, (p 3). This applies not only to small groups of a dozen or so, not only to parliaments of hundreds, but also to societies of millions.

Principles

As noted in the Introduction, this democratic process should enable all concerned not only to debate matters *with* each other, but also to resolve these matters *with* each other. Admittedly, the entire process can be conducted verbally; in large gatherings, however, and/or on any controversial matters, it may be more convenient to use a voting procedure as well.

---

1 The MBC is a decision-making process. Admittedly, it can be used as an electoral system – indeed, many voting procedures can be used both in decision-making and in elections – but the main function of an MBC is in decision-making. The appropriate Borda methodology for an election is the quota Borda system, QBS, the subject of Chapter 2.

2 One such was Le Marquis de Condorcet. McLean and Urken, p 113.

In debate, we normally ask everyone to respect the opinions of everybody else. This needs a caveat, of course, in that all opinions or proposals should first comply with some agreed norm, like the UN Charter on Human Rights. Similarly, in the vote, we may ask all to respect the views of others, that is, to cast a preference on all the options listed - assuming, of course, that the final list is confined to about six to ten options, and seldom if ever more than a dozen.[3]

Accordingly, when I come to vote, I will probably give my own party's proposal my 1st preference. At the same time, however, I should acknowledge that you have the right to support your party's proposal, even if I think it is the worst on offer. I should therefore give your proposal at least my last preference, if only thereby to acknowledge that it is your sincerely held desire and a legitimate aspiration.

Furthermore, in a democracy, we should all agree to abide by the outcome. If, come the count, society thinks your policy option is the best, then of course, I must accept that democratic consensus. By giving it just one point, I am as it were confirming that I will indeed accept such an outcome.

To put the above principles into a mathematical formula - it is called a Borda count or BC - is quite easy (but see also the glossary):

in a vote on n options,   a 1st preference gets n points,
a 2nd preference gets $n-1$ points,
a 3rd preference gets $n-2$ points ... and
a last preference gets 1 point.

Now in *realpolitik*, there may well be those who, for whatever reason, prefer to abstain. In consensus politics, it matters little if someone is sick or whatever, for the calculation of any average will not be rendered too inaccurate if only a few measurements are not taken into account.[4] In similar fashion, some may wish to abstain partially, i.e., to express preferences for some options but not necessarily for all of them. Such is their prerogative.[5] In order to ensure that the count procedure is fair and that those who participate fully in the democratic process are not placed at a disadvantage compared to those who participate partially, those who vote for only m preferences will exercise points as follows:

a 1st preference gets m points,
a 2nd preference gets $m-1$ points
a 3rd preference gets $m-2$ points ... and
a last preference gets 1 point.

---

3   The number 6 is probably enough for any national poll, while 12 is the recommended maximum for any votes in chamber.

4   In majority voting, however, the role of one person may often be crucial! No wonder the stretcher cases are sometimes dragged into the lobbies. Emerson (2002).

5   In any debate on energy and nuclear power, for example, many would probably find some of the options unpalatable.

Whether I vote for just 1 option, or whether I vote for m or even all n options, my 1st preference will thus be 1 point ahead of my 2nd preference (whether I have expressed the latter or not). Similarly, my 2nd preference if expressed will be 1 point ahead of my 3rd preference (whether expressed or not), and so on. The addition of this second formula turns the BC voting procedure into a modified Borda count, MBC. In an MBC, however, it is not so easy to use average preference ratings, so we use consensus coefficients instead: the MBC score divided by the maximum possible score, (V.n).

The Practice

In debate, the procedure should be as follows. All participants should first elect a team of, say, three impartial, non-voting 'consensors', whose task will be twofold.

a) They draw up and maintain a balanced list of all relevant proposals, allowing only those which conform to the UN Charter on Human Rights. If at the end of the debate, the list comes down to just one option, that option can be assumed to represent the *verbal* consensus and the debate may be concluded. If, however, a number of possible options remains, the chairperson asks all parties if they are satisfied that their own proposal is contained in that list, either verbatim or in composite. If that is so, that list becomes the ballot paper for a multi-option preference vote, which could be either the decision-making process or just a straw poll, depending on the outcome. If the most popular option gains a sufficiently high consensus coefficient above a pre-determined level, the consensors may declare this to be the final decision,[6] the *votal* consensus. If not, the vote should be treated as a multi-option straw poll and the debate resumed in a search for other options, based on those which are the more popular.

b) The consensors adjudicate on the outcome of the vote. (In any two-option vote, the two options concerned are invariably regarded as mutually exclusive, even when, as is often the case, they are *not* diametrical opposites.)[7] In a multi-option

---

6 A BC/MBC can be adversely affected if the consensors have not drawn up a list of options which accurately reflects the debate. In mathematical jargon, any additional but unnecessary option, E say, (unnecessary because literally everyone prefers another option, C, which is already on the list), is called an "irrelevant alternative" but, if such an irrelevant alternative were included, it might lead to a different result. More of this in Chapters 4 and 5.

To be sure the outcome is accurate, therefore, the consensors can also do a Condorcet count, which is not so vulnerable. The latter suffers from the paradox (see p 106). So if the outcome is the same in both counts, everyone will know that it truly represents their collective will. If on the other hand the two outcomes are different, then maybe the debate should be resumed, the list of options changed, and another vote held. The conclusion - that for the sake of accuracy, it is better to use a BC/(MBC) as well as a Condorcet count - has been advocated by many: Dodgson, Black and Copeland, for example. Emerson (1998). Furthermore, Nanson proposed a methodology to combine the two - pp 111-2.

7 Protestants and Catholics are both Christian. Serbs and Croats are both Slav. And, as stated by A P Semenov-tian-Shanski during the Russian civil war, both communism and capitalism are creeds based on greed. *Svobodnaya Priroda* (Free Nature), *Priroda*, 1919, nos 4-6, cols 199-216, and quoted in *Models of Nature,* Douglas Weiner, Indiana University, 1988, p 35.

ballot, however, not *all* the options will always be mutually exclusive of *all* the other options. Now sometimes, the first two winning options may be very close to each other in terms of their popularity. In such an instance, the consensors may choose to form a composite, incorporating into the most popular option those aspects of the second most popular option which are compatible. A very simple example might be a vote on six levels of dog-licence, say, and if the most popular option of € 4 is neck-and-neck with the second-placed option of € 5, the consensors may well choose the outcome of € 4.50.[8]

The Milieu

If I know that, at the end of the debate, the success of my own party's proposal will depend on its average preference rating - i.e., it will depend on how *every* voter votes, on *all* the preferences cast by *all* the voters - then I will endeavour to ensure that my own party's proposal is liked by, or at least considered acceptable to, as many participants as possible, including those who, in any majoritarian debate, might well have been my opponents. Gone, therefore, will be the adversarial nature of political debate, as epitomised by the question, "Are you with me or against me?"[9] In its place, a more inclusive atmosphere may prevail.

Subjects of debate and policy proposals can still be controversial, in the best sense of that word, but instead of the discussion deteriorating into a two-sided dialogue, simplistic and divisive, it can remain a multi-optional 'polylogue', sophisticated and civilised.

Majoritarian politics works on the basis of an all-powerful party leadership, and that power is exercised through a system of political patronage and the party whip. In any '*A* versus *B*?' vote, most MPs who are themselves members of the two main parties need little persuasion, for members of 'this' party would hardly want to vote in favour of the supposed opposite proposal from 'that' party.

In a plural democracy, in contrast, when discussion moves beyond the dichotomous banality which is so often associated with binary voting, there will invariably be more than two options on both the agenda and the ballot paper. (Now with two options, there are indeed only 2 ways of casting their preferences: either *AB* or *BA*... which is the same, mathematically, as voting for either *A* or *B*, of course.)

With three options, there are 6 possible ways of voting: *ABC, ACB, BAC, BCA, CAB* and *CBA*. With four options, there are 24 possibilities; with five, 120; six, 720;

---

8   It should be said that every voting procedure is manipulable. But the more sophisticated the procedure, the more difficult it is to manipulate. "The BC is a unique method... to minimise the likelihood that a small group can successfully manipulate the outcome." Saari, 1995, p 14. See also Chapter 4.

9   In posing this question, George W. Bush tried to imply that anyone who opposed Osama Bin Laden therefore supported himself, whereas many disliked the violent policies of both! Here too, therefore, the either/or question does not refer to diametrical opposites!

and so on. The introduction of multi-option voting will herald the demise of the party whip, for while the latter might be able to persuade some to vote for 'this' but not for 'that', he will find it very difficult in, say, a 6-option ballot, to insist on one particular form of 'this' if, in so doing, he tries to argue that all the other 719 possible ways of voting are wrong.

TABLE 1.A	MODIFIED BORDA COUNT BALLOT PAPER

Place a '1' opposite your 1st preference;
you may also place a '2' opposite your 2nd preference,
a '3' opposite your 3rd preference,
a '4' opposite your 4th preference,
a '5' opposite your 5th preference,
and a '6' opposite your 6th preference.

Option (or Candidate)	Preference
A	
B	
C	
D	
E	
F	

The modified Borda count (MBC) is a preferential points voting system in which the option(s) {or candidate(s)} with the most points is(are) the winner(s).

The points may vary as follows:

If you vote for:	1 option	2 options	3 options	4 options	5 options	6 options
your 1st preference gets	1 pt	2 pts	3 pts	4 pts	5 pts	6 pts
your 2nd preference gets		1 pt	2 pts	3 pts	4 pts	5 pts
your 3rd preference gets			1 pt	2 pts	3 pts	4 pts
your 4th preference gets				1 pt	2 pts	3 pts
your 5th preference gets					1 pt	2 pts
your 6th preference gets						1 pt

The Ballot Paper

Let us now look at the practicalities, and let us assume that the consensors have produced a final short list of six options. The appropriate ballot paper is shown in Table 1.A on the previous page; Table 1.B below is an example of a valid full vote, while Table 1.C shows a valid partial vote.

TABLE 1.B		TABLE 1.C		TABLE 1.D	
Three MBC Ballot Papers					
Option	Preference	Option	Preference	Option	Preference
A	2	*A*	2	*A*	2
B	5	*B*		*B*	5
C	1	*C*	1	*C*	1
D	4	*D*		*D*	4
E	3	*E*		*E*	1
F	6	*F*		*F*	6

The Invalid Vote

Before moving on, we should just mention the invalid vote. Where the voter's intentions are unclear, as for example in Table 1.D, the vote must be declared invalid. If, however, someone votes '*A*-2, *B*-5, *C*-1, *D*-4, *E*-3, *F*-4', then his $1^{st}/2^{nd}/3^{rd}$ preferences are unambiguous, so this can be read as a valid partial vote: '*A*-2, - , *C*-1, - , *E*-3, - '.

The Count

In the count, we turn the preferences into points, add up all the points cast for each option, and the option with the most points is the winner.[10] Let us assume, for the moment, that everyone casts a full vote, i.e., that they all express a preference for all six of the options. Well if everyone gives option *B*, say, a 1st preference, option *B* will get an average preference rating of 1. If everyone gives option *E* their 6th preference, *E* will get an average preference rating of 6. And if half the voters give option *F* their 3rd preference while the other half give *F* their 4th, then *F* will get an average preference rating of 3.5, which is of course the mean. Similarly, if half give option *A* their 2nd preference and the other half give *A* their 5th preference, then *A,* obviously a very divisive option, will also get the mean average preference rating of 3.5.

---

10 If every voter submits a full ballot, there is no need to convert the preferences into points, to total these points, and then to re-convert these totals into average preference ratings. Instead, the tellers can examine all the preferences cast for each option and thus calculate each option's average preference rating directly.

  Because of the possibilities of partial voting, however, it is better to rely on a points procedure and a consensus coefficient, (p 17); see also Appendix II.

The chances, in real life, of all six options getting exactly the same mean rating must be very close to zero! Some option(s) will invariably be above the mean, and some option(s) below. "The Borda count... always gives a definite result."[11]

As noted above, p 3, a democratic decision may be a unanimous viewpoint, but those occasions will be rare. At other times, after a process (verbal and/or votal) of give and take, it might be the consensus. And on very controversial topics, the democratic outcome might be the best possible compromise. So, if the winning option has a very good average preference rating - between 1 and 1.5, say - that option can be said to be an almost unanimous viewpoint and the collective wisdom. If its average rating is rather less - round about 2 - we may assume that that option represents the consensus. And if it is less again, with a rating of the order of 2.5, we are talking of the best possible compromise.[12]

Degrees of Consensus

If all participants express their preferences on all the options, then each and every option will enjoy at least some measure of support. If the most popular option receives (an average preference rating and) a consensus coefficient above a certain threshold, it can be assumed to have achieved "a sufficient consensus" to use the expression coined in South Africa's dramatic peace process.[13] Similarly, to use the language of the Belfast Agreement, a different threshold could be laid down as the minimum requirement for a consociational 'key' decision. An obvious advantage of this preference form of voting, therefore, is that there is no longer any need for any sectarian "designations".[14] Instead, we just calculate a sufficiently high consensus coefficient threshold, to ensure cross-community support.

---

11 Reilly, 2002, p 358.

12 In majority voting, a unanimous viewpoint is necessarily the same as a majority opinion (or, for that matter, as any minority opinion). As Jean-Jacques Rousseau himself pointed out, however, a majority opinion is not necessarily the same as a consensus opinion - *The Oxford History of the French Revolution*, William Doyle, OUP, 1990, p 53.

Indeed, we could say that a best possible compromise is invariably *not* the same as a majority opinion, for in most instances of a majority vote, the ballot paper does not even include a compromise!

13 The term, however, was undefined. *Long Walk to Freedom*, Nelson Mandela, Abacus, 1994, p 714.

14 The 1998 Belfast Agreement made provision for a consociational majority vote so that, if a certain number of both unionist and nationalist MLAs, (Members of the Legislative Assembly), supported a particular policy, then that policy would be passed. The trouble is fourfold: such a procedure requires every MLA to be designated either 'unionist' or 'nationalist' (or 'other'); thus, secondly, it perpetuates the very sectarianism a peace process is meant to obviate; furthermore, it renders the 'other' MLAs less powerful than the 'sectarian' ones; and finally, it gives to both sides the power of veto.

A similar system is used rather more successfully in Belgium; and a three-sided version was used, with disastrous consequences, in the early 1990s in Bosnia. Emerson (2000).

Making a Decision

So now let us take an example of a votal consensus decision and, for this purpose, let us imagine that our parliament of a dozen MPs wants to decide how big its executive should be. Accordingly, the politicians come together to hold a debate and, for the sake of simplicity, let us assume that our rather small parliament - of Messrs. *J* to *U* - has drawn up a short list of six proposals, as shown in Table 1.E.

TABLE 1.E	MODIFIED BORDA COUNT BALLOT PAPER ON THE SIZE OF THE EXECUTIVE	
	Option	Preference
A	A cabinet of 5 members	
B	A cabinet of 6 members	
C	A cabinet of 7 members	
D	A cabinet of 8 members*	
E	Another cabinet of 8 members*	
F	A cabinet of all 12 members	

* see below, Table 1.H

Now you might think that all of these options are in some sort of logical order, ranging from small to large, and that therefore he whose 1st preference is for option *A* would vote:

'*A* - 1, *B* - 2, *C* - 3, *D* - 4, *E* - 5, *F* - 6'.

In similar fashion, she whose 1st preference is for option *D* could vote either:

'*D* - 1, *E* - 2, *C* - 3, *F* - 4, *B* - 5, *A* - 6'

or

'*D* - 1, *C* - 2, *E* - 3, *B* - 4, *F* - 5, *A* - 6'

or perhaps

'*D* - 1, *E* - 2, *F* - 3, *C* - 4, *B* - 5, *A* - 6' or '*D* - 1, *C* - 2, *B* - 3, *A* - 4, *E* - 5, *F* - 6'

These are known as "single-peaked preferences" and the first three are shown, diagrammatically, in Table 1.F. If everyone votes with single-peaked preferences, and if all cast preferences on all the options listed, then the collective will of all will also be a single-peaked preference. Furthermore, if we add up the points for the first three sets of preferences used in Table 1.F, we get Table 1.G, and the steeper the subsequent curve, the better the average preference rating and/or the higher the consensus coefficient.

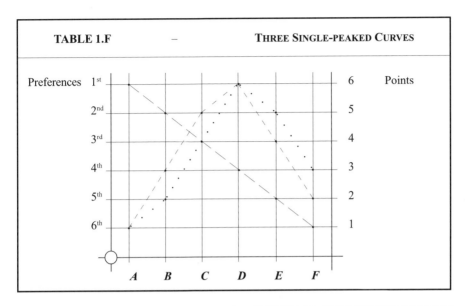

TABLE 1.F — THREE SINGLE-PEAKED CURVES

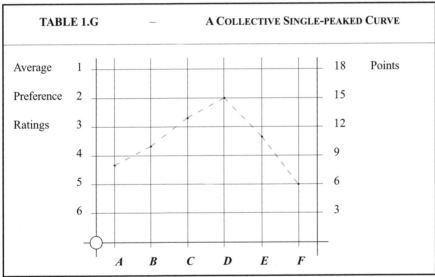

TABLE 1.G — A COLLECTIVE SINGLE-PEAKED CURVE

Politics, however, is not quite as easy. Remember, in our little parliament, we have 12 members, Messrs. *J* to *U*, and there is one big party *W* (4 members), one medium party *X* (3 members), two smaller parties, *Y* and *Z* (2 members each) and one independent, Mr. *U*. Doubtless, each party will vote for what it considers to be in its own vested interest. So, if the executive were to consist of 7 members, option *C*, an obvious breakdown, would be:

$$W - 3, X - 2, Y - 1, Z - 1$$

This could be seen as fairly fair, although not perhaps by Mr. *U*. Secondly, it gives party *W*, which is only *twice* as big as party *Y* or *Z*, *three times* as much influence as these two smaller parties.

If the outcome were to be option *A*, an executive of only 5 members, they would probably get a team of:

$$W\text{-}2, X\text{-}1, Y\text{-}1, Z\text{-}1$$

which might not please *X* very much, because *X*, the medium party, would not wish to be on the same level as the two smaller parties. In contrast, option *B*, an executive of 6 members with a likely breakdown of

$$W\text{-}2, X\text{-}2, Y\text{-}1, Z\text{-}1$$

would give *X* as much power as *W*, and would doubtless please *X* a lot! A full list of the most likely all-party breakdowns is shown in Table 1.H.[15]

	OPTION		*W*	*X*	*Y*	*Z*	*U*
A	A 5-member executive		2	1	1	1	-
B	A 6-member executive		2	2	1	1	-
C	A 7-member executive		3	2	1	1	-
D	An 8-member executive		4	2	1	1	-
E	Another 8-member executive		3	3	1	1	-
F	An all 12-member executive		4	3	2	2	1

TABLE 1.H — PROBABLE ALL-PARTY COALITIONS

---

15 It may often be rather difficult to get a perfectly proportional all-party coalition, not least because human beings cannot be cut up into fractions. All of the possibilities listed here, however, are reasonably fair.

If on the other hand, parliament wanted a majority coalition, there could be considerable confusion: in this setting of 12 MPs, there are five possible ways of forming a minimum majority coalition of 7 or 8 members:

$$W + X \qquad W + Y + Z \qquad W + Y + U$$
$$W + Z + U \qquad \text{and} \qquad X + Y + Z.$$

Furthermore, in any majoritarian analysis, all of these combinations may be considered to be totally 'democratic'!

A fine example occurred in Germany after the Oct. 2005 election. The results in terms of seats in the Bundestag were as follows: CDU/CSU 226, SPD 222, FDP 61, the Left 53, and GP 51. So there were at least 7 'democratic' ways of forming a 'democratic' majority government of a minimum of 308 members: a grand coalition of 226 + 222; or six majority coalitions of 226 (or 222) + 61 + 53, 226 (or 222) + 61 + 51, or 226 (or 222) + 53 + 51.

Example 1A - Choosing the Size of the Executive, The Voters' Profile - Full Ballots

Let us assume the best and the worst: the best, that the MPs have indeed decided to go for an all-party coalition; and the worst, that though they all vote for all 6 options, everyone nevertheless votes for their own vested interest. The ballot paper is as shown:

TABLE 1.I	–	AN MBC BALLOT ON THE SIZE OF THE EXECUTIVE	
	OPTION		PREFERENCE
A	A 5-member executive	2:1:1:1	
B	A 6-member executive	2:2:1:1	
C	A 7-member executive	3:2:1:1	
D	An 8-member executive	4:2:1:1	
E	Another 8-member executive	3:3:1:1	
F	An all 12-member executive	4:3:2:2:1	

Now any member of party *W* would obviously like option *D*, for *D* gives *W* 50% of the seats in government, even though *W* has only got 33% of the seats in parliament. What's more, *D* gives party *W* *twice* as much power as party *X*, and *four times* as much clout as the little parties.

Secondly, party *X*, we know, likes option *B* a lot, and for the same reason of parity with the larger *W* party, it likes option *E* even more. Thirdly, while parties *Y* and *Z* might not like each other very much, on this matter they are agreed: they both prefer option *A* and disagree only on their later preferences. Lastly, out on a limb as usual, the independent Mr. *U* wants option *F*.

It is quite plausible to assume, then, that Ms. *J* of party *W* votes '*D*-1, *C*-2, *A*-3, *F*-4, *E*-5, *B*-6', and Messrs. *K*, *L* and *M* do the same. Ms. *N* and her party *X* colleagues, in contrast, could well vote '*E*-1, *B*-2, *C*-3, *A*-4, *F*-5, *D*-6'.

The two MPs from party *Y* - Messrs. *Q* and *R* - might vote '*A*-1, *F*-2, *C*-3, *B*-4, *D*-5, *E*-6', while Messrs. *S* and *T* of party *Z* are probably just a little different: '*A*-1, *F*-2, *B*-3, *C*-4, *E*-5, *D*-6'.

Finally, the independent Mr. *U*, who is possibly best able to judge the fairness of the various options objectively, could well vote '*F*-1, *C*-2, *B*-3, *E*-4, *D*-5, *A*-6'.

The voters' preferences are shown overleaf in Table 1.J. We can now convert these preferences into points, add up the BC/MBC scores for each option, and then express these totals as average preference ratings and/or consensus coefficients, and this we do in Table 1.K on p 27. The most popular option, with the highest number of points,

TABLE 1.J		EXAMPLE 1A - CHOOSING THE SIZE OF THE EXECUTIVE THE VOTERS' PREFERENCES - FULL BALLOTS					
The electorate and party affiliation		A: 5-members 2:1:1:1	B: 6-members 2:2:1:1	C: 7-members 3:2:1:1	D: 8-members 4:2:1:1	E: 8-members 3:3:1:1	F: 12-members 4:3:2:2:1
W	J	3	6	2	1	5	4
	K	3	6	2	1	5	4
	L	3	6	2	1	5	4
	M	3	6	2	1	5	4
X	N	4	2	3	6	1	5
	O	4	2	3	6	1	5
	P	4	2	3	6	1	5
Y	Q	1	4	3	5	6	2
	R	1	4	3	5	6	2
Z	S	1	3	4	6	5	2
	T	1	3	4	6	5	2
Ind.	U	6	3	2	5	4	1

51, the best average preference rating, 2.75, and the best consensus coefficient, 0.71, is option *C*. Granted, it wins by a very small margin. It is interesting to note, however, that option *C*, the 1st preference of nobody, nevertheless comes out on top - it is, indeed, the best possible compromise.[16]

A Composite?

The runner-up – option *A* – has an average preference rating of 2.83; and when the two leading options are so close together, the consensors might indeed try to form a composite. In this example, a composite of option *C* – a 7-member executive – with option *A* – a 5-member cabinet – would presumably be option *B* – a 6-member government. But option *B* gets a very bad average preference rating, and *B* is not the natural composite of *A* and *C*, for all the tactical considerations of party vested interest we discussed earlier.

So option *C* it is, with a rating of 2.75. Now the maximum possible rating, as always, is an average preference rating of 1; in this instance of a 6-option ballot, the mean is 3.5; so a rating of 2.75, well above the mean, could be said to represent the votal consensus.

---

16 The mathematics for turning a BC/(MBC) score into an average preference rating and/(or consensus coefficient) are in Appendix II.

COLLECTIVE DECISION-MAKING - THE MODIFIED BORDA COUNT

TABLE 1.K		EXAMPLE 1A - CHOOSING THE SIZE OF THE EXECUTIVE THE VOTERS' PROFILE - FULL BALLOTS						
of party:	The Electorate Members of Parliament:	preferences / points	preferences / points	preferences / points	preferences / points	preferences / points	preferences / points	Points Totals:
		THE OPTIONS						
		A: 5-members 2:1:1:1	B: 6-members 2:2:1:1	C: 7-members 3:2:1:1	D: 8-members 4:2:1:1	E: 8-members 3:3:1:1	F: 12-members 4:3:2:2:1	
W	J	3 / 4	6 / 1	2 / 5	1 / 6	5 / 2	4 / 3	21
W	K	3 / 4	6 / 1	2 / 5	1 / 6	5 / 2	4 / 3	21
W	L	3 / 4	6 / 1	2 / 5	1 / 6	5 / 2	4 / 3	21
W	M	3 / 4	6 / 1	2 / 5	1 / 6	5 / 2	4 / 3	21
X	N	4 / 3	2 / 5	3 / 4	6 / 1	1 / 6	5 / 2	21
X	O	4 / 3	2 / 5	3 / 4	6 / 1	1 / 6	5 / 2	21
X	P	4 / 3	2 / 5	3 / 4	6 / 1	1 / 6	5 / 2	21
Y	Q	1 / 6	4 / 3	3 / 4	5 / 2	6 / 1	2 / 5	21
Y	R	1 / 6	4 / 3	3 / 4	5 / 2	6 / 1	2 / 5	21
Z	S	1 / 6	3 / 4	4 / 3	6 / 1	5 / 2	2 / 5	21
Z	T	1 / 6	3 / 4	4 / 3	6 / 1	5 / 2	2 / 5	21
Ind.	U	6 / 1	3 / 4	2 / 5	5 / 2	4 / 3	1 / 6	21
MBC score		50	37	51	35	35	44	252
average preference rating		2.83	3.92	2.75	4.08	4.08	3.33	
		maximum = 1		mean = 3.5		minimum = 6		
consensus coefficient		0.69	0.51	0.71	0.49	0.49	0.61	
		maximum = 1.00				minimum = 0.00		

28   COLLECTIVE DECISION-MAKING - THE MODIFIED BORDA COUNT

Example 1B - Choosing the Size of the Executive, Voters' Profile - Partial Voting

Let us now consider what happens when party members are a little more intransigent and vote only for those options which they consider fully acceptable. In this instance, then, Messrs. *J, K, L* and *M* vote '*D*-1, *C*-2, *A*-3, *F*-4'. Messrs. *N, O, P* vote '*E*-1, *B*-2, *C*-3'. Parties *Y* and *Z* vote '*A*-1, *F*-2'. And Mr. *U* votes '*F*-1, *C*-2, *B*-3'. The voters' profile is in Table 1.L below. The winner is still option *C*, with the highest MBC score of 17, but second place is now shared by options *A* and *D* on 16 points.

TABLE 1.L		EXAMPLE 1B - CHOOSING THE SIZE OF THE EXECUTIVE THE VOTERS' PROFILE - PARTIAL BALLOTS						
of party:	The Electorate Members of Parliament:	preferences / points	preferences / points	preferences / points	preferences / points	preferences / points	preferences / points	Points Totals:
		THE OPTIONS						
		A: 5-members 2:1:1:1	*B*: 6-members 2:2:1:1	*C*: 7-members 3:2:1:1	*D*: 8-members 4:2:1:1	*E*: 8-members 3:3:1:1	*F*: 12-members 4:3:2:2:1	
W	*J*	3 / 2	-	2 / 3	1 / 4	-	4 / 1	10
	K	3 / 2	-	2 / 3	1 / 4	-	4 / 1	10
	L	3 / 2	-	2 / 3	1 / 4	-	4 / 1	10
	M	3 / 2	-	2 / 3	1 / 4	-	4 / 1	10
X	*N*	-	2 / 2	3 / 1	-	1 / 3		6
	O	-	2 / 2	3 / 1	-	1 / 3		6
	P	-	2 / 2	3 / 1	-	1 / 3		6
Y	*Q*	1 / 2	-	-	-	-	2 / 1	3
	R	1 / 2	-	-	-	-	2 / 1	3
Z	*S*	1 / 2	-	-	-	-	2 / 1	3
	T	1 / 2	-	-	-	-	2 / 1	3
Ind.	*U*	-	3 / 1	2 / 2	-	-	1 / 3	6
MBC score		16	7	17	16	9	11	76
consensus coefficient		0.22	0.10	0.24	0.22	0.13	0.15	
		maximum = 1.00			minimum = 0.00			

A Comparison of the MBC with other Voting Procedures
(See also App. I.)

Before we move on, it might be interesting to compare the MBC - Example 1B opposite - with what happens under other voting procedures. Weighted majority voting and plurality voting both look at 1st preferences only, so with an outcome of *A* - 4, *B* - 0, *C* - 0, *D* - 4, *E* - 3 and *F* - 1, both are inconclusive.

Consociational voting requires majority support for one particular proposal from two or more separate electorates, so it is even less likely to produce a clear outcome.

Two-round voting is a plurality vote in the first round, followed by a majority vote in the second round between the two leading options from the first. So options *A* and *D*, the two top scorers on 4 points each, both qualify for the second round, whereupon Messrs. *J, K, L* and *M* all prefer *D* to *A*; Messrs. *N, O, P* are indifferent; Messrs. *Q, R, S* and *T* prefer *A* to *D*; and Mr. *U* is also indifferent. So the outcome is a draw, 4:4, for *A* and *D*.

In approval voting, the first few preferences count as 'approvals'. If we consider all 1st and 2nd preferences thus, the outcome is *A* 4, *B* 3, *C* 5, *D* 4, *E* 3, *F* 5; a draw for *C* and *F*.

But if we consider all 1st, 2nd and 3rd preferences thus, the outcome is *A* 8, *B* 4, *C* 8, *D* 4, *E* 3, *F* 5; a draw for *A* and *C*.

Serial voting consists of a series of majority votes, until only one option remains unbeaten. With the options in order, small to large - *A B C D E F* - the first majority vote is *A* v *F*, and *A* defeats *F* by 8:1.
In the second vote, *A* v *E*, *A*'s margin of victory is 8:3.
The third round, *A* v *D*, is a draw, 4:4.
If the fourth round is *A* v *C*, then *C* wins 8:4, for a final of *C* v *B*, which *C* wins 5:3; while if the fourth round is *D* v *B*, it is a 4:4 draw as well, and *D* v *C* is yet another.

We examine the alternative vote, AV, overleaf. Let us first do a BC, which of course gives no effect to partial voting: *A* gets four 1st and four 3rd preferences at 6 and 4 points each respectively, which is 24 and 16 points, a total of 40 points. The totals are:

A 40, *B* 19, *C* 37, *D* 24, *E* 18 and *F* 38   -   a win for option *A*.

The MBC comes next, and this does take partial voting into account; as shown in Table 1.L, it gives:

A 16 *B* 7, *C* 17, *D* 16, *E* 9 and *F* 11   -   a victory for *C*.

A Condorcet count examines all the pairings in turn. When we look at *A* v *B*, we see Messrs. *J, K, L* and *M* all prefer *A* to *B*, as too do *Q, R, S* and *T*. The threesome, *N-O-P*, however, along with Mr. *U*, prefer *B* to *A*. The ratio, then is 8:4, and *A* wins that pairing.

We already know that *A:D* is 4:4, *A:E* is 8:3, *A:F* is 8:1, *B:C* is 3:5 and both *B:D* and *C:D* are 4:4. The full tally is as shown overleaf - and *C* comes out on top with 4 $^{1}/_{2}$.

TABLE 1.M			A CONDORCET COUNT					
			A	B	C	D	E	F
A:B	=	8:4	1					
A:C	=	4:8			1			
A:D	=	4:4	½			½		
A:E	=	8:3	1					
A:F	=	8:1	1					
B:C	=	3:5			1			
B:D	=	4:4		½		½		
B:E	=	1:3					1	
B:F	=	3:9						1
C:D	=	4:4			½	½		
C:E	=	5:3			1			
C:F	=	7:5			1			
D:E	=	4:3				1		
D:F	=	4:5						1
E:F	=	3:9						1
		Totals:	3½	½	4½	2½	1	3

Finally, AV, in which the least popular option is eliminated and its votes are transferred in accordance with its voters' 2nd preferences, until one option gets 50%. The first round score was: *A* 4, *B* 0, *C* 0, *D* 4, *E* 3, *F* 1, which puts *B* and *C* out of the contest. In the second round, we eliminate *F*, the 1st preference vote of Mr. *U*, but it only goes to *C* and then *B* so it is non-transferable. Next, we eliminate *E*'s total, from Messrs *N*, *O* and *P*, but these votes go to *B* and then *C*, so they too become non-transferable. The outcome is therefore a draw, 4-4, between *A* and *D*.

A Second Comparison of the BC/MBC with other Voting Procedures

If we go back to the full ballots of example 1A, (Table 1.K on p 27), we can see what happens in that scenario as well. The outcome of a plurality vote is the same, of course, for the 1st preferences are unchanged. In a second round vote between *A* and *D*, we see that Messrs. *N*, *O*, *P* prefer *A* to *D*, albeit marginally, while Mr. *U* prefers *D* to *A*, just, and the outcome is option *A* by a margin of 7:5.

In an approval vote of example 1A, a count of just the 1st and 2nd preferences gives the same tally of *A* 4, *B* 3, *C* 5, *D* 4, *E* 3, *F* 5, a draw between *C* and *F*, which is as expected; after all, all the voters expressed at least two preferences. Serial voting also produces a similar result in both examples: *A* now beats *F* by 11:1, it beats *E* by 8:4 and *D* by 7:5, but *C* then wins over *A* by 8:4, and in the final *C* wins over *B* by 7 to 5. When everyone submits a full vote, the outcomes of a BC and an MBC are the same, of course: *A* 50, *B* 37, *C* 51, *D* 35, *E* 35, *F* 44. In a Condorcet count, the final tally is *A* 4, *B* 1, *C* 5, *D* 0.5, *E* 1.5, *F* 3. And lastly, under AV, we again eliminate *F*; then, with *B* and *C* already out of the race, *U*'s vote transfers to his 4th preference, *E*, which leaves options *A*, *D* and *E* all on a score of 4.

All the outcomes are in Table 1.N. If Tables 1.K and 1.L are examined by eye, the reader may reasonably surmise that option **C** is, indeed, a fair outcome and that option **A** is the most probable runner-up in both profiles. So, if but in these examples, we may conclude that the MBC and Condorcet counts, which give (almost) the same outcome, are accurate measures of collective opinion. Indeed, in both theory and practice, the outcomes of an MBC count and a Condorcet count often coincide; (p. 17n).

TABLE 1.N	–	A COMPARISON		
VOTING PROCEDURE	Full Ballots		Partial Ballots	
	Winner	Runner-up	Winner	Runner-up
plurality	(**A** – 4 and **D** – 4)		(**A** – 4 and **D** – 4)	
weighted/consociational majority	-	-	-	-
two-round voting	**A** – 7	**D** – 5	(**A** – 4 and **D** – 4)	
approval voting (1st and 2nd prefs)	**C** – 5 and **F** – 5		**C** – 5 and **F** – 5	
approval voting (1st /2nd/3rd prefs)	**C** – 10 and **A** – 8		**A** – 8 and **C** – 8	
AV or STV	**A, D, E** – 4		**A, D** – 4	
serial voting	**C** – 7	**B** – 5	**C** – 5,	**B** – 3
BC	**C** – 51	**A** – 50	**A** – 40	**F** – 38
MBC	**C** – 51	**A** – 50	**C** – 17	**A, D** – 16
Condorcet count	**C** – 5	**A** – 4	**C** – 4.5	**A** – 3.5

Consensus

If everyone had been really intransigent, each voting for only their 1st preference, the outcome would have been: **A** - 4, **B** - 0, **C** - 0, **D** - 4, **E** - 3, and **F** - 1. In effect, of course, this would be the same as a plurality vote, a voting procedure which allows the voter to express only one preference. So the outcome, in this instance, would have been an impasse.[17]

When people express more than one preference, however, they are more likely to influence the outcome. Mr. **U**, for example, could well have concluded that he was unlikely to get a consensus for his favourite, option **F**. He might therefore have decided to give a preference to option **C**. Indeed, if he chose to cast a full ballot with a 1st preference for **C**, he would have given **C** a larger winning margin. In like manner, others too might have been persuaded, by the voting procedure itself, not only to participate more fully in the democratic process, but also to vote in favour of that option which they felt might indeed represent the consensus.

---

17 If in an MBC everyone did resort to a 1st preference only (plurality) vote, the resulting consensus coefficients would be derisory. See p 92.

Plurality voting in decision-making is the same as FPP in elections. When there are more than two options/candidates, the winner may get not a majority but only the largest minority.

Example 1C - Setting the Agenda

Now let us take a different example, one in which people are making not a single but a compound decision, as in choosing an agenda. If, for instance, the UN Security Council wanted to hold a debate on international affairs, it could well consider a number of urgent topics, as suggested by the 15 member states. I have drawn up a list of ten possible subject headings in Table 1.P, arranged in alphabetical order, and in this sort of situation, there are again probably *no* single-peaked preferences.

TABLE 1.P		AN MBC BALLOT PAPER ON THE AGENDA FOR A MEETING OF THE UN SECURITY COUNCIL	
		Option	Preference
	A	Africa - Aids	
	B	Antarctica	
	C	Caucasus and Chechnya	
	D	India/Pakistan and Kashmir	
	E	Iraq	
	F	Iran, North Korea; nukes	
	G	Israel/Palestine	
	H	Rwanda and the DRC	
	I	Sudan and Darfur	
	J	Tsunami	

TABLE 1.Q		— MBC RESULTS - POINTS AND AVERAGE PREFERENCE RATINGS		
	OPTION	Points Scores	Average Preference Ratings	
A	Africa - Aid	75	6	
B	Antarctica	90	5	Max = 1
C	Caucasus and Chechnya	60	7	
D	India/Pakistan and Kashmir	90	5	
E	Iraq	105	4	Mean = 5.5
F	Iran, North Korea; nukes	75	6	
G	Israel/Palestine	90	5	
H	Rwanda and the DRC	60	7	Min = 10
I	Sudan and Darfur	75	6	
J	Tsunami	105	4	

Let us assume that the outcome of a BC/MBC is as shown, (Table 1.Q), in which case it would be possible to arrange, not only the order of the agenda, but also to allocate the time to be given to each topic, let us say 5 minutes for every 15 points.

TABLE 1.R			–	AGENDA
		10.00		Iraq
		10.35		Tsunami
		11.10		Antarctica
11.40		break		
		12.00		India/Pakistan
		12.30		Israel/Palestine
13.00		break		
		14.00		Africa - aids
		14.25		Iran, North Korea
		14.50		Sudan
15.15		break		
		15.30		Caucasus
		15.50		Rwanda and DRC
		16.10	AOB	

Similar compound decisions can be taken on budget allocations, planning proposals, and policy priorities. Take, for example, a budget. In a majoritarian milieu, one person produces a budget, and parliament then debates various sections and, if need be, takes a number of majority votes. Under a more consensual structure, each party could produce an entire budget, or perhaps just entire clauses, and then, after a suitable debate, all could cast their preferences on the various options listed.

Committees

If the list of possible items for the agenda is very long, it may be more practical to agree beforehand, firstly, on how many items are to be included on the final agenda, and secondly, on just how many preferences people are to be asked to vote for. If the final agenda is to include 10 options, they could agree to vote, either for the full list of 10, or on just their first 6 preferences; in all probability, the final outcome would not be very different.

When working in small groups, however, it is always advisable to ask all concerned to cast their preferences on all the options listed. In this way, every option will receive a definite MBC score and a definite average preference rating. And given that each option has doubtless come from one or more individuals, all may thus participate, and be seen to participate.

The MBC as an Electoral System

In the footnote on page 1, it was noted that a decision-making process may sometimes be used as an electoral system, and this is also the case with a BC/MBC. It must be pointed out, however, that this form of election is not proportional and that if proportionality is required, one should refer to QBS and Chapter 2, (p 58).

Let us take the example of the election of a sub-committee of six people. The ballot paper can be prepared in one of two ways, either by listing the preferences and asking the voters to name their candidates from a given list of those eligible, or by listing all the candidates and asking the voters to state their preferences. In a parliamentary setting, it is better for the election to take place with every MP eligible for election to the sub-committee, with the possible exception a) of those who are already serving on too many committees, and b) of those who have already served, let us say, two terms. In the present example, we shall assume that Ms. *J* and Ms. *P* are both disqualified for this reason. Sample ballot papers are shown in Tables 1.S and 1.T.

TABLE 1.S		TABLE 1.T	
BALLOT PAPERS FOR AN MBC ELECTION OF A SUB-COMMITTEE			
List of candidates: Messrs. *K, L, M, N, O, Q, R, S, T, U*		Candidate	Preference
Preference	Candidate	*M*	
1st		*Q*	
2nd		*S*	
3rd		*L*	
4th		*T*	
5th		*O*	
6th		*R*	
		U	
		K	
		N	

Example 1D - The MBC as an Electoral System - Choosing a Sub-committee

To see how the MBC works in practice, let us consider an election in which the MPs choose a sub-committee of 6 members of equal status[18] by casting up to 6 preferences

---

18 By the term 'equal status', I mean that all persons elected to this sub-committee will be on a par with each other. If parliament wishes to elect a sub-committee with members of different statuses - with one person the chair, another the secretary, and so on - a matrix vote should be used, as in Chapter 3.

from a selection of 10 candidates. Again, we assume that members vote in accordance with their vested interests.

Ms. *J*, then, gives her first three preferences to her Party colleagues, Messrs. *K, L* and *M*, her later preferences to her associates in party *Y*, and her 6th preference to the independent Mr. *U*. In like manner, Ms. *P* votes for Ms. *N* and Mr. *O*, and then for Mr. *S* and Ms. *T*, and if there is no one else she likes, so she may opt to submit a partial vote, '*N*-1, *O*-2, *T*-3, *S*-4'. The full profile of preferences and points are in Table 1.U, overleaf.

In this example, Ms. *P* submits a partial vote and exercises only 10 points. Ms. *J*, meanwhile, hands in a full vote, so she exercises all 21 points. The MBC scores received by each candidate are shown in the bottom row and, in this instance, the six most popular, and therefore the six chosen members of our sub-committee, are Messrs. *M, S, L, N, O* (shown in horizontal stripes) and either *Q* or *U* (in diagonals), who tie for sixth place.

In case of a tie like this, we choose the candidate who scores the most 1st preferences, and Mr. *Q* gets 2 whereas Mr. *U* gets only 1, so the final seat goes to Mr. *Q*. The outcome, then, is Messrs. *M, S, L, N, O* and *Q;* 2 for Party *W*, 2 for *X*, 1 for *Y* and 1 for *Z*.

A More Consensual Approach

If parliament wished to be really consensual, it could use the ballot paper in Table 1.T - which, you will notice, is in random rather than alphabetical order - and ask everyone to list all ten preferences. In this way, everyone would be able to acknowledge the candidatures of everyone eligible. Furthermore, if every member listed all ten preferences, all ten candidates would receive a score greater than zero.

As noted on p 33, such an outcome would help to create a less adversarial milieu, which is so essential for a truly all-inclusive democracy. While asking the MPs to express just six preferences may nevertheless be adequate, the former approach all but guarantees that many will vote across the party political or even sectarian divide.

It is also beneficial to operate on the basis that every member of parliament is eligible to serve on every sub-committee (unless, as previously indicated, they are already serving on too many other committees or have already served two terms). There is little to admire in those who nominate themselves for certain posts; and there is something commendable in being chosen for a position for which one has not campaigned.

TABLE 1.U — EXAMPLE 1D - ELECTING A SUB-COMMITTEE
THE VOTERS' PROFILE - PARTIAL BALLOTS

of party:	The Electorate: Members of Parliament	K preferences / points	L preferences / points	M preferences / points	N preferences / points	O preferences / points	Q preferences / points	R preferences / points	S preferences / points	T preferences / points	U preferences / points	Points Totals:
		of party W			of party X		of party Y		of party Z		Ind.	
W	J	3 / 4	2 / 5	1 / 6	- / -	- / -	4 / 3	5 / 2	- / -	- / -	6 / 1	21
W	K	3 / 4	2 / 5	1 / 6	- / -	- / -	4 / 3	5 / 2	- / -	- / -	6 / 1	21
W	L	3 / 2	2 / 3	1 / 4	- / -	- / -	- / -	- / -	- / -	- / -	4 / 1	10
W	M	2 / 5	3 / 4	1 / 6	- / -	- / -	6 / 1	- / -	4 / 3	- / -	5 / 2	21
X	N	- / -	- / -	- / -	1 / 6	2 / 5	6 / 1	- / -	4 / 3	3 / 4	5 / 2	21
X	O	- / -	- / -	- / -	1 / 6	2 / 5	6 / 1	- / -	3 / 4	5 / 2	4 / 3	21
X	P	- / -	- / -	- / -	1 / 4	2 / 3	- / -	- / -	4 / 1	3 / 2	- / -	10
Y	Q	5 / 2	4 / 3	3 / 4	- / -	- / -	1 / 6	2 / 5	- / -	- / -	6 / 1	21
Y	R	4 / 2	3 / 3	- / -	- / -	- / -	1 / 5	2 / 4	- / -	- / -	5 / 1	15
Z	S	- / -	- / -	- / -	3 / 4	4 / 3	- / -	5 / 2	1 / 6	2 / 5	6 / 1	21
Z	T	- / -	- / -	- / -	3 / 3	4 / 2	- / -	- / -	1 / 5	2 / 4	5 / 1	15
Ind.	U	- / -	- / -	5 / 2	- / -	4 / 3	- / -	3 / 4	2 / 5	6 / 1	1 / 6	21
MBC score		19	23	28	23	21	20	19	27	18	20	218
consensus coefficient		0.26	0.32	0.39	0.32	0.29	0.28	0.26	0.38	0.25	0.28	

The Plebiscite

There is absolutely no reason at all why the same consensual method of multi-option decision-making should not be used in community groups, trades unions, company boardrooms and elsewhere or, indeed, in society as a whole, especially whenever the matter in question is controversial. The most obvious instances are plebiscites on sovereignty. As often as not, these are adversarial majority votes, pitting one lot of people against another on the basis of an ethnic or pseudo-ethnic/religious divide.[19]

Such referendums should never be restricted to just two options. Newfoundland, after all, held a 3-option vote on her constitution. Singapore did the same. While Guam held a 6-option ballot, or should I say 7-options: six options were proposed, but a further seventh slot was left blank, just in case a (group of) voter(s) came up with a different idea. In similar fashion, Sweden held a 3-option poll on nuclear power, and New Zealand had a 5-option vote on electoral reform.[20] All of the above referendums were conducted under a version of the rules laid down for a plurality vote or a two-round vote. If the political will had been there, however, they could just as easily have been held under an MBC.

Furthermore, the word "No" should never be an option. Germany uses "a constructive vote of no confidence" to ensure that any member of the Bundestag who wishes to vote out the existing government must first propose, and name, an alternative administration.[21] In like manner, societies voting on their constitutional status should always be given a number of positive concrete proposals to choose from, and hopefully more than two! Occasions when voters may just reject something, without suggesting an alternative, should be avoided.[22]

---

19 The 1991 referendum in Croatia allowed the Catholic Slavs to be independent of the Orthodox Slavs in what had been the state of all the Southern (i.e. Yugo-) Slavs. Similarly, though the Indonesian invasion of 1975 and other atrocities should not be forgotten, the plebiscite in East Timor enabled the Catholic Timorese to separate from their Moslem Timorese neighbours in the West of the island.

20 Emerson, 2002.

21 This and a ban on national referendums were introduced after WWII as lessons from Weimar.

22 On 8.11.2003, by 99% to 1%, Gibraltar said "No" to one possible solution, and thus perpetuated the problem.

On 24.4.2004, 76% of the Greek Cypriots rejected, while 65% of the Turkish Cypriots accepted, Kofi Annan's proposal; because the methodology was consociational, the proposal was lost, and this problem also remains unsolved. See p 129.

Before signing the Belfast Agreement, some of the Unionists had continually said "No!" to pretty well everything, as did many Bosnian Serbs, both before and after Slobodan Milošević said 'yes' on their behalf to the Dayton accords.

Similarly, in the French referendum on Europe in May, 2005, instead of asking, at the very least, a two-option question, "European constitution, *comme ci* or *comme ça?*" they asked only one, "European constitution *comme ci, oui ou non?*" As a result, those who opposed any EU constitution, or Jacques Chirac, or Turkish accession, or Macdonalds... or *anything*... all voted 'Non'!

The Future

There are some who suggest the MBC formulae for the points awarded for a full vote,

$$n, n-1 \ldots 2, 1$$

and a partial vote,

$$m, m-1 \ldots 2, 1$$

are too rigid. After all, while most people might feel pretty strongly about their 1st and 2nd preferences, many do not feel so passionately about the relative merits of their 5th and 6th preferences. Accordingly, one of the smallest democracies in the world - Nauru - has adopted her own variation of the BC for parliamentary elections.[23] Instead of the formula:

$$n, n-1 \ldots 2, 1$$

they use:

$$1, \frac{1}{2} \ldots \frac{1}{n-1}, \frac{1}{n}$$

Thus, in a 6-option ballot, a 1st preference gets 1 point; a 2nd preference gets $\frac{1}{2}$ a point; a 3rd preference $\frac{1}{3}$; a 4th preference $\frac{1}{4}$, and so on. Brilliant... except, as Donald Saari has pointed out,[24] such a count is not strictly a BC and may not therefore possess the same good characteristics. See also Appendix III.

---

23 The current population of Nauru is about 10,000. The use of their variation of BC is discussed in Reilly (2001) and Emerson (2002).

24 Private correspondence.

Chapter 2

A Pluralist Parliament for a Plural Society
The Quota Borda System, QBS

PURPOSE

The aim of this Chapter is to devise an electoral system by which the electorate can elect a parliament which fairly represents every sizeable minority in society. This means, *inter alia,* the system should be proportional. Furthermore, such proportionality should be based upon *what the voters* consider to be important. If as happens in many post-conflict societies, people are concerned about religious and/or ethnic backgrounds, then the system should cater for such strongly held feelings. If, however, albeit in time, other topics not necessarily covered by the 'main' political parties take precedence - issues such as GM foods or whatever - then the electoral system should again be able to cater for such opinions.[1]

Furthermore, as noted on page 5, every elected representative should represent the constituency in its entirety; accordingly, the system should also be preferential. So, in a multi-member constituency of, say, 6 members, the voter should be enabled to express a full 6 preferences.[2]

Principles

Several principles are involved. In a win-win electoral system, almost by definition, there should always be more than one winner. Instead, therefore, of electing a chairperson or a president *only*, those concerned should also elect a deputy chair or a vice-president as well,[3] if not indeed a complete executive.

Secondly, there is the question of size. For any given parliament of *x* members, under a non-PR system in single-seat constituencies, the size of that constituency (in terms of its population) can be relatively small. Because there is only one winner, however, the threshold - i.e., the average percentage of the valid vote needed for success in systems such as FPP, AV or a two-round election - is obviously quite high.

---

1   As we shall see later on, the two main systems which do this without direct resort to party or any other labels are PR-STV and QBS.

2   In small groups of a dozen or less, people can be asked to cast their preferences on all who are eligible to stand, (i.e., on all 'candidates'). In a general election where there could well be up to 20 candidates or more, it is only wise and practicable to ask the voters in a multi-member constituency of 6 seats, to list a limited number of 6 candidates.

3   The original US presidential system was like this: the winner became the president, the runner-up the vice-president.

With these electoral systems, smaller parties and independents are at a distinct disadvantage.

Multi-member constituencies, on the other hand, can cater for several elected representatives and have a correspondingly smaller threshold,[4] but the size of the electorate is then much larger.

Many argue that the elected representative should be a local person, identifiable with his/her constituency; this implies the use of small constituencies. At the same time, consideration must be given to overall proportionality, which requires larger populations. On balance, then, for general or local council elections, a 6-seater multi-member constituency should suffice. This still involves quite a high threshold, so the best way of combining the constituency principle with a low threshold is by using a two-tier or top-up system: 6-seater constituencies with, say, a 2% regional/national top-up.[5]

For a top-up to work effectively, every voter should be able to vote for whatever party is standing in that society, even if that particular party is not standing in every constituency. Accordingly, for any party standing in not all but a certain minimum number of constituencies, a ballot paper may, in one of the other constituencies, contain some "un-candidated parties". In similar fashion, it may also include some non-party candidates or independents.

Given the principles of MBC, a top-up should be based not only on the voters' 1st preferences, but on an MBC count of the voters' first three 'party-preferences'.[6] The MBC total received by each party could also be used as the basis of party funding.

Finally, if society so wishes, a gender quota may be applied, something like a rule to the effect that every party nominating three or more candidates in any election must ensure that 1 of 3, 2 of 4, 40% of any number greater than 4, or 45% of any number greater than 6 are male and the same minimum number female. This does not guarantee equal representation but, in time, it will often help to facilitate such an outcome.

---

4   The word 'threshold' refers to the approximate percentage required to win a seat and, to a large extent, it depends on the quota. (When electing 1 person, a quota is c. 50% + 1); when electing 2 representatives, it is about 33% + 1; for 3, it is roughly 25% + 1; for 4, it's close to 20%; and for 5 and 6, approximately 17% and 14% respectively. As noted in the glossary, however, there is a choice of precise formulas.

5   A top-up features in many electoral systems, such as in the MMP system (sometimes confusingly called AMS) which is used, for example, in Germany and New Zealand.

6   A single 'party-preference' is defined as a vote for one particular party. Accordingly, a vote of 'W - 1, W - 2, W - 3' contains only 1 party-preference, so in an MBC top-up procedure, such a count would mean that W gets 1 point.

  A vote of 'X - 1, X - 2, W - 3, W - 4' contains 2 party-preferences, so X would get 2 points and W 1 point.

  Thirdly, a vote of 'Y - 1, U - 2, X - 3, W - 4' may be regarded as a 3 (or rather 4) party-preferences, so Y would get 3 points, the independents 2, and X 1 point.

The Milieu

As we have seen, (p 31), the MBC procedure encourages the voters to exercise all their preferences. In the setting of an election, because the quota acts as a restraint on the number of candidates each party chooses to nominate, so QBS in effect encourages them to vote across party, across gender, and even across the religious-cum-ethnic-cum-racial divide.

A QBS election consists of two elements: a quota and an MBC. The quota works like this. Any candidate gaining a quota of 1st preferences gets elected. In a constituency of 3 or more seats, any pair[7] of candidates gaining 2 quotas gets 2 candidates elected. And in a constituency of 5 or more seats, any triplet[7a] of candidates which gets 3 or just 2 quotas gets 3 or 2 candidates elected.

Now if, in let us say a 6-seater constituency, a party expects to win 2 seats or, at the most, 3 seats, it would be wise for that party to nominate either 2 or a maximum of 3 candidates. Obviously, if it nominates 4 candidates and yet gains only 2 quotas of 1st preferences, the voters' profile of 1st preferences cast might show each candidate with only half a quota... and the party might thus fail to get anyone elected at an early stage.

An Outline of the Count

As we shall see on pp 44-5, the count is conducted in two parts and up to seven stages, with the proviso that those candidates successfully elected in Part I are not taken into further consideration in Part II. In Part I of the count:

When there are just 2 candidates, any candidate gaining 1 quota of 1st preferences wins that 1 seat.

When there are 3 or 4 candidates, any candidate gaining 1 quota of 1st preferences wins that 1 seat; and any pair of candidates gaining 2 quotas wins those 2 seats.

When there are 5+ candidates, any candidate gaining 1 quota of 1st preferences wins that 1 seat; any pair of candidates gaining 2 quotas wins those 2 seats; any triplet of candidates gaining 3 quotas wins those 3 seats; and any triplet of candidates gaining 2 quotas wins those 2 seats, the actual seats going to those 2 candidates of the triplet with the highest MBC scores.

If seats are still to be filled, then, in Part II of the count, any pair of candidates gaining 1 quota wins 1 seat, the actual seat going to the candidate with the higher MBC score; next, any triplet gaining 1 quota gains 1 seat, the actual seat going to the candidate with the highest MBC score; and finally, seats are awarded to the candidate(s) with the highest MBC scores.

---

7   If x voters vote *A* - 1, *B* - 2 ...; if y voters vote *B* - 1, *A* - 2 ...; and if $x + y \geq 1$ quota, then the pair *A-B* is said to gain 1 quota.

7a Similarly, if u voters vote *D* - 1, *B* - 2, *E* - 3... or *D* - 1, *E* - 2, *B* - 3...; if v voters vote *B* - 1, *D* - 2, *E* - 3... or *B* - 1, *E* - 2, *D* - 3...; if w voters vote *E* - 1, *B* - 2, *D* - 3... or *E* - 1, *D* - 2, *B* - 3...; and if $u + v + w \geq 1$ quota, then the triplet *B-D-E* is said to gain 1 quota.

TABLE 2.A	Quota Borda System - Ballot Paper for the 6-seater Constituency of ...

Place a '1' opposite your 1st preference;
you may also place a '2' opposite your 2nd preference,
a '3' opposite your 3rd preference,
a '4' opposite your 4th preference,
a '5' opposite your 5th preference,
and a '6' opposite your 6th preference.

Candidate	Party	Preference
O	*X*	
K	*W*	
S	*Z*	
-	*Y*	
J	*W*	
U	-	
L	*W*	
N	*X*	

The quota Borda system is a two-part electoral system, in which candidates may get elected, on the basis of either a quota of $1^{st}/2^{nd}/3^{rd}$ preferences and/or a high points total.

For the calculations of the quota, a 1st preference is always a 1st preference, regardless of how many other candidates you give other preferences for.

The points, however, may vary as follows:

If you vote for:	1 candidate	2 candidates	3 candidates	4 candidates	5 candidates	6 candidates
your 1st preference gets	1 pt	2 pts	3 pts	4 pts	5 pts	6 pts
your 2nd preference gets		1 pt	2 pts	3 pts	4 pts	5 pts
your 3rd preference gets			1 pt	2 pts	3 pts	4 pts
your 4th preference gets				1 pt	2 pts	3 pts
your 5th preference gets					1 pt	2 pts
your 6th preference gets						1 pt

The Ballot Paper

If, as we decided, society consists of Messrs. *j, k, l ... u*, with Messrs. *j - m* in party *W*, *n - p* in *X*, etc., then in a multi-member constituency of 6 representatives:

> party *W* can expect to win 2 or at best 3 seats,
> party *X* can expect to win 1 or at best 2 seats,
> party *Y* can expect to win 1 seat at best,
> party *Z* can expect to win 1 seat at best, and
> the independent candidate *U* can also expect to win 1 seat at best.

In our own example, then, let us assume that parties *W, X, Y* and *Z* are hoping to win 3, 2, 1 and 1 seats respectively, that Mr. *U* is also standing, and that party *Y* is standing in this particular constituency as an "un-candidated party". The ballot paper, here presented in random (non-alphabetical) order, will look as shown in Table 2.A.

A Valid Vote

An example of a valid full vote is shown in Table 2.B, but even if the voter lists 8 preferences, as in Table 2.C, it will still count as a valid full vote as per Table 2.B.

TABLE 2.B			TABLE 2.C
A QBS VOTE (FOR EXAMPLE OF MS. *j*, A *W* PARTY SUPPORTER)			
Candidate	Party	Preferences	Preferences
O	*X*		7
K	*W*	2	2
S	*Z*	6	6
-	*Y*	4	4
J	*W*	1	1
U	-	5	5
L	*W*	3	3
N	*X*		8

The Invalid Vote

Before we move on, we will again pause to consider the invalid vote. In Table 2.D overleaf, the 1st preference intentions of the voter are unclear, so the entire vote must be declared invalid.

The 1st/2nd/3rd preferences in Table 2.E, however, are clear enough, so this would be a valid partial vote, as shown in Table 2.F.

TABLE 2.D			TABLE 2.E	TABLE 2.F
\multicolumn{5}{c}{Examples of Valid and Invalid QBS Votes}				
Candidate	Party	Preferences	Preferences	Preferences
O	X			
K	W	2	2	2
S	Z	6	6	
-	Y	4	4	
J	W	1	1	1
U	-	5	4	
L	W	1	3	3
N	X			

The Count

It must be emphasised that regardless of how many valid preferences a voter casts, a 1st preference is always a 1st preference. It is only the MBC score which varies according to how many preferences the voter exercises.

The first task for the tellers is to:

a) count V, the valid vote, and calculate the quota by dividing this number, V, by the number of seats + 1, i.e., 7 in our example, and then taking the next highest integer. 12 divided by 7 is 1.7 so the quota is 2.[8]

b) count up all the 1st preferences for each candidate, and

c) count all the MBC scores for each candidate.

The count then falls into two Parts and up to seven stages. If, at any stage, all the seats have been filled, the count is terminated and the results declared. Stages i) and v), vi) and vii) apply to all QBS elections which must, of course, elect at least 2 persons. Stages i), ii), v), vi) and vii) relate to all QBS elections in constituencies of 3 or 4 seats. While all stages are relevant in QBS elections in constituencies of 5 or more seats.

Part I of the count proceeds as follows.

Stage

i) all candidates gaining the quota of 1st preferences are elected;

ii) all pairs of candidates gaining 2 quotas of 1st/2nd preferences get both candidates elected;

---

8 This particular formula is known as the Droop quota. It is also used in PR-STV elections.

iii) all triplets of candidates gaining 3 quotas of 1st/2nd/3rd preferences[9] get all 3 candidates elected;

iv) all triplets of candidates gaining 2 quotas of 1st/2nd/3rd preferences get 2 candidates elected, the 2 seats going to the 2 candidates of the triplet with the highest MBC scores.

In Part II of the count, any candidates elected during Part I are no longer taken into consideration.

v) all pairs of candidates gaining 1 quota of 1st/2nd preferences gain 1 seat, which goes to the candidate of the pair with the higher MBC score;

vi) all triplets of candidates gaining 1 quota of 1st/2nd/3rd preferences gain 1 seat, which goes to the candidate of the triplet with the highest MBC score;

vii) any remaining seats are awarded to those candidates with the highest MBC scores.

By a similar logic, you might suppose that a quadruplet of candidates gaining 4 quotas should get 4 candidates elected; that a quintuplet gaining 5 quotas should get 5 elected; and that a sextet gaining 6 quotas should get 6 elected candidates. The last scenario, however, would represent a one-party state, which is hardly a democratic ideal for a plural society. To suggest a limit of a triplet and 3 quotas for a 5+seater constituency (with a limit of a pair and 2 quotas for a 3/4-seater), therefore, and to insist that the candidates' MBC scores must be the criterion for any further electoral success is wise, not only for so-called stable democracies, but especially for countries such as Rwanda. Indeed, there are those in Kigali who have already suggested that no one party should ever have more than 50% of the seats in parliament.[10]

A 2% Top-up

In a regional/national top-up, the MBC scores for all parties, based on the voters' first 3 'party-preferences' (see p 40), are calculated. If, then, a particular party gains, say, more than 2% but less than 4% of the regional/national MBC total, but does not yet have representation in the parliament, then that party shall be awarded one top-up seat. The seat will be awarded to the candidate of that party who gains the highest MBC score in terms of a percentage of the MBC total in his/her constituency. Similarly, if any party gains more than 4% of the regional/national MBC total but less than 6%, and yet has only 1 elected candidate or maybe none at all at the constituency level, that party shall be awarded 1 or 2 top-up seats respectively. And so on.

---

9 See also footnote 7a on p 41. If, to take a second example, a quota (or more) of voters votes '*B*-1, *C*-2, *E*-3' or '*B*-1, *E*-2, *C*-3' or '*C*-1, *B*-2, *E*-3' or '*C*-1, *E*-2, *B*-3' or '*E*-1, *B*-2, *C*-3' or '*E*-1, *C*-2, *B*-3', then the *B*-*C*-*E* triplet is said to have one (or more) quotas.

10 Report on a visit to Rwanda, Emerson, March 2003, is available on www.deborda.org which is the de Borda Institute website.

Precursor I - A Hypothetical Case, a Voters' Profile with Partial Ballots

In our first precursor, just to show how the count works, we have 12 voters and, to keep it simple, just ten candidates standing for 6 seats; in this instance, I have omitted Ms. *J* and Mr. *S*. As might be expected, Messrs. *j, k, l* and *m* give their first 3 preferences to their party candidates: *K, L* and *M*.

So Ms. *j* votes: '*K*-1, *L*-2, *M*-3',
and Mr. *k* votes: '*L*-1, *K*-2, *M*-3',
while Mr. *q* votes: '*Q*-1, *R*-2'.

The voters' profile is shown in Table 2.H. Apart from Mr. *u*, every voter submits a partial vote. So, with the quota of 1st preferences equal to 2, the count proceeds as in Table 2.G. In the light-tinted Part II, stages v) to vii), remember, candidates who have already been elected in Part I, stages i) to iv), are no longer taken into account.

STAGE	TABLE 2.G – A QBS COUNT, PRECURSOR I	ELECTED
i)	Mr. *L* gains the quota of two 1st preferences, and so does Ms. *T*, (both shown in bold reverse), but *L* comes first because *L* has more 2nd preferences.	*L* and *T*
ii)	There are no pairs of candidates gaining 2 quotas.[11]	-
iii)	And there are no triplets with 3 quotas.	-
iv)	There is, however, a triplet with 2 quotas: candidates *K, L* and *M* are just such a trio, gaining as they do the 1st/2nd/3rd preferences of four voters: Messrs. *j, k, l* and *m*, (shown in tint). *L* is already elected, and *M* has a higher MBC score than *K*, so this seat goes to *M*.	*L, T* and *M*
v)	A pair of unelected candidates, *Q* and *R*, (shown in diagonal stripes) has one quota, so this seat goes to Mr. *Q* because of his higher MBC score.	*L, T, M* and *Q*
vi)	A triplet of unelected candidates also has a quota - Messrs. *N, O* and *P* (vertically striped) - so this seat goes to the highest MBC score of the three, namely, Ms. *P*.	*L, T, M, Q* and *P*
vii)	There is one seat still to fill, so we take the unelected candidate with the highest MBC score, and it is Ms. *N*.	*L, T, M, Q, P* and *N*

The result, then, is the election of Messrs. *L, T, M, Q, P* and *N*, which means that parties *W, X, Y* and *Z* have 2, 2, 1 and 1 person(s) elected... which is fair.

---

11 The *K-L* pair of candidates - and we are now looking at the number of voters who have voted either '*K*-1, *L*-2' or '*L*-1, *K*-2' - get two 1st preferences, i.e., one quota, (as indicated in small cross-hatch), from Messrs *j* and *k*, and the *L-M* pair get two 1st prefs as well (in large cross-hatch). So too does *Q-R*, as we see in stage v). But, as stated, no pair gets 2 quotas.

TABLE 2.H — **PRECURSOR I - A HYPOTHETICAL CASE. A VOTERS' PROFILE WITH PARTIAL BALLOTS**

of party:	The Electorate:	K	L	M	N	O	P	Q	R	T	U	Total number of points exercised:
		of party W			of party X			of party Y		of Z	Ind.	
W	j	1 / 3	2 / 2	3 / 1								6
	k	2 / 2	1 / 3	3 / 1								6
	l	3 / 1	2 / 2	1 / 3								6
	m	3 / 1	1 / 3	2 / 2								6
X	n				1 / 3	2 / 2	3 / 1					6
	o				3 / 1	1 / 3	2 / 2					6
	p				2 / 2	3 / 1	1 / 3					6
Y	q							1 / 2	2 / 1			3
	r							2 / 1	1 / 2			3
Z	s									1 / 1		1
	t									1 / 1		1
Ind.	u	6 / 1		5 / 2	4 / 3		3 / 4	2 / 5		1 / 6		21
MBC score		8	10	9	9	6	10	8	3	2	6	71
singles 1st prefs		1	**2**	1	1	1	1	1	1	**2**	1	} QUOTAS
pairs 1st prefs*		1 quota	1 quota					one quota 2				
triplets 1st prefs		**two quotas 4**			**one quota 3**							

* The 2 pairs in hatch fail to qualify for stage ii) of the count; the **Q-R** pair qualifies in stage v).

TABLE 2.I		PRECURSOR II - A HYPOTHETICAL CASE ANOTHER VOTERS' PROFILE WITH PARTIAL BALLOTS										
of party:	The Electorate:	preferences / points	preferences / points	preferences / points	preferences / points	preferences / points	preferences / points	preferences / points	preferences / points	preferences / points	preferences / points	Total number of points exercised:
		THE CANDIDATES										
		K	L	M	N	O	P	Q	R	T	U	
		of party W			of party X			of party Y		of Z	Ind.	
W	j	1 / 3	2 / 2	3 / 1								6
	k	2 / 2	1 / 3	3 / 1								6
	l	1 / 3	2 / 2	3 / 1								6
	m	1 / 3	3 / 1	2 / 2								6
X	n				1 / 2	2 / 1						3
	o				1 / 2	2 / 1						3
	p				1 / 2	2 / 1						3
Y	q	3 / 1	2 / 2	1 / 3								6
	r	3 / 1	2 / 2	1 / 3								6
Z	s				2 / 2	1 / 3				3 / 1		6
	t									1 / 2	2 / 1	3
Ind.	u						4 / 1	3 / 2		2 / 3	1 / 4	10
MBC score		13	12	11	8	6	0	1	2	5	6	64
singles 1st prefs		**3**	1	**2**	**3**	1	0	0	0	1	1	QUOTAS
pairs 1st prefs*		1½ quotas / 1 quota		two quotas / 4						one quota / 2		
triplets 1st prefs		three quotas / 6										

* Both of the pairs shown in hatch fail to qualify for stage ii) of the count.

Precursor II - A Hypothetical Case, Another Voters' Profile with Partial Ballots

In our second presursor, the parties have formed into blocs: parties *W* and *Y* on the one hand, *X* and *Z* on the other, but Mr. *u* is still acting independently. The voters' profile is shown opposite in Table 2.I. Every voter submits a partial vote, and the quota of 1st preferences is still 2. The count proceeds as follows:

STAGE	TABLE 2.J – A QBS COUNT, PRECURSOR II	ELECTED
i)	*K*, *N* and *M* all have a quota of two or more 1st preferences, (in bold reverse). Messrs. *K* and *N* both have three 1st preference votes, and they both have one 2nd preference vote, but *K* comes out on top with two 3rd preferences. So the exact order of election is *K N M*.	*K, N* & *M*
ii)	There is one pair of candidates with 2 quotas, i.e., four 1st preferences, (shown in two separate boxes of vertical stripes) for *N* and *O* have the 1st/2nd preferences of four voters: Messrs *n, o, p* and *s*. *N* has already been elected, so the second seat goes to *O*.[12]	*K, N, M* and *O*
iii)	One triplet has 3 quotas, i.e., six 1st preferences, (shown in two boxes of tint): candidates *K, L* and *M* have the 1st/2nd/3rd preferences of six voters - Messrs. *j, k, l, m, q* and *r*. *K* and *M* have already been elected, so this third seat goes to *L*.	*K, N, M, O* and *L*
iv)	-	
v)	From here onwards, none of the candidates who have been elected so far is taken into account. There is one pair of candidates, *T* and *U*, (diagonal stripes), who share one quota of voters, Messrs. *t* and *u*, so they get one seat which goes to the candidate with the higher MBC score, Mr. *U*.	*K, N, M, O, L* and *U*
vi) - vii)	-	-

The Result

The result in this instance is the election of messrs *K, N, M, O, L* and *U*. So, party *W* gets 3 elected members, *X* gets 2, and the last member is Mr. *U*. This would suggest that if parties *Y* and *Z* are going to let themselves be absorbed into blocs, they would be well advised to come to some sort of arrangement by which members of the larger party commit themselves to spread their 1st preferences, not just among Messrs *K, L* and *M*, as seen here, but rather, let us say, among *K, L* and *Q*.

---

12 The *K-L* pair, (in small cross-hatch), has '*K*-1, *L*-2' or '*L*-1, *K*-2' votes from 3 persons - Messrs *j, k* and *l* - but that, of course, is only 1½ quotas. And the *L-M* pair, (in large cross-hatch), has just 1 quota.

TABLE 2.K — EXAMPLE 2A - ELECTING A PARLIAMENT
THE FIRST VOTERS' PROFILE - PARTIAL BALLOTS

The Electorate: of party:		J (prefs/points)	K (prefs/points)	L (prefs/points)	N (prefs/points)	O (prefs/points)	Q (prefs/points)	S (prefs/points)	U (prefs/points)	Total points exercised
		of party W			of party X		of Y	of Z	Ind.	
W	j	2 / 4	1 / 5	3 / 3			4 / 2		5 / 1	15
	k	2 / 4	1 / 5	3 / 3			4 / 2		5 / 1	15
	l	3 / 2	2 / 3	1 / 4			4 / 1			10
	m	3 / 1	1 / 3	2 / 2						6
X	n				1 / 4	2 / 3		3 / 2	4 / 1	10
	o				2 / 3	1 / 4		3 / 2	4 / 1	10
	p				2 / 2	1 / 3		3 / 1		6
Y	q	3 / 3	2 / 4	4 / 2			1 / 5		5 / 1	15
	r	4 / 1	2 / 3	3 / 2			1 / 4			10
Z	s				3 / 2	2 / 3		1 / 4	4 / 1	10
	t				3 / 1	2 / 2		1 / 3		6
Ind.	u		5 / 2		4 / 3	6 / 1	3 / 4	2 / 5	1 / 6	21
MBC score		15	25	16	15	16	18	17	12	134
singles 1ˢᵗ prefs		0	3	1	1	2	2	2	1	
pairs 1ˢᵗ prefs*		1 quota			1½ quotas			quota		QUOTAS
			1 quota			1		quota		
				1			quota			
triplets 1ˢᵗ prefs		two quotas 4			two... 3 +			quotas 2		

* With less than 2 quotas each, these five pairs in hatch or stripes fail to qualify for stage ii).

Example 2A - Electing a Parliament, the First Voters' Profile - Partial Ballots

Let us now consider three rather more realistic examples in which a society of *j* to *u*, in one 6-seater constituency, elects 6 representatives to a parliament. As noted earlier, given party strengths and potential alliances, the parties can be expected to nominate only a limited number of candidates; let us say, they choose as follows:

W - *J*, *K* and *L*;   *X* - *N* and *O*;
Y - *Q*;   *Z* - *S*;   and the independent Mr. *U*.

That is a total of 7 party candidates, no un-candidated parties[13] and 1 independent - 8 candidates altogether. In this profile, most voters submit a partial list of preferences. Ms. *j* votes '*K* - 1, *J* - 2, *L* - 3, *Q* - 4, *U* - 5'; Ms. *n* votes '*N*- 1, *O* - 2, *S* - 3, *U* - 4'; and only Mr. *u* casts all six preferences. Please note that, while the ballot may be displayed in random order, the candidates here are listed alphabetically and therefore by parties. The valid vote is 12; the number of seats to be elected is 6; so the quota, (the integer greater than 12 divided by 7), is again 2.

STAGE	TABLE 2.L – A QBS COUNT, EXAMPLE 2A	ELECTED
i)	Four candidates each gain 1 quota (bold reverse) of 2 or more 1st preferences. So *K, O, S,* and *Q* are elected, their order of election determined by the number of 2nd preferences each receives.	*K, O, S* and *Q*
ii) - iii)	-	-
iv)	There are two triplets with two quotas, i.e., 4 or more 1st preferences. The *O-S-N* trio share the 1st/2nd/3rd preferences (in diagonal stripes) of five voters: Messrs. *n, o, p, s* and *t*. While candidates *J, K* and *L* are supported by four voters: Messrs. *j, k, l* and *m,* (in tint). The triplet *O-S-N* already has two candidates elected, *O* and *S,* so no change. But the *J-K-L* trio has only one elected member, *K,* so the second seat goes to *L* (who has the higher MBC score of 16 compared to *J*'s 15).	*K, O, S, Q* and *L*
v) - vi)	-	-
vii)	The next to be elected is either Ms. *J* or Ms. *N,* for both have an MBC score of 15, but because Ms. *N* has a 1st preference, the latter is elected.	*K, O, S, Q, L* and *N.*

The result is the election of Messrs. *K, O, S, Q, L* and *N,* which again means party *W* wins 2 seats, party *X* wins 2 seats, party *Y* wins 1 seat, and party *Z* wins 1 seat, so the outcome is reasonably proportional.

---

13 In real life, there will be very few 'un-candidated parties' which actually win a constituency seat. Obviously, if a party thinks it is in with a chance, it will find and field a candidate. And in those counts where an 'un-candidated party' does win a constituency seat and then forfeits it because it is 'un-candidated', all is not lost; it will doubtless gain a seat in the top-up stage.

| TABLE 2.M | \multicolumn{9}{c}{EXAMPLE 2B - ELECTING A PARLIAMENT
THE SECOND VOTERS' PROFILE - FULL BALLOTS} |

The Electorate: of party:		J	K	L	N	O	Q	S	U	Total number of points exercised:
		\multicolumn{3}{c	}{of party W}	\multicolumn{2}{c	}{of party X}	of Y	of Z	Ind.	
W	j	1 / 6	3 / 4	2 / 5			4 / 3	6 / 1	5 / 2	21
	k	2 / 5	3 / 4	1 / 6	6 / 1		4 / 3		5 / 2	21
	l	3 / 4	2 / 5	1 / 6			5 / 2	6 / 1	4 / 3	21
	m	2 / 5	3 / 4	1 / 6			5 / 2	6 / 1	4 / 3	21
X	n		6 / 1		1 / 6	2 / 5	5 / 2	3 / 4	4 / 3	21
	o		6 / 1		2 / 5	1 / 6	5 / 2	3 / 4	4 / 3	21
	p	6 / 1			2 / 5	1 / 6	5 / 2	3 / 4	4 / 3	21
Y	q	3 / 4	4 / 3	2 / 5			1 / 6	6 / 1	5 / 2	21
	r	5 / 2	4 / 3	2 / 5			1 / 6	6 / 1	3 / 4	21
Z	s		6 / 1		3 / 4	2 / 5	5 / 2	1 / 6	4 / 3	21
	t		6 / 1		3 / 4	2 / 5	4 / 3	1 / 6	5 / 2	21
Ind.	u	6 / 1	5 / 2		4 / 3		3 / 4	2 / 5	1 / 6	21
\multicolumn{2}{|l|}{MBC score}	28	29	33	28	27	37	34	36	252
\multicolumn{2}{|l|}{singles 1st prefs}	1	0	**3**	1	**2**	**2**	**2**	1	QUOTAS
\multicolumn{2}{	l	}{pairs 1st prefs*}	\multicolumn{2}{c	}{1½}	\multicolumn{2}{c	}{quotas 1}	\multicolumn{2}{c	}{1 / 1½ quotas}	\multicolumn{2}{c	}{quota / quota}	
\multicolumn{2}{	l	}{triplets 1st prefs}	\multicolumn{3}{c	}{**two quotas 4**}	\multicolumn{3}{c	}{two ... 3 +}	\multicolumn{2}{c	}{**quotas 2**}	

* With less than 2 quotas each, the four pairs shown in hatch or stripes fail to qualify for stage ii) of the count.

Example 2B - Electing a Parliament, the Second Voters' Profile - Full Ballots

Taking a slightly different scenario, with voters now submitting full votes, Ms. *j*, might well vote '*J* - 1, *L* - 2, *K* - 3, *Q* - 4, *U* - 5, *S* -6'. Ms. *n*, on the other hand, might vote '*N* - 1, *O* - 2, *S* - 3, *U* - 4, *Q* - 5, *L* - 6'. And so on.

STAGE	TABLE 2.N — A QBS COUNT, EXAMPLE 2B	ELECTED
i)	Candidates *L, O, S* and *Q* all gain the necessary quota of two 1st preferences, (bold reverse) and they are placed in this order because, where they tie on 1st preferences {as do *O, S* and *Q*} we consider the number of 2nd preferences {*O* gets 3, *S* 1 and *Q* 0}.	*L, O, S* and *Q*
ii) - iii)	- [14]	-
iv)	There are two triplets with 2 quotas. Five voters - Messrs. *n, o, p, s* and *t* (in diagonal stripes) - give their $1^{st}/2^{nd}/3^{rd}$ preferences to candidates *N, O* and *S*, so this triplet gains 2 quotas. And four voters - Messrs. *j, k, l* and *m* (in tint) - give their $1^{st}/2^{nd}/3^{rd}$ preferences to candidates *J, K,* and *L*, so this triplet of candidates also gains 2 quotas. The first *N-O-S* triplet already has 2 elected members - *O* and *S* - so no change here. The second *J-K-L* triplet - already has one elected candidate - *L* - so this second seat goes to either *J* or *K*, and therefore it goes to *K*, for he has the higher MBC score of 29.	*L, O, S, Q* and *K*
v) - vi)	-	-
vii)	The last seat goes to Mr. *U*, with an MBC score of 36.	*L, O, S, Q, K* and *U*.

The Result

The result is therefore the election of Messrs. *L, O, S, Q, K* and *U*, which means:

    party *W* wins 2 seats,   party *X* wins 1 seat,
    party *Y* wins 1 seat   party *Z* wins 1 seat
    and Mr. *U* also wins 1 seat.

which, again, is fair.

---

14 The *J-L* pair (tint and hatch) has the $1^{st}/2^{nd}$ preferences of only 3 voters, i.e., $1^{1}/_{2}$ quotas, from Messrs. *j, k* and *m.* So too, the *N-O* pair of candidates (diagonal stripes) has the $1^{st}/2^{nd}$ preferences of *n, o* and *p*. In like manner, the *L-Q* pair (vertical stripes) has just 1 quota from Messrs. *q* and *r*, while the *O-S* pair (also diagonal) has similar support from Messrs. *s* and *t*.

TABLE 2.P	EXAMPLE 2C - ELECTING A PARLIAMENT THE THIRD VOTERS' PROFILE - FULL BALLOTS									
of party:	The Electorate:	preferences / points	preferences / points	preferences / points	preferences / points	preferences / points	preferences / points	preferences / points	preferences / points	Total number of points exercised:
		\multicolumn{8}{c	}{THE CANDIDATES}	
		J	**K**	**L**	**N**	**O**	**Q**	**S**	**U**	
		\multicolumn{3}{c	}{of party W}	\multicolumn{2}{c	}{of party X}	of Y	of Z	Ind.	
W	j	3 / 4	1 / 6	5 / 2			2 / 5	6 / 1	4 / 3	21
W	k	3 / 4	1 / 6	5 / 2			2 / 5	6 / 1	4 / 3	21
W	l	3 / 4	1 / 6	5 / 2			2 / 5	6 / 1	4 / 3	21
W	m	3 / 4	1 / 6	5 / 2			2 / 5	6 / 1	4 / 3	21
X	n			6 / 1	3 / 4	1 / 6	5 / 2	2 / 5	4 / 3	21
X	o			6 / 1	3 / 4	1 / 6	5 / 2	2 / 5	4 / 3	21
X	p			6 / 1	3 / 4	1 / 6	5 / 2	2 / 5	4 / 3	21
Y	q	3 / 4	1 / 6	5 / 2			2 / 5	6 / 1	4 / 3	21
Y	r	3 / 4	1 / 6	5 / 2			2 / 5	6 / 1	4 / 3	21
Z	s			6 / 1	3 / 4	1 / 6	5 / 2	2 / 5	4 / 3	21
Z	t			6 / 1	3 / 4	1 / 6	5 / 2	2 / 5	4 / 3	21
Ind.	u	3 / 4	1 / 6	5 / 2			2 / 5	6 / 1	4 / 3	21
\multicolumn{2}{|c|}{MBC score}	28	42	19	20	30	45	32	36	252
\multicolumn{2}{|c|}{singles 1st prefs}	0	**7**	0	0	**5**	0	0	0	QUOTAS
\multicolumn{2}{|c|}{pairs 1st prefs}		**7 +**			**5 +**	**0**	**0**		QUOTAS
\multicolumn{2}{|c|}{triplets 1st prefs}	**7 +**			**5 +**		**0**	**0**		QUOTAS

Example 2C - Electing a Parliament, the Third Voters' Profile - Full Ballots

Finally, we look at the situation which arises if parties *W* and *Y* along with Mr. *u* gang up against the *X* and *Z* bloc, that is, if the election turns into a divisive and polarised contest between two opposing factions. So all of the *W-Y-u* voters vote:

'*K* - 1, *Q* - 2, *J* - 3, *U* - 4, *L* - 5, *S* - 6'

while the *X-Z* group vote

'*O* - 1, *S* - 2, *N* - 3, *U* - 4, *Q* - 5, *L* - 6'

as in Table 2.P. In this scenario, everyone is voting for a full slate of 6 candidates in order to maximise their MBC scores.

STAGE	TABLE 2.Q – A QBS COUNT, EXAMPLE 2C	ELECTED
i)	In this instance, only two candidates gain a quota, *K* and *O*, (in black and grey bold reverse).	*K* and *O*
ii)	There are two pairs of candidates (in black and grey reverse) which both gain two quotas (i.e., at least four 1st preferences), with 7 + 0 and 5 + 0 totals of 1st preferences, respectively: *K* and *Q* is the first pair, (black reverse and dark tint) which is supported by seven voters: Messrs. *j, k, l, m, q, r* and *u*; *O* and *S* make up the second pair, (grey reverse and dark diagonal stripes) with the help of the other five: Messrs. *n, o, p, s* and *t*. So *Q* and *S* are elected.	*K, O, Q* and *S*
iii)	There is one triplet of candidates which has 3 quotas (in black reverse plus dark and light tint) - candidates *K, Q* and *J* are all supported by the seven: Messrs. *j, k, l, m, q, r* and *u*. So this means *J* is elected.	*K, O, Q, S* and *J*
iv)	There is one triplet with 2 quotas, (in grey reverse plus dark and light stripes) - candidates *O, S* and *N* are all supported by *n, o, p, s* and *t*. But *O* and *S* are already elected, so no change at this stage.	-
v) - vi)	-	-
vii)	Finally, Mr. *U*, with an MBC score of 36, is elected.	*K, O, Q, S, J* and *U*

The Result

The third result is the election of Messrs. *K, O, Q, S, J* and *U*, which also means:

        party *W* wins   2 seats,   party *X* wins   1 seat
        party *Y* wins   1 seat   party *Z* wins   1 seat
and   Mr. *U* also   wins   1 seat,

and yet again, the outcome is a fair one.

An Analysis

A review of the three examples - 2A, 2B and 2C - is shown in Table 2R.

TABLE 2.R		AN ANALYSIS OF QBS ELECTIONS				
		PARTY REPRESENTATIVES				
EXAMPLE	ELECTED	W	X	Y	Z	U
2A	*K, O, S, Q, L* and *N*	2	2	1	1	0
2B	*L, O, S, Q, K* and *U*	2	1	1	1	1
2C	*K, O, Q, S, J* and *U*	2	1	1	1	1

This suggests QBS is a fairly stable electoral system, but further experimentation will perhaps help to confirm this supposition.

A COMPARISON OF QBS WITH OTHER ELECTORAL SYSTEMS

To weigh up the relative merits of different electoral systems is rather more difficult than any comparison of various decision-making processes, (pp 29-31 and Appendix I, p 149 *et seq.*). This is because some electoral systems use single-member constituencies, whereas others use PR in multi-member constituencies, which therefore have more than one winner. The referred to comparisons, however, do apply to non-PR electoral systems.

In this instance, then, taking example 2B in one 6-seater constituency, (pp 52-3), it is appropriate to contrast just the different types of PR. Most PR-list systems consider only the 1st preferences cast, of which the scores are:

$L - 3, J - 1$ (so party *W* gets 4 votes)
$N - 1, O - 2$ (so party *X* gets 2 votes)
$Q - 2$ (so party *Y* gets 2 votes)
$S - 2$ (so party *Z* gets 2 votes)
and $U - 1$ (so Mr.   *U* gets 1 vote).

This means, according to nearly all the formulas used in PR-list elections – the divisors d'Hondt and Sainte Laguë along with the quotas Droop and Hare are the most common – the outcome in terms of seats would be:

$W = 2, X = 1, Y = 1, Z = 1$ and $U = 1$.

Under PR-STV, as the quota is 2, *L, O, Q* and *S* would all get elected, and *L*'s surplus of 1 would mean that *J* also gets elected. The final seat would go to *N* or *U*, so again, the overall result would be:

$W = 2, X = 2, Y = 1$ and $Z = 1$

or
$$W = 2, X = 1, Y = 1, Z = 1 \text{ and } U = 1.$$

So, on the face of it, QBS is at least as good as other forms of PR, and because it takes all the preferences cast into account, it is probably rather better.

Practical Guidelines

In real life, when electorates of thousands are electing their representatives, the count is, needless to say, a little more complicated. The obvious procedure is to divide all the votes cast into bunches as per their 1st preference candidates; next, to sub-divide each bunch into batches in line with their 2nd preferences; and then, to divide each batch into bundles according to their 3rd preferences.

Once this has been done - the totals of 1st preferences established, the single candidates and solid coalitions of pairs and triplets with one or more quotas identified, and the MBC scores calculated - the votes may be left in their bundles, batches and bunches, ready for any re-counts if required. Meanwhile, the computer can do the maths, the tellers can display the data on their computer screens, with pairs and triplets of candidates in suitably coloured rows, and the party hacks can check all this data on their lap-tops.

Example 2D - Electing a Sub-committee, the Voters' Profile, Partial Ballots

As was said on p. 34, QBS can also be used to elect a sub-committee, if, as will often be the case, it is necessary to guarantee proportionality. In this instance, the 12 MPs choose, from amongst 10 of their number, a sub-committee of six persons, and let us assume that they vote, as usual, with vested interest in mind.

For this we may copy Table 1.U from p. 36 into Table 2.T, and we can then do a QBS count on that voting profile, as follows.

STAGE	TABLE 2.S – A QBS COUNT, EXAMPLE 2D	ELECTED
i)	Candidates *M, N, S* and *Q* all gain a quota (shown in reverse), and are therefore elected.	*M, N, S* and *Q*
ii) - iii)	-	-
iv)	The (tinted) triplet *of K-L-M* gains the $1^{st}/2^{nd}/3^{rd}$ preferences of four voters - Messrs. *J, K, L* and *M* - and therefore gains 2 quotas. Ms. *L* has a higher score than Mr. *K*, so *L* is elected.	*M, N, S, Q* and *L*
v) - vi)	-	-
vii)	Finally, Mr. *O* picks up the sixth seat.	*M, N, S, Q, L* and *O*

The Result

The result of this last QBS election - Messrs. *M, N, S, Q, L* and *O*, with parties *W, X, Y* and *Z* gaining 2, 2, 1 and 1 seat(s) respectively, is about the same as the result of the MBC election we did on p 35, when the order of election was *M, S, L, N, O* and *Q*.

Conclusion

The author has tried to promote this voting mechanism in a number of settings, and while he received a fair hearing in Bosnia from the National Working Group, he has had little response in his own Northern Ireland where the best that can be hoped for is a top-up version of PR-STV.[15]

Admittedly, PR-STV *allows* the voter to cross the sectarian divide. A QBS election goes one further: it actually *encourages* the voter so to act. Both PR-STV and QBS use the same voting procedure in that the voters vote 1, 2, 3... according to their preferences, so in both types of election, the voter may vote for both Catholic and Protestant candidates. The main difference between the two systems is in how the counts treat these votes. In PR-STV, the vote may well be transferred, literally, from one candidate

---

15 The author first drew up a Green Party document on such a proposal in 1996, and re-visited this idea as part of the GP 2004 Review of the Belfast Agreement.

A PLURALIST PARLIAMENT - THE QUOTA BORDA SYSTEM 59

TABLE 1.U and 2.T

EXAMPLE 2D - ELECTING A SUB-COMMITTEE THE VOTERS' PROFILE, PARTIAL BALLOTS

of party:	The Electorate, Members of parliament:	K (prefs/points)	L (prefs/points)	M (prefs/points)	N (prefs/points)	O (prefs/points)	Q (prefs/points)	R (prefs/points)	S (prefs/points)	T (prefs/points)	U (prefs/points)	Total points exercised
		K	**L**	**M**	**N**	**O**	**Q**	**R**	**S**	**T**	**U**	
		of party *W*			of party *X*		of party *Y*		of party *Z*		Ind.	
W	J	3 / 4	2 / 5	1 / 6			4 / 3	5 / 2			6 / 1	21
	K	3 / 4	2 / 5	1 / 6			4 / 3	5 / 2			6 / 1	21
	L	3 / 2	2 / 3	1 / 4							4 / 1	10
	M	2 / 5	3 / 4	1 / 6			6 / 1		4 / 3		5 / 2	21
X	N				1 / 6	2 / 5	6 / 1		4 / 3	3 / 4	5 / 2	21
	O				1 / 6	2 / 5	6 / 1		3 / 4	5 / 2	4 / 3	21
	P				1 / 4	2 / 3			4 / 1	3 / 2		10
Y	Q	5 / 2	4 / 3	3 / 4			1 / 6	2 / 5			6 / 1	21
	R	4 / 2	3 / 3				1 / 5	2 / 4			5 / 1	15
Z	S				3 / 4	4 / 3		5 / 2	1 / 6	2 / 5	6 / 1	21
	T				3 / 3	4 / 2			1 / 5	2 / 4	5 / 1	15
Ind.	U			5 / 2		4 / 3		3 / 4	2 / 5	6 / 1	1 / 6	21
MBC score		19	23	28	23	21	20	19	27	18	20	218
singles 1st prefs		0	0	**4**	**3**	0	**2**	0	**2**	0	1	
pairs 1st prefs*		1½ quotas				1 quota						QUOTAS
					1½ quota				1 quota			
triplets 1st prefs		**two quotas 4**										

* With less than 2 quotas each, the four pairs in hatch or stripes fail to qualify for stage ii).

to another. In QBS, however, there are no transfers, and all points cast for each candidate go to those candidates' individual MBC scores. In PR-STV, then, while the voter may vote for both a Catholic *and* a Protestant, it can happen that, in the count, the vote is awarded to a Catholic *or* a Protestant. In QBS, in contrast, if the voter votes for both candidates, then, in the count, both will benefit.[16]

The other electoral system which is worthy of note in this regard is the Lebanese system[17] where the voting procedure caters for, if not indeed encourages, cross-confessional voting profiles. Its main disadvantage lies in the fact that, in order for the system to work, candidates have to be 'designated' according to their religious background, so in this regard, it is not unlike the consociational decision-making procedures in the Belfast Agreement.

To the best of my knowledge, the only other system which enables the voter to cross the party if not the sectarian divide is the particular type of PR-open-list system which is used in Luxembourg and Switzerland. Here, as can happen in QBS, the voter is entitled to vote for as many candidates as there are seats to be filled, but this form of list system does not necessarily encourage the voter to vote across the political divide. On balance, therefore, the system most suited for a plural and integrated society, and certainly for any post-conflict society engaged in a peace process, is a top-up version of QBS.

A Consensual Society

In society at large, and certainly in any smaller organisations, it might be easier to allow the entire citizenry or membership - or at least those who have not already served, say, two terms - to be candidates. Those with political ambition will doubtless campaign, but the electoral system should allow society, if it so wishes, to choose the more modest; hopefully, if elected, the modest will agree to serve; and all concerned may then commend them for so doing (p 35).

---

16 For a full analysis of the PR-STV procedure, see Emerson (1998).

17 The Lebanese electoral system consists of so many FPP elections. If, in one constituency, the population ratio of Druze:Maronite:Shia:Sunni is 1:1:2:1, then in any general election, that constituency will hold five simultaneous FPP votes, and in effect, every voter will vote five times. Accordingly, if party *W* wishes to stand, it must find five candidates with the same ratio of religious backgrounds, all to stand on the one *W* ticket. Khazen (1998).

If this system were used in Northern Ireland, then someone like Mr. Paisley of the DUP would first have to find a like-minded Catholic to stand as his running-mate!

Chapter 3

Electing a Power-sharing Executive
The Matrix Vote

PURPOSE

Having decided on the size of cabinet (Chapter 1), and having elected a truly representative parliament (Chapter 2), it is now time for that parliament to elect its executive. In such an election, members may choose an entire cabinet: a prime minister, a minister of finance, another of foreign affairs, and so on.

Even at a humble level, where local committees consist of a chairperson, a secretary and a treasurer, etc., a wide variety of talents and skills is involved. In other words, those elected will be of a different status to each other. Accordingly, we move from a linear to a tabular ballot paper. And our task is to construct a proportional and preferential voting mechanism by which a larger number of people can elect a smaller number of persons, a team, each of whom is to perform a different function.

Principles

In theory, all members of parliament - all, that is, who have not already served, let us say, two terms in the executive - shall be eligible for election, regardless of whether they are members of a large or small political party, or for that matter independent members. Secondly, all MPs shall be able to vote on an equal basis, regardless of their party political affiliations. And thirdly, the voting procedure shall ensure that the choice for each individual MP is high and that, *ipso facto*, the degree of manipulation which any 'leader' may exercise shall be severely restricted.

If all participate on an equal basis in such a proportional electoral system, the outcome is bound to be a broad-based, 'all-party', power-sharing, coalition government of national unity, (to use an amalgam of all the expressions associated with this type of administration).

Many consider such a mixed executive to be a *sine qua non* of any post-conflict peace agreement, but it could also be argued that such is also a pre-requisite of any truly democratic government. After all, as noted in the Introduction (p 2), parliament should represent *all* the people; and in similar vein, the government should represent the *entire* parliament. Such is surely a minimum for any plural society... which describes just about everywhere these days.

The Matrix Vote

The matrix vote is based on a QBS count which in turn is based on an MBC. Thus the parties concerned will almost certainly decide to limit the number of candidates they ask to stand (pp 41 and 43); even then, party members and others may well choose to vote for MPs who have not been so nominated. In an un-whipped House, such freedom of choice will come to be the norm.

The Northern Ireland Assembly consists of 108 members. If we assume that two of them have already been elected to serve as First Minister and Deputy First Minister, then, in electing an executive of ten ministers, any one MLA may choose any one of 106 members as their 1st preference; any one of 105 members to be their 2nd preference; any one of 104 members to be their 3rd preference; and so on. In addition, each MLA may nominate his/her 1st preference to any one of ten ministries; their 2nd preference to any one of nine; their 3rd to any one of 8; and so on. This means that every MLA will have a choice of millions of different ways of voting.[1] It is called pluralism.

As implied earlier, (pp 18-9), within such a milieu of choice, it would be very difficult for any party whip (if such still existed) to impose that particularly undemocratic phenomenon known as "party discipline".

The Ballot Paper

Let us imagine our parliament of 12 persons - the same Messrs. *J* to *U* - has decided to elect an executive of six persons: a prime minister plus five ministers of *A, B, C, D* and *E*. In such a situation, the ballot paper could look like Table 3.A.

Secondly, we may assume that the parties nominate the following candidates for ministerial office:

W	3	*J, K* and *L*
X	2	*N* and *O*
Y	1	*Q*
Z	1	*S*
-	1	*U*

Thirdly, it is assumed that most people regard the post of PM as key, and that the *B, C* and *D* ministries are also considered to be very important.[2] Now party *W*, being the largest, will probably hope to get the post of PM, as well as, let's say, either the *C* or *D* ministries. Party *X* will probably not even bother with the premiership, but will try to get, let us say, the *A* and *D* ministries. While everybody else will aim to get their nominee elected to the post for which they think he/she is most suited.

---

1   The figures are in Appendix IV.

2   A Minister of Finance is usually regarded as being powerful, while the Minister of Sport, for example, is not normally seen as being so influential.

TABLE 3.A	A QBS MATRIX VOTE - BALLOT PAPER FOR THE ELECTION OF A 6-PERSON EXECUTIVE

Place the name of your 1st preference in the 1st column, opposite the ministerial post in which you wish him/her to serve;
you may also place the name of your 2nd preference in the 2nd column, opposite the ministerial post in which you wish him/her to serve;
you may also place the name of your 3rd preference in the 3rd column, opposite the ministerial post in which you wish him/her to serve; and so on.

Ministries	P R E F E R E N C E S					
	1st	2nd	3rd	4th	5th	6th
Prime Minister						
Minister of A						
Minister of B						
Minister of C						
Minister of D						
Minister of E						

The QBS Matrix Vote is an electoral system in which, firstly, candidates are elected on the basis of their popularity as measured in a QBS count; and secondly, successful candidates are appointed to that ministry to which, in the consensus of those voting as measured by the individual candidates' MBC sums, they are most suited.

For the calculations of the quota, a 1st preference is always a 1st preference, regardless of how many other candidates you vote for.

The points, however, may vary as follows:

If you vote for:	1 candidate	2 candidates	3 candidates	4 candidates	5 candidates	6 candidates
your 1st preference gets	1 pt	2 pts	3 pts	4 pts	5 pts	6 pts
your 2nd preference gets		1 pt	2 pts	3 pts	4 pts	5 pts
your 3rd preference gets			1 pt	2 pts	3 pts	4 pts
your 4th preference gets				1 pt	2 pts	3 pts
your 5th preference gets					1 pt	2 pts
your 6th preference gets						1 pt

Finally, let us assume that it is generally accepted that:

> Ms. *J* would make a good Minister of *C*;
> Ms. *N* has the talents for the Ministry of *D*;
> Mr. *Q* is a potential Minister of *B*; and
> Mr. *S* has the necessary for the Ministry of *E*.

Table 3B shows an example of a valid vote, where a *W* party member is voting. A full valid vote has one name in each column and one name in each row, with all six names referring to different candidates.

TABLE 3.B – THE MATRIX VOTE, A VALID VOTE

Ministries	\multicolumn{6}{c}{PREFERENCES}					
	1st	2nd	3rd	4th	5th	6th
Prime Minister	*J*					
Minister of *A*					*U*	
Minister of *B*				*Q*		
Minister of *C*		*K*				
Minister of *D*			*L*			
Minister of *E*						*S*

The Invalid Vote

As usual, we pause to discuss the invalid vote, i.e., the vote in which the voters' 1st preference intentions are unclear. Tables 3.C and 3.D show two examples. In 3.C, the

TABLE 3.C | **TABLE 3.D**

VALID/INVALID VOTES

	\multicolumn{6}{c}{PREFERENCES}					
	1st	2nd	3rd	4th	5th	6th
PM	*J*					
A					*U*	
B				*Q*		
C		*J*				
D			*L*			
E						*S*

	\multicolumn{6}{c}{PREFERENCES}					
	1st	2nd	3rd	4th	5th	6th
PM	*J*					
A					*U*	
B				*Q*		
C	*K*					
D			*L*			
E						*S*

voter has given Ms. *J* both a 1st and a 2nd preference; and in 3.D, there are 1st preferences for both *J* and *K*.

The Partial Vote

As before, the voter who so wishes may submit a partial vote, as, say, in Table 3.E. In like manner, any vote in which not the 1st but some later preference intentions are unclear, as in Table 3.F, can also be regarded as a valid partial vote - in this instance, as in table 3.E.

TABLE 3.E						TABLE 3.F					
PARTIAL VOTES											
	PREFERENCES						PREFERENCES				
	1st	2nd	3rd	4th	5th	6th		1st	2nd	3rd	4th	5th	6th
PM	J						PM	J					
A							A					U	
B							B			Q			
C		K					C		K				
D							D			L			
E							E						S

The Count

Initially, the tellers must:

a) count the valid vote and calculate the QBS quota.

Then they

b) count all the 1st preferences for each individual candidate,

c) count all the MBC sums for each candidate to each post,

d) count all the MBC scores for each candidate, and

e) count all the MBC totals for each ministerial post.

With that done, they next

f) conduct a QBS election, so as to identify the six most popular members;

and finally,

g) identify those ministerial posts in which each of the six elected members will serve.

Precursor - A Very Hypothetical Case

Imagine, for the sake of argument, a game which involves just three players - one goalkeeper, one back and one forward - and that a sports club has decided to choose their three-person team democratically. The players in the club, Messrs. *j* to *u*, are all eligible; Messrs *j, k, l* and *m* are all pretty good goalies, Messrs. *n, o, p* and *q* are excellent backs, and the rest, Messrs. *r, s, t* and *u*, are brilliant forwards.

The appropriate ballot paper will look like this:

TABLE 3.G	A MATRIX VOTE		
	1st preference	2nd preference	3rd preference
Goalie			
Back			
Forward			

Now obviously, each voter will want to choose a team which consists of one goalie, one back, and one forward. Granted, players can sometimes swop positions, but the best possible team will surely consist of the best in each position.

Accordingly, if I think *j* is the best goalie, *p* the best back, and *s* the best forward, and if I think that of these three, *p* is the most talented player, followed by *s* and *j*, then my preferences would be *p* 1st, *s* 2nd, and *j* 3rd. I would therefore vote as follows:

TABLE 3.H	MY PREFERENCES		
	1st	2nd	3rd
Goalie			*j*
Back	*p*		
Forward		*s*	

You might have a different opinion and vote:

TABLE 3.I	YOUR PREFERENCES		
	1st	2nd	3rd
Goalie		*m*	
Back			*p*
Forward	*s*		

And a third person may think that all the designated backs are not so good, and may therefore prefer to put one of the forwards in defence:

ELECTING A POWER-SHARING EXECUTIVE - THE MATRIX VOTE

TABLE 3.J	A THIRD PERSON'S PREFERENCES		
	1st	2nd	3rd
Goalie		j	
Back			s
Forward	t		

If we add these three votes together, we get the following:

TABLE 3.K	ALL OUR PREFERENCES		
	1st	2nd	3rd
Goalie		m, j	j
Back	p		p, s
Forward	s, t	s	

When we turn this round, with the players on top and the preferences in the body of the table, we get:

TABLE 3.L	ALL OUR PREFERENCES				
	j	m	p	s	t
Goalie	3, 2	2			
Back			1, 3	3	
Forward				2, 1	1

On turning these preferences into points - a 1st preference is 3 points, a 2nd preference is 2, and 3rd is 1 - we get the following totals:

TABLE 3.M	ALL OUR POINTS				
	j	m	p	s	t
Goalie	1+2=3	2			
Back			3+1=4	1	
Forward				2+3=5	3
TOTAL	3	2	4	6	3

That is it. In the consensus of admittedly only three voters, the final team should consist of the two with the most points, *s* and *p*, (dark tint), and either one or other of the two in third place, *j* or *t*, (light tint). Then, in order of popularity, we choose their positions of play by looking at the biggest sums (striped); so *s* who has 5 pts is the forward, and *p* with 4 is the back. There is a bit of a dispute about the third player, because both *j* and *t* are equally popular on 3 points. But the problem is quickly solved: we already have a forward and, in our tripartite consensus, *j* is the best goalie. So the final team is *s, p* and *j*. And *s* is the captain.

Example 3A - Electing an Executive, the First Voters' Profile - Full Ballots

As in Chapter 2, we will now consider an example in which every member of parliament - Messrs. *J* to *U* - votes in their order of preference for the six ministers whom each would like to be a member of the executive. In this first profile, members tend to follow the party line, with just a little variation on the laid down theme: they all vote for themselves first! So, Ms. *J* gives herself her 1st preference, for instance, but so too do Messrs. *K, L, N* and *O*, and only the likes of Mr. *M*, who is not a nominated candidate, are not egocentric.

We assume the four parties are still acting according to their vested interests, and that they nominate 8 candidates:

TABLE 3.N	–	MATRIX VOTE NOMINATIONS
Party *W* nominates Messrs. *J, K* and *L*,	and	Ms. *J* would be a good Min. of *C*
X nominates Messrs. *N* and *O*,	and	Ms. *N* would be a good Min. of *D*
Y nominates Mr. *Q*,	and	Mr. *Q* would be a good Min. of *B*
Z nominates Mr. *S*,	and	Mr. *S* would be a good Min. of *E*
and there is the one independent,		Mr. *U*.

In such a setting, Ms. *J* could well vote as in Table 3.P; her party colleague, Mr. *K* would probably differ but slightly, Table 3.Q; while Ms. *N*, from an opposing party, might vote as in Table 3.R.

TABLE 3.P	Ms *J*	PREFERENCES					
		1st	2nd	3rd	4th	5th	6th
A BALLOT FROM MS. *J*	PM		*L*				
	A			*K*			
	B				*Q*		
EXAMPLE 3A	*C*	*J*					
	D					*U*	
	E						*S*

Interestingly enough, however, because the very voting procedure encourages all to submit a full ballot - i.e., to cast preferences for a full slate of 6 candidates - and because the procedure suggests it is wise for each party to limit their number of nominees to a realistic level, everyone (in our example) who does submit a full ballot crosses the party divide. In real life, MPs might not be so consensual: it is possible, for example, for members to cast their lower preferences for some of their other party colleagues, even though they know those persons are unlikely to get elected. See Chapter 4.

| TABLE 3.Q | TABLE 3.R |

TWO MORE FULL VALID VOTES, EXAMPLE 3A

Mr K	PREFERENCES					
	1st	2nd	3rd	4th	5th	6th
PM	L					
A		K				
B			Q			
C		J				
D					U	
E						N

Ms N	PREFERENCES					
	1st	2nd	3rd	4th	5th	6th
PM	O					
A						K
B					Q	
C		N				
D				U		
E			S			

Let us hope common sense prevails; if it does not, only they will be the losers, for thus they will lose the opportunity to influence part of the outcome. The confidence remains, however, that even in plural societies like Northern Ireland and Bosnia, the system itself will encourage all concerned to vote across the party divides. Furthermore, this characteristic of the voting procedure is achieved without any resort to sectarian designations.

But back to our example. The full list of the ballots cast by all the MPs is shown in Annex A, (pp 82-3). First, let us add the three votes already cast, the votes of Messrs. *J, K* and *N,* as in Table 3.S. Three full votes were cast. So, needless to say, we now have 3 nominees in each column, and 3 in each row. Already, then, we have an idea about who may win, and who may become what.

TABLE 3.S

A TRIO OF VOTES

EXAMPLE 3A

	PREFERENCES					
	1st	2nd	3rd	4th	5th	6th
PM	L	L, O				
A			K, K			K
B				Q, Q	Q	
C	J, N	J				
D				U	U, U	
E			S			S, N

Now we can shuffle this around slightly, so that the candidates are on top, and the preferences cast are in the main body of the table in chronological order: Messrs. *J-K-N.*

TABLE 3.T			—		A Matrix Vote Count of Three Votes, Example 3A						
CANDIDATES AND THEIR PREFERENCES											
	J	K	L	M	N	O	P	Q	R	S	T	U
PM			2, 1			2						
A		3,3,6										
B								4,4,5				
C		1, 2			1							
D												5,5,4
E					6					6, 3		

When we do this with all the votes cast - (which, may I remind you, are in Annex A) - we get the voters' profile of preferences in light tint and sums in bold, as in Table 3.V opposite. The points per preference are not included, but *K*, for example, gets a 5th preference for PM, i.e., a sum of 2 pts. The next stage is to do a QBS election, based on a) the candidates' singletons/pairs/triplets of quotas of 1st/2nd/3rd preferences, and b) their MBC scores. The example given is the same as Example 2B shown in Table 2.M on p. 52, so the quota is still 2 and the calculations are the same as in Table 2.N on p. 53, which is therefore repeated here.

STAGE	TABLE 2.N and 3.U — A QBS Count, Example 2B/3A	ELECTED
i)	Candidates *L*, *O*, *S* and *Q* all gain the quota of two 1st preferences, (in bold reverse) and they are placed in this order because, where they tie on 1st preferences {as do *O*, *S* and *Q*} we consider the number of 2nd preferences {*O* gets 3, *S* 1 and *Q* 0}.	*L*, *O*, *S* and *Q*
ii) - iii)	-	-
iv)	There are two triplets with 2 quotas. Five voters - Messrs. *N*, *O*, *P*, *S* and *T* [in Annex A] - give their 1st/2nd/3rd preferences to candidates *O*, *S* and *N*, (horizontal stripes, Table 3.V opposite), so this triplet gains 2 quotas. And four voters - Messrs. *J*, *K*, *L* and *M* [Annex A] - give their 1st/2nd/3rd preferences to candidates *J*, *K*, and *L*, (vertical stripes), so this triplet of candidates also gains 2 quotas. The first *O-S-N* triplet already has 2 elected members - *O* and *S* - so no change here. The second *J-K-L* triplet has one elected candidate, *L*, so this second seat goes to either *J* or *K*, and therefore it goes to *K*, with the higher MBC score of 29.	*L*, *O*, *S*, *Q* and *K*
v) - vi)	-	-
vii)	The last seat goes to Mr. *U*, with an MBC score of 36.	*L*, *O*, *S*, *Q*, *K* and *U*.

* With less than 2 quotas each, the 4 pairs in hatch or diagonal stripes fail to qualify for stage ii).

TABLE 3.V — **EXAMPLE 3A - ELECTING AN EXECUTIVE, THE FIRST VOTERS' PROFILE - FULL BALLOTS**

THE CANDIDATES (WHO ARE ALSO THE VOTERS) - THE MEMBERS OF PARLIAMENT

Ministers		J	K	L	M	N	O	P	Q	R	S	T	U	MBC post totals
PM	Prefer-ences		5	2,1,1 1,2,2			2,1,1						4,5	
	Sums		2	33			17						5	57
Min. of **A**	Prefer-ences		3,3,2 3,6,4				2,2						4,4 5,1	
	Sums		21				10						14	45
Min. of **B**	Prefer-ences								4,4,5,5,5 5,1,1,5,4,3					
	Sums								37					37
Min. of **C**	Prefer-ences	1,2,3,2 6,3,5,6	6,6,6			1								
	Sums	28	3			6								37
Min. of **D**	Prefer-ences		4			2,2,3, 3,4							5,5,4 4,4,3	
	Sums		3			21							17	41
Min. of **E**	Prefer-ences					6					6,6,6,3,3,3 6,6,1,1,2			
	Sums					1					34			35
MBC scores		28	29	33	0	28	27	0	37	0	34	0	36	252
singles 1st prefs		1	-	**3**	-	1	**2**	-	**2**	-	**2**	-	1	QUOTAS
pairs 1st prefs*		1½		1 quotas			1 ½ quotas		quota		quota			
triplets 1st prefs			two quotas of 4			two quotas of 3 +								

The outcome at this stage, therefore, is that the following candidates have been elected to the executive:

Messrs. **L, O, S, Q, K** and **U**.

Then, on the basis of the above, and omitting the unsuccessful candidates - Messrs. **J** and **N** as well as those who scored nothing - Messrs. **M, P, R** and **T** - we now have to see who takes which ministry. To do this, we simplify Table 3.V into Table 3.W; the latter shows the MBC sums in the body of the table, as well as the candidates' MBC scores and the MBC totals for each post. We also introduce another row - popularity - to show the order of election as per the QBS count.

TABLE 3.W	–	THE NEXT STAGE OF THE MATRIX VOTE COUNT, EXAMPLE 3A					
	CANDIDATES						Relative Import
Minister	*K*	*L*	*O*	*Q*	*S*	*U*	MBC post totals
PM	2	33	17			5	57
Min. of *A*	21		10			14	45
Min. of *B*				37			37
Min. of *C*	3						37
Min. of *D*	3					17	41
Min. of *E*					34		35
MBC scores	29	33	27	37	34	36	
Popularity	5th	1st	2nd	4th	3rd	6th	

Next, we place the candidates in their order of popularity, 1st to 6th, left to right; and we re-arrange the ministerial posts in order of importance, as defined by the MBC post totals in the right hand column, top to bottom. The result is Table 3.X, where the biggest sums have been tinted.

Finally, we examine the individual MBC sums, starting with the biggest. In our own example, Mr. **Q** with 37 points (in the darkest tint) is the first to be appointed, and he becomes the Minister of **B**. Mr. **S** on 34 points is next, as Minister of **E**. Then Ms. **L**, with 33 points, becomes PM. And the fourth highest sum, 21, means Mr. **K** becomes the Minister of **A**.

We have a draw for the fifth position, for there are two sums of 17, both in stripes: Mr. **O** has 17 for the premiership, while Mr. **U** has 17 to suggest he should be the Minister of **D**. In such instances, priority is given to the more popular candidate, and if still there is a draw, to the more important ministerial post.

In fact, in this instance, there is no dispute at all: Mr. **O** cannot be PM, for that post has already been filled. Accordingly, Mr. **U** becomes Minister of **D**, and Mr. **O** the Minister of **C**.

TABLE 3.X — THE FINAL STAGE OF THE MATRIX VOTE COUNT, EXAMPLE 3A

Minister	ELECTED CANDIDATES						Relative Importance MBC post totals
	L	O	S	Q	K	U	
PM	33	17		2	5		57
Min. of A		10			21	14	45
Min. of D					3	17	41
Min. of C					3		37
Min. of B				37			37
Min. of E			34				35
MBC scores	33	27	34	37	29	36	
Popularity	1st	2nd	3rd	4th	5th	6th	

The final result is shown in Table 3.Y. It is a power-sharing executive consisting of 2 members of party *W*, one each of parties *X*, *Y* and *Z*, and the independent member Mr. *U*. Furthermore, by voting for Mr. *Q* to be the Minister of *B*, the voters have ensured that he does indeed get that job. Similarly, the talents of Mr. *S*, as noted in Table 3.N, have been recognised, and he is now the Minister of *E*. Ms. *J* and Ms. *N*, however, were pipped at the post - with 28 points, they were joint 7th in the QBS election - though they too were recognised for their specialist skills.

TABLE 3.Y — THE MATRIX VOTE RESULTS, EXAMPLE 3A

Minister	ELECTED CANDIDATES						Relative Importance MBC post totals
	L	O	S	Q	K	U	
PM	33						57
Min. of A					21		45
Min. of D						17	41
Min. of C		0					37
Min. of B				37			37
Min. of E			34				35
MBC scores	33	27	34	37	29	36	

One of the advantages of the matrix vote is that, while there are still winners and losers as there are in any election, any possible causes of dissatisfaction invariably relate to the least popular persons and the least important ministries.

Example 3B - Electing the Executive, the Second Voters' Profile, Partial Ballots

We now consider the slightly different scenario of persons voting partially. Two of the ballot papers are shown in Table 3.Z – the votes of Messrs. **J** and **K** – and all of them are in Annex B, pp 84-5. The voters' profile - with preferences in light tint, points in darker tint, and sums in bold - is shown opposite. Looking at Mr. **K** again, he gave himself a 1st preference for the post of PM, but because he expressed just 5 preferences, he here gets a sum of 5 points. The QBS count proceeds as per Table 3.AA.

TABLE 3.Z							—	THE VOTES OF MESSRS. *J* AND *K*, EXAMPLE 3B					
Ms. *J*	PREFERENCES						Mr. *K*	PREFERENCES					
	1st	2nd	3rd	4th	5th	6th		1st	2nd	3rd	4th	5th	6th
PM	*J*						PM	*K*					
A							A					*T*	
B			*Q*				B				*P*		
C		*L*					C		*J*				
D		*K*					D			*L*			
E							E						

STAGE	TABLE 3.AA — A QBS COUNT, EXAMPLE 3B	ELECTED
i)	There are four candidates with the quota (in bold reverse) - *J, N, S* and *Q* - and an inspection of their 2nd and 3rd preferences puts them in this order.	*J, N, S* and *Q*
ii) - iii)	-	-
iv)	The *J-K-L* trio (in diagonal stripes) has 2 quotas from Messrs. *J, K, L* and *M* [Annex B], giving *L* a seat, and so too, from Messrs. *N, O, P* and *S* [Annex B], the *N-O-S* threesome (vertical stripes) qualifies, but they already have 2 seats.	*J, N, S, Q* and *L*
v) - vi)	-	-
vii)	The highest MBC score of the unelected candidates gives this last seat to either *K* or *U*, but *K* wins for he has more 3rd preferences.	*J, N, S, Q, L* and *K*

Taking the successful candidates from above - *J, N, S, Q, L* and *K* - and the MBC post totals of the ministries from the right hand column of Table 3.AB, we can now produce Table 3.AC overleaf, with some of the biggest sums shown in various tints.

---

* The 3 pairs in hatch or horizontal stripes fail to qualify for stage ii) of the count.

ELECTING A POWER-SHARING EXECUTIVE - THE MATRIX VOTE 75

TABLE 3.AB		EXAMPLE 3B - ELECTING THE EXECUTIVE, THE SECOND VOTERS' PROFILE, PARTIAL BALLOTS THE CANDIDATES (WHO ARE ALSO THE VOTERS) - THE MEMBERS OF PARLIAMENT													MBC post totals	QUOTAS
Ministers		J	K	L	M	N	O	P	Q	R	S	T	U			
PM	Prefs	1,2,1	1	2,3,6									4,4,4			
	points	4,4,3	5	4,2,1									1,1,1			
	Sums	**11**	**5**	**7**									**3**	**26**		
Min. of A	Prefs						2,1,2,3	5,3				5	4,4,1			
	points						3,4,2,2	1,1				1	2,1,6			
	Sums						**11**	**2**				**1**	**9**	**23**		
Min. of B	Prefs							4	4,4,1,1,3							
	points							2	1,2,5,4,4							
	Sums							**2**	**16**					**18**		
Min. of C	Prefs	2,3,2		2,1,2	5											
	points	4,3,3		3,5,2	2											
	Sums	**10**		**10**	**2**									**22**		
Min. of D	Prefs		3,3,3,5	3		1,2,1,2,2		4								
	points		2,3,1,1	3		4,3,3,3,2		3								
	Sums		**7**	**3**		**15**		**3**						**28**		
Min. of E	Prefs										3,3,3,1,1,2					
	points										2,2,1,4,3,5					
	Sums										**17**			**17**		
MBC scores		**21**	**12**	**20**	**2**	**15**	**11**	**7**	**16**	**0**	**17**	**1**	**12**	**134**		
singles 1st prefs		**2**	1	1	-	**2**	1	-	**2**	-	**2**	-	1			
pairs 1st prefs*}		1½		quotas		1½ quotas					quota					
triplets 1st prefs		two quotas: 4 × 1st prefs					two quotas: 3 +				1					

TABLE 3.AC — THE NEXT STAGE OF THE MATRIX VOTE COUNT, EXAMPLE 3B

Minister	ELECTED CANDIDATES						Relative Importance MBC post totals
	J	*N*	*S*	*Q*	*L*	*K*	
Min. of *D*		**15**			3	7	28
PM	**11**				7	5	26
Min. of *A*							23
Min. of *C*	10				10		22
Min. of *B*				**16**			18
Min. of *E*			**17**				17
MBC scores	21	15	17	16	20	12	

There is little doubt as to ministerial appointments. The tinted sums 17, 16, 15 and 11 mean that Messrs. *S, Q, N* and *J* become the Ministers of *E, B, D*, and Prime Minister. The two 10s (in stripes) suggest Ms. *L* must be Minister of *C*, because Ms. *J* is already busy. And this all means that Mr. *K* must take the last post, the Minister of *A*. The final outcome is in Table 3.AD.

TABLE 3.AD — THE MATRIX VOTE RESULTS, EXAMPLE 3B

Minister	ELECTED CANDIDATES						Relative Importance MBC post totals
	J	*N*	*S*	*Q*	*L*	*K*	
Min. of *D*		15					28
PM	11						26
Min. of *A*						0	23
Min. of *C*					10		22
Min. of *B*				16			18
Min. of *E*			17				17
MBC scores	21	15	17	16	20	12	

Now in this example, Mr. *K* finishes up as the Minister of *A*, even though, in the opinion of those voting, he has no especial talents for this post. He is still, however, the sixth most popular MP in parliament, and it is only right that he should get this remaining ministry. In practice, of course, when far more than a dozen MPs are voting, the chances of any one MP being appointed to a post with a sum of zero must also be just about zero.

Example 3C - Electing the Executive, the Third Voters' Profile, Full Ballots

In our third example, the various parties form into two opposing blocs and vote accordingly. Table 3.AG overleaf shows the preferences in light tint and the sums in bold. As in Example 3A, with full ballots, there is no need to show the rows of points; Mr. **K** now gets seven 5th preferences for the **D** Ministry, and in a full ballot, a 5th preference is worth 2 pts; 7 x 2 = 14, so he gets a sum for **D** of 14 points.

TABLE 3.AE — TWO MORE MATRIX VOTES, EXAMPLE 3C

	PREFERENCES					
	1st	2nd	3rd	4th	5th	6th
PM	L					
A			U			
B		Q				
C			J			
D				K		
E						S

The votes of *J, K, L, M, Q, R* and *U*.

	PREFERENCES					
	1st	2nd	3rd	4th	5th	6th
PM				U		
A		O				
B						Q
C						K
D	N					
E		S				

The votes of *N, O, P, S* and *T*.

In this example, we need hardly be surprised that there are again some candidates who do not get any scores at all! In the QBS count, the following get elected:

STAGE	TABLE 3.AF — A QBS COUNT, EXAMPLE 3C	ELECTED
i)	Only two candidates gain a quota, (bold reverse), *L* and *N*.	*L* and *N*
ii)	There are two pairs (one in diagonal and the other in vertical stripes) which both gain two quotas: *L* and *Q* (diagonal) form the first pair, supported by Messrs. *J, K, L, M, Q, R* and *U*; while *N* and *S* make up the second pair, (vertical) with the help of Messrs. *N, O, P, S* and *T*. So *Q* and *S* are elected.	*L, N, Q* and *S*
iii)	The triplet *L-Q-J* (cross-hatch) has 3 quotas, so *J* is next to be elected.	*L, N, Q, S* and *J*
iv)	The triplet *N-O-S* has 2 quotas, (horizontal) but *N* and *S* have already been elected, so there is no change.	-
v) - vi)	-	-
vii)	Finally, *U* is the unelected candidate with the highest MBC score, so he too gets elected.	*L, N, Q, S, J* and *U*

TABLE 3.AG — EXAMPLE 3C - ELECTING THE EXECUTIVE, THE THIRD VOTERS' PROFILE, FULL BALLOTS

THE CANDIDATES (WHO ARE ALSO THE VOTERS) - THE MEMBERS OF PARLIAMENT

Ministers		J	K	L	M	N	O	P	Q	R	S	T	U	MBC post totals
PM	Prefer-ences			1,1,1,1 1,1,1									4,4,4 4,4	
	Sums			42									15	57
Min. of A	Prefer-ences						3,3,3 3,3						4,4,4,4 4,4	
	Sums						20						21	41
Min. of B	Prefer-ences								2,2,2,2,2,2 2,6,6,6,6					
	Sums								40					40
Min. of C	Prefer-ences	3,3,3,3,3 3,3,3	5,5,5 5,5											
	Sums	28	10											38
Min. of D	Prefer-ences		5,5,5,5 5,5			1,1,1 1,1								
	Sums		14			30								44
Min. of E	Prefer-ences										6,6,6,6,6 6,2,2,2,2,2			
	Sums										32			32
MBC scores		28	24	42	0	30	20	0	40	0	32	0	36	252
singles 1st prefs		-	-	7	-	5	-	-	-	-	-	-	-	QUOTAS
pairs 1st prefs				7		5								
triplets 1st prefs				7		5								

Taking the successful candidates from p 77 - **L, N, Q, S, J** and **U** - and taking the relative importance of the ministries from the MBC post totals in the right hand column of p 78, we then produce the table below:

TABLE 3.AH	THE MATRIX VOTE RESULTS, EXAMPLE 3C						
Minister	ELECTED CANDIDATES						Relative Importance MBC post totals
	L	*N*	*Q*	*S*	*J*	*U*	
PM	42						57
Min. of *D*		30					44
Min. of *A*						21	41
Min. of *B*			40				40
Min. of *C*					28		38
Min. of *E*				32			32
MBC scores	42	30	40	32	28	36	

Example 3D - Electing a Sub-committee

Needless to say, the election of a sub-committee in which each of the various members has a different status or function - a chairperson, secretary and treasurer, for example - can also be done by a QBS matrix vote. Furthermore, in theory, the election part of the matrix vote can be done by any one of a number of systems - PR-list, PR-STV or whatever, there are over 300 different electoral systems to choose from[3] - but for the reasons given in Chapter 2, I think QBS is the most inclusive.

An Analysis

Table 3.AI shows the three outcomes, their relative party strengths, and, in tint, those candidates who were successfully appointed to the specific post for which they were considered to be most suited. This suggests that the matrix vote, like QBS, is pretty robust, but again, more research would do no harm. Doubtless, too, when politicians learn to be less self- or party-centred, the system will prove itself to be even more consensual.

A COMPARISON OF THE MATRIX VOTE WITH OTHER PROCEDURES

At the time of writing, the matrix vote is the only electoral mechanism known to the author by which a group of people - a parliament or an AGM - can elect persons to a

---

3   Bogdanor, p 209.

TABLE 3.AI		–	A Matrix Vote Analysis	
		Example 3A	Example 3B	Example 3C
PM		L	J	L
Min. of A		K	K	U
Min. of B		Q	Q	Q
Min. of C		O	L	J
Min. of D		U	N	N
Min. of E		S	S	S
Party	W	2	3	2
	X	1	1	1
	Y	1	1	1
	Z	1	1	1
Independent		1	0	1

team - a government or an executive committee - in which each elected team player is chosen to perform a different function - ministerial post or executive office.

There are other ways in which governments can be chosen, of course. In some countries - the UK, for instance - the PM alone is responsible for choosing who is to be in his/her cabinet; furthermore, he can then hire and fire at will or whim, if not re-shuffle the entire pack! It is a methodology which gives this one individual almost dictatorial powers. Elsewhere, in the Ukraine, for example, the president appoints but only if parliament approves.

In spheres less political, at the AGMs of community groups and public associations, members usually resort to a series of majority/plurality votes - one for chair, one for secretary, and so on - but in those groups where there is one dominant faction, this can and does lead to much abuse. So back to politics.

In some elected chambers, persons are appointed to committees and so forth, in rough proportion to their relative strengths in chamber. This is happening in many local councils in Northern Ireland, a similar process of selection is written into the Belfast Agreement for the NI Assembly, but it also happens in many parliaments. In some instances, they use the d'Hondt formula, which from a party point of view, is possibly fair enough,[4] but this methodology means that members of small parties and Independents rarely get a fair chance.

---

4 In most applications, the d'Hondt formula tends to favour the bigger parties, while the Sainte Laguë formula is a little fairer. In like manner, when used in PR-list systems, the Hare quota is fairer than the Droop - Lijphart, 1994, p 158.
   With PR-STV, however, the Droop quota allows for more transfers - Lakeman, p 147. Similarly, in QBS, Droop gives smaller parties a greater chance of success in the earlier stages of the count.

Where pluralism and power-sharing are important, and where proportionality must be maintained at all costs, electorally or otherwise, many countries tend to concoct a non-electoral mechanism. The Belfast Agreement turns what should be the election of the First and Deputy First Ministers into a yes-or-no decision, a ratification at best. The Dayton Agreement in Bosnia stipulates a 3-person presidency, which is actually more sectarian than the arrangement that had been in place before the 1992-95 war.[5] And finally, in the Lebanon, the Taif Accord stipulates that the President shall be a Maronite, the Prime Minister a Sunni, and the Speaker a Shia.[6]

Practical Guidelines

The matrix vote is designed for the committee, the local council, the national parliament and the international gathering. Admittedly, it could be used by a general electorate, if indeed they decided to elect not only their parliament directly, but also their government. In practice, however, it will usually be used in indirect elections only. The corresponding electorate will therefore be measured in tens or, at most, a few hundreds, so any mathematical complications will be relatively small and easily surmountable.

Conclusions

The Belfast Agreement uses a d'Hondt mechanism, not for the *election* of the executive, but rather for its *selection*. It is a procedure which disenfranchises any member of the Assembly who is not in one of the four 'big' parties; secondly, it is not a methodology by which it can be hoped that every future minister will be in a post to which he/she is best suited; and thirdly, it means that anyone not in one of the 'big' four parties need not aspire to ministerial office.

In our own example of the QBS matrix vote, however, all three profiles facilitated the appointment of at least two ministers to the posts for which, in the consensus of those voting, they were the most suitable.

At the very least, in small organisations, the matrix vote allows people in AGMs etc. to vote for whomsoever they wish to serve in whatever position they wish, without the win-or-lose nonsense of umpteen majority votes. In a word, the matrix vote is very much a win-win methodology, suitable for use in committees and parliaments alike, and most certainly for application in any elected chamber associated with a peace process.

---

5   The Dayton Agreement stipulates that the Presidency shall consist of 1 person from each of the three religious groups, Catholic, Moslem and Orthodox, (though it uses the term 'ethnic'). Before the war, there were seven members, two each of the above, plus one Yugoslav.

6   el-Khazen, 1991, p 64.

Ms *J*	1st	2nd	3rd	4th	5th	6th
PM		*L*				
A			*K*			
B				*Q*		
C	*J*					
D					*U*	
E						*S*

Mr *K*	1st	2nd	3rd	4th	5th	6th
PM		*L*				
A			*K*			
B				*Q*		
C		*J*				
D					*U*	
E						*N*

PARTY *W*

Ms *L*	1st	2nd	3rd	4th	5th	6th
PM	*L*					
A		*K*				
B				*Q*		
C			*J*			
D					*U*	
E						*S*

Mr *M*	1st	2nd	3rd	4th	5th	6th
PM	*L*					
A			*K*			
B					*Q*	
C		*J*				
D					*U*	
E						*S*

Ms *N*	1st	2nd	3rd	4th	5th	6th
PM		*O*				
A					*K*	
B				*Q*		
C	*N*					
D					*U*	
E		*S*				

Mr *O*	1st	2nd	3rd	4th	5th	6th
PM	*O*					
A				*U*		
B				*Q*		
C						*K*
D		*N*				
E			*S*			

PARTY *X*

Ms *P*	1st	2nd	3rd	4th	5th	6th
PM	*O*					
A			*U*			
B				*Q*		
C						*J*
D		*N*				
E			*S*			

In a 6-candidate (BC)/MBC with full ballots:

a 1st preference gets 6 points,

a 2nd preference gets 5 points,

a 3rd preference gets 4 points,

a 4th preference gets 3 points,

a 5th preference gets 2 points,

and a 6th preference gets 1 point.

ELECTING A POWER-SHARING EXECUTIVE - THE MATRIX VOTE

Mr Q	1st	2nd	3rd	4th	5th	6th
PM		L				
A					U	
B		Q				
C			J			
D				K		
E						S

Ms R	1st	2nd	3rd	4th	5th	6th
PM		L				
A				K		
B		Q				
C					J	
D			U			
E						S

PARTY Y

Mr S	1st	2nd	3rd	4th	5th	6th
PM			U			
A		O				
B				Q		
C						K
D				N		
E	S					

Ms T	1st	2nd	3rd	4th	5th	6th
PM					U	
A		O				
B				Q		
C						K
D				N		
E	S					

PARTY Z

Mr U	1st	2nd	3rd	4th	5th	6th
PM					K	
A	U					
B			Q			
C						J
D				N		
E		S				

Independent Mr. U

ANNEX A
EXAMPLE 3A - THE INDIVIDUAL VOTES, FULL BALLOTS

PARTY W

Ms *J*	1st	2nd	3rd	4th	5th	6th
PM	*J*-4					
A						
B				*Q*-1		
C		*L*-3				
D			*K*-2			
E						

Mr *K*	1st	2nd	3rd	4th	5th	6th
PM	*K*-5					
A					*T*-1	
B				*P*-2		
C			*J*-4			
D			*L*-3			
E						

Ms *L*	1st	2nd	3rd	4th	5th	6th
PM	*J*-4					
A				*P*-1		
B				*Q*-2		
C	*L*-5					
D			*K*-3			
E						

Mr *M*	1st	2nd	3rd	4th	5th	6th
PM	*J*-3					
A						
B						
C		*L*-2				
D			*K*-1			
E						

PARTY X

Ms *N*	1st	2nd	3rd	4th	5th	6th
PM				*U*-1		
A		*O*-3				
B						
C						
D	*N*-4					
E			*S*-2			

Mr *O*	1st	2nd	3rd	4th	5th	6th
PM				*U*-1		
A	*O*-4					
B						
C						
D		*N*-3				
E			*S*-2			

Ms *P*	1st	2nd	3rd	4th	5th	6th
PM						
A		*O*-2				
B						
C						
D		*N*-3				
E			*S*-1			

The points awarded per preference vary according to the MBC formula: $m, m-1 \ldots 2, 1$. So points awarded are as shown in each box.

ELECTING A POWER-SHARING EXECUTIVE - THE MATRIX VOTE

Mr *Q*	1st	2nd	3rd	4th	5th	6th
PM		*L*-4				
A				*U*-2		
B	*Q*-5					
C			*J*-3			
D					*K*-1	
E						

Ms *R*	1st	2nd	3rd	4th	5th	6th
PM			*L*-2			
A				*U*-1		
B	*Q*-4					
C			*J*-3			
D						
E						

PARTY Y

Mr *S*	1st	2nd	3rd	4th	5th	6th
PM			*U*-1			
A			*O*-2			
B						
C						
D		*N*-3				
E	*S*-4					

Ms *T*	1st	2nd	3rd	4th	5th	6th
PM						
A		*P*-1				
B						
C						
D		*N*-2				
E	*S*-3					

PARTY Z

Mr *U*	1st	2nd	3rd	4th	5th	6th
PM					*L*-1	
A	*U*-6					
B			*Q*-4			
C				*M*-2		
D			*P*-3			
E	*S*-5					

Independent Mr. *U*

ANNEX B
EXAMPLE 3B - THE INDIVIDUAL VOTES, PARTIAL BALLOTS

Chapter 4

The Art or Science of Manipulation

DECISION-MAKING

The question of *how* society takes its decisions is fundamental... yet seldom discussed. Imagine, then, a simple debate: which, of ten different policies, each one represented by a sports team, is the best? Well in politics, as in sport, there are many methodologies.

In many majority votes, the captain of last year's champions picks his own club to play the weakest of the ten opponents, and he just ignores the other teams. Furthermore, he chooses the time and venue, and sometimes, he is also the ref!

A plurality vote is a first-past-the-post relay race. But no-one knows where the post is![1] It could be anywhere, from 10% + 1 of the vote to 50% + 1. Then, in two-round voting, members of the losing teams from the plurality vote first round can join up with one or other of the two finalists for a majority vote play off.

Approval voting is a ball game played on a circular pitch with as many goals as there are teams, but teams are not allowed to score more than once in any one goal. An alternative vote is a plurality relay race of many posts and intervals, and each time the ref. blows the whistle, the team which is lying last disbands itself, and its members can then join other teams. While serial voting is a gladiatorial knock-out, where one team stays on the pitch until it is beaten, whereupon another takes over, until only one remains.

Finally, in both Borda and Condorcet counts, all teams play the ball game against each other in turn: in a BC/MBC, the ultimate winner is the team with the most goals; under Condorcet, it is the team with the most wins (and/or draws). Now in most seasons, the team which wins the league (Condorcet) is also the team with the most goals (Borda). There is the outside chance that a Condorcet runner-up wins one of its matches with a massive score like 23-nil and becomes the BC/MBC winner; so in theory, the BC/MBC winner may not be the Condorcet winner. Usually, however, the two winners are one and the same; and when the two outcomes do coincide, all concerned may rest assured that the process was indeed fair.

Interestingly enough, quite a few sporting organisations use variations of the more sophisticated methodologies. Most sports leagues are a form of Condorcet count, and other events like grand-prix racing are a form of BC - so a driver who never comes first may nevertheless win the championship! It is only knock out tournaments such as many tennis competitions which are binary processes - like umpteen majority votes - where so much depends on the luck of the draw. In majoritarian politics, these variables of chance are often replaced by acts of manipulation.

---

[1] Dummett, 1997, p 39.

The Political Game

One obvious form of manipulation relates to the fact that politicians in power are often able to choose whichever form of voting best suits their vested interests. No wonder they like majority voting, for this allows them to manipulate still further, especially if their political regime enables them to control the agenda. They write the motion and, as noted earlier, it is this motion (plus an amendment or two, perhaps) which is then put to the vote. From the referendums of Napoleon and Hitler[2] to the vote in the UN Security Council on Iraq (Resolution 1441, of Oct. 2002), experience shows the question is usually the answer, (p 2).

In many circumstances, then, politicians are able to manipulate things, a) by choosing the voting methodology, and b) by controlling the agenda. In addition, they usually help themselves c) by deciding the timing. And in parliamentary circles, if they still need some assistance, they get it d) by cracking the party whips!

An Example of Manipulation in Decision-making

The vote just mentioned - the UN resolution on Iraq - is a case in point. Only the US and Britain proposed a resolution. France, for one, did not like it; in particular, she objected to the phrase "serious consequences". Nevertheless, she voted in favour. Which begs the question: why? Did she actually support the motion? Or did she think that, well, it was better than nothing? Or again, was she concerned about the need for international solidarity or some other factor?

We do not know. The outcome of the vote does not tell us. In other words, that vote meant very little, and even though it was unanimous, the actual will of the Council was still unclear, let alone their level of enthusiasm. For Messrs. Bush and Blair then to talk of overwhelming support and so forth was at best illogical.

A Better Methodology

If instead of the existing majoritarian procedure, the Security Council had allowed all fifteen members to participate fully in that decision-making process, then France (with, perhaps, Germany, and maybe Russia as well) might have proposed her own wording. Syria, too, might have put forward a third variation. And maybe, at the end of the debate, the number of options on the table might have been, let us say, five.

Now to reduce a multi-option debate to a two-option vote is itself an act of manipulation. If the debate is multi-optional, the vote, too, should be multi-optional.

If, then, all fifteen members had cast their preferences on these 5 options in an MBC, it would have been possible to analyse the collective opinion with a little more accuracy.

---

2   A full list of 'democratic dictators' is in Emerson (2002).
      There are some *good* ways of taking majority votes, of course, and one of the best is the citizens' initiative, in which the question on the ballot paper is not so open to manipulation by the politician in power.

Let us assume all fifteen had submitted full ballots. If, then, in the count, the Bush/ Blair proposal had actually come out on top with an average preference rating of 1.5 or even higher, the two sponsors could indeed have spoken of unanimity. If their option had got a rating of about 2.5, then, as suggested on p 21, they could have called it a good compromise. And if their option had not come out on top, they could have at least accepted the winning option as the democratic consensus of Council, and described the decision-making process as free and fair.

After all, and certainly when the subject matter is on such a complicated topic, a free vote ought to be a multi-option vote, so that those concerned are free, literally, to choose their 1st (and subsequent) preferences. Secondly, if the vote is to be fair and the analysis accurate, it must also be preferential.

Multi-option voting, almost by definition, reduces the power of the politician to manipulate. When New Zealand had a problem with its FPP electoral system, they decided it just had to be changed. In the event, they appointed a Royal Commission, which drew up a short list of five possible electoral systems, and this short list was then the basis of a 5-option referendum, albeit counted in a rather unusual plurality-cum-two-round voting system. Both the major political parties opposed this more pluralist approach to politics and, although the exercise was a success, neither party has sought to introduce this more sophisticated methodology into parliament. No surprises there, of course.[3]

In the light of Chapter 1, we can lay down the following criteria for a democratic form of decision-making. In any organisation, large or small, the debate should be plural. If and when, at the end of the debate, there are a number of options 'on the table' (or computer screen), all concerned should be allowed to express their preferences on (one, some or, better still) all the options, in an MBC vote.

MANIPULATING A BC/MBC

A BC/MBC is not beyond manipulation, of course. Indeed, every voting procedure is manipulable. It is probably fair to say, however, that the more sophisticated the methodology, the more difficult it is to manipulate.

Even in a simple majority vote, prospects for manipulation depend upon a knowledge of, or at least an accurate speculation of, how the other voters intend to vote. In majority voting, this task is tricky enough. In preference voting, however, it is obviously more difficult. And on those occasions when the outcome is not just the single option which is collectively most popular, but a combination of those options (plural) which form the basis of a compound decision - as in an agreed agenda, a budget proposal, or when the consensors opt to form a composite - the difficulties for the manipulator are probably insurmountable. Nevertheless, let us consider the possibilities.

---

3 *Reform of New Zealand's Voting System,* Malcolm Mackerras in *Representation*, Summer 1994, p 36. See also Colin Hughes in Butler and Ranney, p 171.

If we take the simple case of a discussion on dog license fees, we could well imagine a situation in which the debate concludes with a set of six possible options, as follows:

Option *A*	zero	Option *D*	€ 5
Option *B*	€ 1	Option *E*	€ 10
Option *C*	€ 2	Option *F*	€ 25

In most cases, those whose 1st preference is, let us say, option *C*, will probably have a 2nd/3rd preference for either options *B/D* or options *D/B*. Furthermore, those with a 1st plus 2nd preference profile of '*C* - 1, *B* - 2' will probably have a 3rd preference of either *A* or *D*. And so on.

Life would be a little more complicated if, for instance, one of the options was "€2 for little dogs and €5 for big ones". Nevertheless, if everyone votes sincerely, most of their preferences will fall into single-peaked curves like the ones we saw on p 23.

What's more, if the persons voting are MPs, their preferences should all be in the public domain, not least via the pages of Hansard, and if there are signs that someone has been voting tactically - for whatever reason, honest or otherwise - then the press and others may wish to ask why.

Tactical voting is, of course, a possibility. So let us see what could happen. In regard to the above canine conundrum, let us assume that my sincere preferences are:

'*C* - 1, *D* - 2, *E* - 3, *B* - 4, *F* - 5, *A* - 6'.

Well if I reckon option *D* is probably going to win, and that there is no danger at all of *A* winning, I could cast a tactical vote, a twin- or rather triple-peaked curve, like this -

'*C* - 1, *A* - 2, *E* - 3, *B* - 4, *F* - 5, *D* - 6'.

This would boost the chances of *C* while at the same time diminishing *D*'s prospects. There may be trouble ahead, however. If too many think and act in this way, and if the *D* supporters use the same tactic to bolster *D* and hamper *C*, they might all finish up with option *A*!

When the subject is more serious, the chances of such blatant manipulation are not so strong. If the ballot concerned the constitutional future of Northern Ireland, for example, and if Mr. Paisley thought the option of a federal Ireland could actually do rather well whereas the unitary state united Ireland option would probably not, then he could try to persuade his faithful to cast their 2nd preferences for a united Ireland! Well, if he did, that would spell the end for Mr. Paisley!

So, back to the world of *realpolitik*. While there are countless occasions for tactical voting in many majority votes, especially when the voter's particular 1st preference aspiration is not even on the ballot paper, there will be relatively few temptations in an MBC vote, not least because a multi-option ballot is almost bound to include the 1st preferences of most. There will still be some tactical voting, of course, and doubtless too quite a lot of partial voting.

The Irrelevant Alternative

Manipulation may initially be attempted during the debate stage. Let us say there are 4 options on the ballot paper – **A, B, C,** and **D** – and three people intend to vote like this:

TABLE 4.A		Ms J	Mr K	Ms L
	1st preference	A	C	B
A VOTERS' PROFILE	2nd preference	B	D	D
	3rd preference	C	B	C
	4th preference	D	A	A

In this instance, the points would be $A = 6, B = 9, C = 8$ and $D = 7$. So A would lose. Now suppose that I, an option A supporter, managed to get another option E onto the agenda, an E which is close to, but not as good as A. So everyone would be expected to put E just behind A, as shown in Table 4B.

TABLE 4.B		Ms J	Mr K	Ms L
	1st preference	A	C	B
PLUS AN IRRELEVANT ALTERNATIVE	2nd preference	E	D	D
	3rd preference	B	B	C
	4th preference	C	A	A
	5th preference	D	E	E

The new scores would be: $A = 9, B = 11, C = 10, D = 9$ and $E = 6$, and A would tie for third place. This is the theory of the so-called irrelevant alternative: E is 'irrelevant', because everyone prefers A to E, but its inclusion can screw the result.

Indeed, add another similar option, F, as in Table 4.C, and A would then become joint second. The scores in this contest would be $A = 12, B = 13, C = 12, D = 11, E = 9$ and $F = 6$. Add yet another irrelevance, G, and A would be a joint winner! In all three scenarios, however, the Condorcet winner is B.

TABLE 4.C		Ms J	Mr K	Ms L
	1st preference	A	C	B
PLUS ANOTHER IRRELEVANT ALTERNATIVE	2nd preference	E	D	D
	3rd preference	F	B	C
	4th preference	B	A	A
	5th preference	C	E	E
	6th preference	D	F	F

Now, as already noted (p 17n), a Condorcet count can sometimes suffer from the paradox of voting, (where, in a quite different example, option $A > B > C > A > B$ .... *ad nauseam,* as in Maurice Salles' p 106 and Hannu Nurmi's pp 114-6). A BC/MBC, however, cannot. Instead, a BC/MBC can suffer from the irrelevant alternative, but a Condorcet count cannot. This is why parliamentary votes should be subject to a combined MBC/Condorcet count, (pp 17n, 31 and 86), especially if the subject matter is controversial. If both counts give the same outcome, all may know that the chosen democratic process was accurate.

There again, if the consensors are doing a good job – in other words, if they are ensuring that the final list of options is balanced and fair, and truly representative of the debate as a whole – there will not be any irrelevant alternatives on the ballot paper. It is for this reason that the rules for an MBC are concerned, not only with the voting procedures and the rules for the count, but also with the process by which the consensors formulate the list of options, (p 17).

Practical Considerations

We said earlier that elected politicians should be perfectly capable of voting on a ballot of anything up to 10 or 12 options, (p 16n). What's more, they should be able to do so electronically, by texting their vote on their special-issue mobile phones to a computer in which the program, *Decision-maker,*[4] is ready to analyse the resulting voters' profile. In other ballots such as regional or national referendums, a short list of 4 or 5 options will normally suffice.

So in any elected chamber or small committee, it should be possible to allow all concerned to express their preferences on an (electronic) 'ballot paper' of up to 10-12 options. Asking them to express their preferences on just 6 of them might actually lead to the same result. As was stated on pp 33 and 35, the advantage of a full ballot is that every option then gets a score, and thus every proposer will feel that they have participated in the process.

The Effects of Partial Voting

The purpose of the MBC is to facilitate the identification of a consensus, if and when one exists. If all concerned cast all their preferences, then it will be possible to identify (the points total and) the average preference rating or consensus coefficient of the winning option. This, if you like, is a measure of the level of consensual support with which the electorate regards this option.

If some people submit only partial votes, however, the effect on the results can be fairly dramatic. As will be seen in Appendix III, she who in a 6-option ballot casts preferences on all 6 options, in effect, exercises 21 points; whereas he who casts only a 1st preference exercises just 1 point. The discrepancy is understandable, the effect is

---

[4] This program is on the CD-ROM enclosed inside the front cover. See also p 4.

fair, but it does mean that the overall points totals of *all* the options are lower than what they would otherwise have been.

On a really divisive issue, therefore, a minority could decide to submit a partial vote of only 1 preference. This would reduce the level of support for *all* the options, including of course that of the winning option. In societies where the attainment of "a sufficient consensus" is considered crucial,[5] and where such sufficiency has been defined in terms of a minimum consensus coefficient, this could mean that the outcome fails and that the minority, in effect, vetoes that particular proposal... by participating!

If a minority does vote in this way, it obviously means that the overall level of consensus is indeed low; it is only right, therefore, that the maths of the result should reflect this. It must also be remembered that the rules of an MBC count actually encourage all concerned to participate, and to participate as fully as their principles allow, (p 31). If the minority abstains, they have no influence on the democratic process. If they do participate, even but partially, they can thereby affect the average opinion, and maybe moderate what would otherwise be, for them at least, an unpalatable outcome. Now they might participate - indeed, they will be much more likely to participate - if they can do so, not only in the vote, but also in the debate beforehand; if, that is, they can also put forward their own proposal. And if, as a result, their particular proposal is included on the ballot paper, they will want it to do well. In which case, they will be tempted to participate more fully in the vote.

The situation is much better than that which prevails in a majoritarian milieu. On really contentious majority votes, the minority often does not participate at all and instead, they do the very opposite and organise a boycott. In some cases, indeed, the minority has often resorted to war.[6]

MANIPULATING A QBS ELECTION

If the quota element of QBS is working in the way it is designed to work, a party will tend to nominate only one more candidate than the number it may reasonably expect to be elected, (p 41). Given, then, that the MBC part encourages the voter to express a full range of preferences - and in a 6-seater constituency, voters would normally be

---

5   The South African term - p 21.

6   In the 1973 border poll in Northern Ireland, the 'mainly Catholic' SDLP organised a regional boycott.
    In the Balkans, it was worse. In 1991 in Croatia, the Catholics boycotted a poll run by the Orthodox in the *'krajina'* - (three areas of Croatia which were largely populated by Serbs) - and one week later, in a nation-wide ballot, it was *vice versa*; the combined result was war.
    In the 1992 referendum in Bosnia, the Orthodox organised a similar boycott; so, on a 63% turnout, they lost, by 99%; the result was another war. Emerson (2000). See p 142.
    Referendums in the Caucasus, in both Abkhazia and Nagorno-Karabakh, were retrospective and post-war... by which time, in each case, the minority was in exile and disenfranchised. Emerson, 2002, p 12.

asked to cast their preferences for 6 candidates, and so a full ballot would be one containing six preferences - the effect is a boost to pluralism and tolerance in society: voters are encouraged to vote across gender, party, and even sectarian divides.

Imagine, then, that the number of candidates is quite high, and that two of the candidates are very popular and almost bound to get elected. For a voter to vote tactically in such circumstances is perhaps only sensible: he/she can ignore these two favourites, and vote instead for the six whom he/she feels are nevertheless in with a good chance of being in the top six.

There again, the voters could have other motivations. They could vote for their party favourites, and then cast their lower preferences for some of the other parties' "no-hopers" - the equivalent of option *A* in our earlier canine example, (p 89). If such a tactic is going to be successful, however, it will need some publicity... but the same Mr. Paisley is unlikely to encourage his DUP faithful to give a high preference to a federal Ireland candidate rather than a united Ireland proponent; (cf. p 89).

The Irrelevant Alternative

The MBC part of QBS is, of course, subject to the same mathematical anomalies as a straight MBC vote. In decision-making, there is normally a limited number of options on the table. In an election, however, there may be lots and lots of candidates, and who is to know whether or not, mathematically speaking, one or more of them is an 'irrelevant alternative'. Given the quota element of QBS, however, there is no need to worry about this unduly.

Practical Considerations

A QBS election may, however, exhibit another anomaly. Consider, for example, a 3-seater constituency with the following voters' profile:

TABLE 4.D	Preferences	NUMBER OF VOTERS				
		5	4	4	4	4
A QBS ANOMALY	1st preference	*A*	*B*	*C*	*C*	*D*
	2nd preference	*B*	*C*	*B*	*D*	*C*
	3rd preference	*C*	*A*	*A*	*A*	*A*
	4th preference	*D*	*D*	*D*	*B*	*B*

the valid vote, V = 21
the number of seats = 3,
so the quota = 6,
and the MBC scores are: *A* – 52, *B* – 51, *C* – 66 and *D* – 41.

No single candidate gains a quota, {stage i) from p 44}, and no pairs get two quotas {stage iv)}. So we move to stage v). And there are two pairs – **BC** in tint and **CD** in stripes – both of which gain 1 quota of 1st preferences on the basis of an equal number of eight 1st preferences gained. There are two possible scenarios at this point.

Scenario 1. If we take the **BC** pair first of all, the seat goes to the more popular **C**. So we then take the **CD** pair and, because **C** has already been elected, the seat goes to **D**. In this contest, no consideration is given to the **ABC** triplet of thirteen 1st preferences because one of the triplet, **C**, is now elected, so the final seat depends on the MBC scores only, which means it goes to **A**. The overall result, then, is **C, D** and **A**.

Scenario 2. If, however, we take the **CD** pair first, then candidate **C** is still the first elected, whereupon **B** will be chosen from the other pair and, once again, option **A** will pick up the third seat. So, in this instance, the outcome is **C, B** and **A**.

To overcome this dilemma, it is important, at each stage of a QBS count, to consider *all* possibilities simultaneously and, in stages v) to vii) inclusive, only those candidates elected at a *strictly earlier* stage are not taken into any further consideration.

In the situation of Table 4.D, therefore, the correct procedure is to treat the two pairs, **BC** and **CD**, simultaneously. Each pair, in its own right, deserves one seat; so, taken together, the two pairs deserve two seats, and the two most popular candidates of the three individuals concerned - **B, C** and **D** - are **B** and **C**. The third seat, based as said above on the MBC scores only, goes to **A**. Accordingly, the correct outcome is **C, B** and **A**.[7]

Quasi-chaotic

A voting system is said to be quasi-chaotic if, at least in theory, an outcome might be very different simply because just a few voters decide to change their preferences, perhaps only slightly.

In some circumstances, the vacillation of just one person can swing a majority vote; so the latter can be very chaotic. At the same time, a voting system which involves eliminations and transfers - AV and PR-STV, for example - can be quasi-chaotic. A BC/MBC, however, relying as it does on points totals, is monotonic and not so capricious. Nevertheless, there will undoubtedly be occasions when two or more candidates are neck-and-neck, in which case one voter's change of mind may effect a *slightly* different result; but this is as it should be.

A QBS, however, is not just a BC/MBC, so there could be instances in QBS when one voter's shift of opinion will mean a pair or triplet loses or gains the full quota, and will

---

7 This observation was prompted by a paper from Markus Schulze - *On Dummett's Quota Borda System*, published in *Voting Matters*, No 15, June 2002. His observation is valid, but his criticism is to a large extent obviated by restricting, in Part I of the count, the use of pairs of candidates with 2 quotas to constituencies of 3 or 4 seats, and the use of triplets with 2 or 3 quotas to constituencies of 5+ seats.

thus change the overall result quite drastically.[8] Because of the emphasis in QBS on the MBC, it is nevertheless fair to suggest that QBS is "less 'quasi-chaotic'" than PR-STV, as Professor Dummett is quoted as claiming.[9]

It must also be said that both QBS and PR-STV are very good systems. How sad it is that the question of which electoral system should be used is so often based on a binary choice... which takes us back to Chapter 1.

Small Is Beautiful

Finally, we return from the political world to the small committee. If there are 10 candidates competing for 6 places, and if all 10 are known to the voters concerned, it is better to ask all to cast their preferences on (one, some or hopefully) all 10 candidates. As in decision-making, (p 35), the process *could* be conducted by asking the voters to cast just (a maximum of) 6 preferences, but again, a more inclusive atmosphere will be created by the former methodology.

Given the large constituencies which are the norm in politics, not to mention the invariably large number of candidates, the more pragmatic approach in general elections and so forth is to ask the voters to list just as many preferences as there are seats to be contested; (p 39n).

MANIPULATING A MATRIX VOTE ELECTION

In a parliamentary setting, manipulation of a matrix vote can be very difficult. If a parliament of hundreds is to elect a cabinet of a dozen or so, the degree of choice will be huge, (see Appendix IV). As we saw on pp 18-9, there are 720 different ways of voting in a 6-option BC. In a matrix vote for a cabinet of 6 members from a parliament of just a dozen members, there are millions of possible ways of voting. *Ergo*, the power of any one political leader or party whip to manipulate things is minimal. Nevertheless, some possibilities may be tempting and attempted.

As noted above, if members are prepared to waste part of their vote, they can use some of their preferences on "no-hopers". If I really want Ms. *J*, say, to be a minister, I could give my 1st preference to her, and all my other preferences to individuals who I know have no chance at all of ever getting elected to cabinet; this would perhaps boost the prospects for Ms *J*, but it would also mean that I would thus loose any influence on the election of the other ministers. For many politicians, this would be a price too high, and not least because it would mean that, if elected, Ms. *J* would be ideologically alone in cabinet.

Indeed, if we return to the three-person football teams of pp 66-7, and if I really wanted goalkeeper *m* to play, I could give him my 1st preference, for sure; then, at the

---

8   An example from Nicolaus Tideman is included in the paper by Markus Schulze (p 95n) and it demonstrates the point quite clearly.

9   *Ibid.*

same time, I could give my other two preferences to "no-hoper" goalkeepers in both back and forward positions. But thus I too would lose my chance of participating fully in choosing the complete team.

Consider, though, another problem: imagine that there are lots of forwards to choose from and quite a few backs on offer, but that only two goalies, *m* and *n*, have passed their fitness tests. Preferences, then, may be spread thinly amongst a multitude of forwards and backs, while the two goalies pick up a huge bundle of preferences, even if they are only 3rd preferences. The result could well be that both of them get chosen!

The obvious remedy is to ensure that there are roughly the same number of players in each category. In political teams, when the number of MPs campaigning to high office is always gargantuan, and when most of them would accept *any* ministerial post - goalie, back or forward - any fears of this sort of aberration are unfounded.

On the Smaller Scale

Consider a small gathering, where a group of x members prepares to elect a committee from a field of y candidates - (where $x \geq y$) - and the committee is to consist of z persons. In this instance, it is again better if every member of x is asked to cast their preferences for all the y candidates, for this means that every member of y will finish with a positive score.

The matrix vote can be used even when $y = z$, i.e., when it has already been decided that so many persons are to serve on the committee, but not yet decided who is to perform which function. Thus the committee itself will vote on who is to hold which office.

The voting procedure, therefore, can be twofold. Either x persons use (an MBC or, preferably) a QBS election to elect the z committee members; and then, either all x or maybe just z vote in a matrix vote, to see who serves in which office. Or x persons can elect the executive committee in just the one QBS matrix vote. The former procedure, though a little more long-winded, may be the more inclusive, for it allows all x members to vote on all y candidates whereas, in the latter procedure, some of the less popular candidates may well get a score of 0.

Conclusion

The conclusion is similar to our earlier observations: like MBC and QBS, the matrix vote has huge potential when smaller numbers of persons are aiming to work in consensus. Indeed, in such situations, and especially when all options and/or all candidates are to be voted on, nearly everyone will feel encouraged to vote sincerely, and few will be the temptations to manipulate.

Even in the political arena, however, the catalytic effect of these consensual voting procedures is almost bound to dominate proceedings.

PART II

A CRITIQUE

Chapter 5

The Theory of Voting and the Borda Systems
Maurice Salles

Abstract

The birth (or should we say the re-birth) of voting theory at the end of 18th century in France exemplifies the victory of Condorcet over Borda. This victory was confirmed by the rebirth of voting theory in the 1940s with the magisterial works of Arrow and Black. Only since publications by Dummett, Young and Saari, did Borda systems recover their importance. In this chapter, I will explain how and why this happened. I am grateful to Peter Emerson and Louis Aimé Fono for helpful comments.

INTRODUCTION

In the *Discours Préliminaire* of the *Essai sur l'Application de l'Analyse à la Probabilité des Décisions Rendues à la Pluralité des Voix* (1785) Condorcet criticizes Borda (*un Géomètre célèbre*) and his method. In particular, he gives a simple example where a Condorcet (majority) winner is not elected by some scoring rules, including Borda's rule. Obviously, this was for Condorcet a major default of Borda's rule. Implicitly, majority rule under its binary form (*a* is socially preferred to *b* if the number of voters who prefer *a* to *b* is greater than the number of voters who prefer *b* to *a*) is recommended even if this method can *'former un système qui renferme des propositions contradictoires'*[1] (a clear allusion to what is known today as the Condorcet paradox). Nevertheless, it seems rather obvious that Condorcet had in mind some procedure to escape from the paradox, a procedure which nowadays is called the generalized Condorcet procedure - the equivalent to Kemeny's rule {see Guilbaud, Kemeny, Monjardet, Risse and Saari (2006)}.

The rebirth of modern social choice theory and voting theory can be fixed to the publications of Black's and Arrow's papers at the end of the 1940s and the beginning of the 1950s {see Black (1948, 1958), Arrow (1950, 1963)}. Black's analysis is principally about the existence of a Condorcet winner under majority rule, a Condorcet winner that is the median voter's best alternative, given that the voters' preferences have been appropriately restricted (single-peaked preferences). Arrow's famous (im)possibility theorem is about the impossibility to always obtain a transitive social preference, given individual rational (transitive) preferences, when one uses an aggregation procedure satisfying a list of properties. Among these properties, the so-called independence of irrelevant alternatives excludes that the aggregation procedure be Borda's rule.

---

1 "...form a system which contains contradictory propositions." See *Discours Préliminaire*, pages clxxvij-clxxix.

In this chapter, I will first present formal definitions, then present Arrow's theorem, Black's analysis, and some further developments, outlining the exclusion of scoring rules in general and Borda's rule in particular.

BASIC DEFINITIONS AND ARROW'S THEOREM

Let X be the set of social states. Although nothing specific has to be assumed for this set, we will assume in general (to simplify) that it is finite. A binary relation, a *preference*, over X is a subset of $X \times X$. It will be denoted by $\succeq$. I will write $x \succeq y$ rather than $(x, y) \in \succeq$. All binary relations considered in this chapter are supposed to be *complete* (for all x and $y \in X$, $x \succeq y$ or $y \succeq x$) and, consequently, *reflexive* (for all $x \in X$, $x \succeq x$).

The *asymmetric* part of $\succeq$, denoted $\succ$ is defined (since $\succeq$ is complete) by $x \succ y$ if $\neg y \succeq x$. The *symmetric* part of $\succeq$ is defined by $x \sim y$ if $x \succeq y$ and $y \succeq x$. Intuitively, $x \succeq y$ will mean 'x is at least as good as y', $x \succ y$ will mean 'x is preferred to y' and $x \sim y$ will mean 'there is an indifference between x and y'.

We say that $\succeq$ is *transitive* if for all x, y and $z \in X$, $x \succeq y$ and $y \succeq z \Rightarrow x \succeq z$;

$\succ$ is transitive if for all x, y and $z \in X$, $x \succ y$ and $y \succ z \Rightarrow x \succ z$; and

$\sim$ is transitive if for all x, y and $z \in X$, $x \sim y$ and $y \sim z \Rightarrow x \sim z$.

If $x \succeq$ is transitive, $\succ$ and $\sim$ are transitive too. We say that $\succeq$ is *quasi-transitive* if $\succ$ is transitive (then $\sim$ is not necessarily transitive). A complete and transitive binary relation is a *complete preorder* (sometimes called 'weak ordering'). Let **B** denote the set of complete binary relations over X, **P** denote the set of complete preorders over X, and **Q** denote the set of complete and quasi-transitive binary relations over X.

Let N be the set of individuals. We will assume that it is finite. Individual $i \in N$ has her preference given by a complete preorder $\succeq_i$ over X. A *profile* π is a function from N to **P**′, $\pi : i \mapsto \succeq_i$, where **P**′ $\subseteq$ **P** with **P**′ $\neq \phi$. Let Π' be the set of profiles when the $\succeq_i$'s are in **P**′ and Π be the set of all profiles (when the $\succeq_i$'s are in **P**). Since N is finite and $\#X = n$, a profile is an n-list $(\succeq_1, ..., \succeq_n)$ with each $\succeq_i$ in **P**′. Then $\Pi' = \mathbf{P}'^n$ and $\Pi = \mathbf{P}^n$ (**P**′^{n} and **P**^{n} are n-times Cartesian products of **P**′ and **P**).

Definition 1

An *aggregation function* is a function $f : \Pi' \to \mathbf{B}$.

An aggregation function associates a unique complete binary relation, a social preference, denoted by $\succeq_S$, to individual preferences (one preference for each individual).

To obtain Arrow's and other impossibility theorems, the domain of the aggregation function f must be rich enough. This will be taken care of (with some excess) by the following condition U.

THE THEORY OF VOTING AND THE BORDA SYSTEMS

Definition 2

(Universality, U.) Let f be an aggregation function. *Universality* requires that $\mathbf{P'} = \mathbf{P}$.

This means that an individual preference can be any complete preorder. There is no restriction imposed by some kind of upper rationality or the existence of inter-individual constraints. The next condition is the most important from the viewpoint considered in this chapter.

Definition 3

(Independence–binary form, I.) Let π and $\pi' \in \Pi'$ with $\pi : i \mapsto \succeq_i$ and $\pi' : i \mapsto \succeq'_i$. Consider any $x, y \in X$. If $\succeq_i |\{x,y\} = \succeq'_i |\{x,y\}$ for all $i \in N$, then $\succeq_S |\{x,y\} = \succeq'_S |\{x,y\}$ where $\succeq_S = f(\pi)$ and $\succeq'_S = f(\pi')$. ($\succeq_S |\{x,y\}$ is the restriction of $\succeq_S$ to $\{x,y\}$.)

The underlying idea is that if the preferences between say alternatives a and b in the first profile π and the second profile π' coincide for each individual, that is if Ms. j has the same preference between a and b in the first and the second profile, and if Mr. k has the same preference between a and b in the first and the second profile, etc., then the social preference between a and b must be identical in the two cases. Consider for instance that $X = \{a, b, c, d, e\}$ and $N = \{j, k, l\}$ and that the two profiles are given by $(\succeq_j, \succeq_k, \succeq_l)$ and $(\succeq'_j, \succeq'_k, \succeq'_l)$ with:

$(\succeq_j, \succeq_k, \succeq_l)$ $\qquad\qquad\qquad (\succeq'_j, \succeq'_k, \succeq'_l)$

$b \succ_j c \sim_j a \succ_j d \sim_j e \qquad c \succ'_j d \sim'_j b \sim'_j e \succ'_j a$
$c \succ_k d \succ_k a \sim_k b \sim_k e \qquad d \succ'_k c \succ'_k e \succ'_k a \sim'_k b$
$a \succ_l c \succ_l d \succ_l e \succ_l b \qquad c \succ'_l d \succ'_l a \succ'_l b \succ'_l e$

Consider now the subset $\{a, b\}$. We have:

$(\succeq_j, \succeq_k, \succeq_l)$ $\qquad\qquad\qquad (\succeq'_j, \succeq'_k, \succeq'_l)$

$b \succ_j - \sim_j a \succ_j - \sim_j - \qquad -\succ'_j - \sim'_j b \sim'_j - \succ'_j a$
$-\succ_k - \succ_k a \sim_k b \sim_k - \qquad -\succ'_k - \succ'_k - \succ'_k a \sim'_k b$
$a \succ_l - \succ_l - \succ_l - \succ_l b \qquad -\succ'_l - \succ'_l a \succ'_l b \succ'_l -$

Considering only preferences over a and b, one obtains:

$(\succeq_j, \succeq_k, \succeq_l)$ $\qquad\qquad\qquad (\succeq'_j, \succeq'_k, \succeq'_l)$

$b \succ_j a \qquad\qquad\qquad\qquad b \succ'_j a$
$a \sim_k b \qquad\qquad\qquad\qquad a \sim'_k b$
$a \succ_l b \qquad\qquad\qquad\qquad a \succ'_l b$

The independence condition indicates that in this case the social preference over $\{a, b\}$ must be the same in both cases. If, for instance, we have $a \succ_S b$, we must also have $a \succ'_S b$.

Majority rule as described in the introduction satisfies this independence condition. In fact, all aggregation functions where the social preference between two alternatives is uniquely defined from individual preferences over these two alternatives will satisfy this condition. It is true in particular for voting games where winning coalitions are *a priori* defined and where an alternative x is socially preferred to an alternative y if every individual in a winning coalition prefers x to y. In some cases winning coalitions are defined relative to a quota (the game is then anonymous or symmetric) that can be a majority or some *super* majority (see among others Dummett and Farquharson or, recently, Banks *et al.*).

In proofs, this condition of independence plays a major rôle in what Sen has called an epidemic result. If for a specific profile π, one obtains say $a \succeq_s b$ for two options a and $b \in X$, then for all profiles π' in which the individual preferences over a and b are identical with the individual preferences over a and b in the initial profile, we will have the same preference: $a \succeq'_s b$.

As mentioned previously this condition excludes scoring rules including, of course, Borda's rule and forbids that the aggregation function takes some form of intensity of preferences into account. Regarding Borda's rule, consider an example with $X = \{a, b, c, d\}$ and $N = \{j, k, l\}$, and the following two profiles: $(\succeq_j, \succeq_k, \succeq_l)$ and $(\succeq'_j, \succeq'_k, \succeq'_l)$:

$(\succeq_j, \succeq_k, \succeq_l)$ $(\succeq'_j, \succeq'_k, \succeq'_l)$

$a \succ_j b \succ_j c \succ_j d$ $a \succ'_j c \succ'_j d \succ'_j b$
$b \succ_k a \succ_k d \succ_k c$ $b \succ'_k a \succ'_k d \succ'_k c$
$c \succ_l b \succ_l a \succ_l d$ $c \succ'_l b \succ'_l a \succ'_l d$

3 points are attributed to an alternative ranked 1st, 2 points to an alternative ranked 2nd, 1 point to an alternative ranked 3rd and 0 to an alternative ranked last. If we consider $\{a, b\}$, a gets 6 points and b gets 7 points for the first profile and a obtains 6 points and b only obtains 5 points for the second profile. But preferences of Messrs. k and l are entirely identical and for Ms. j we have $a \succ_j b$ and $a \succ'_j b$. Independence would require that the social preference between a and b be identical, but Borda's rule gives $b \succ_s a$ and $a \succ'_s b$. The fact that Ms. j ranked a 1st and b 2nd in the first profile and a 1st and b last in the second profile should not have any effect according to the independence condition. One can easily imagine that Ms. j's preference in favour of a is a lot stronger in $\succeq'_j$ than in $\succeq_j$. It is certain that using majority rule, even when a Condorcet winner exists, must not conceal that obvious difficulties could be solved by using Borda's rule instead. For instance, suppose that we have 101 individuals and 15 options, $\{x_1, ..., x_{15}\}$, and that 51 individuals rank the options from x_1 to x_{15} in the natural order: $x_1 \succ x_2 \succ x_3 ... \succ x_{15}$, and that 50 individuals rank them in the following manner: $x_2 \succ x_3 \succ x_4 ... \succ x_{15} \succ x_1$. Obviously, x_1 is a Condorcet winner, and, in fact x_1 would be the winner under many voting procedures (in particular voting procedures used in the real world). However, x_1 is 'hated' by nearly 50% of the individuals and x_2 is preferred by nearly 50% and is either ranked 1st or 2nd by all (see Michael Dummett's foreword to this volume for further comments).

The next condition (condition P) is a weak form of unanimity (Pareto principle).

Definition 4

(Pareto principle, P.) Let f be an aggregation function, $\pi \in \Pi'$ and $x, y \in X$.[2] *If for all $i \in N$, $x \succ_i y$, then $x \succ_s y$ where $\succ_s$ is the asymmetric part of $\succeq_s = f(\pi)$.*

This condition or its variants are easily admissible and pervade the microeconomic literature leading to the concept of Pareto optimality (in the weak form of the above definition, an alternative is Pareto optimal if there is no other alternative that everyone prefers).

Definition 5

A *dictator* is an individual $i \in N$ such that for all $x, y \in X$ and all $\pi \in \Pi'$, $x \succ_i y \Rightarrow x \succ_s y$ where $\succ_s$ is the asymmetric part of $\succeq_s = f(\pi)$.

Definition 6

(Condition D⁻, non-dictatorship.) There is no dictator.

Arrow's theorem holds for aggregation functions that are social welfare functions.

Definition 7

A **P**-*valued aggregation function* (or *social welfare function*) is a function $f: \Pi' \to \mathbf{P}$.

The theorem states basically that the four conditions are inconsistent with a transitive social preference $\succeq_s$, more precisely and formally we have the following statement.

Theorem 1

{Arrow (1950, 1951, 1963).} *If $n \geq 2$ and $\#X \geq 3$, there is no **P**-valued aggregation function (social welfare function) satisfying U, P, I and D⁻.*

One may wonder why, in the second part of the 20th century in particular, economists in general and probably the greatest of them all found these conditions attractive. I will be slightly caricatural in my comments, but I strongly believe that these comments are basically correct. The development of economic theory in the 19th century was mainly a British affair. Among the concepts that were crucial for this development, the concept of utility was prominent. The use of Bentham's utilitarianism was rather unsophisticated. Utilities are real numbers and, in some sense, all standard properties of real numbers were employed to derive results. For instance, one can say that a given individual is twice happier with x than with y, that the difference of utility between w and x is twice greater than the difference between y and z etc.. Also, one can say that Mr. i is twice happier with x than Ms. j with y and so on. The notion of Pareto optimum is one of the first notions that goes against this flexibility. If we consider the weak version of the Pareto principle, we can say that x is Pareto superior to y if every individual prefers x to y. Then being Pareto superior is a binary relation that is transitive

---

2 Both x and y are necessarily distinct.

if individual strict preferences are transitive. This binary relation is a partial order whose maximal elements are the Pareto optima. With Pareto (and with Walras[4]), economic theory became essentially a continental affair, and it is this theory that became the dominating paradigm in American microeconomics, and to some extent in Britain, in the first part of the 20th century. Pareto optimality was even the only admissible welfare criterion. Moral philosophers could perhaps go beyond, but economists were not supposed to deal with this kind of question. This view is generally associated with Robbins {for perceptive comments Sen (1987) is highly recommended}. It seems that to use only ordinal utilities that are non comparable across individuals is a corollary of this view. Incidentally, there is no need to make stronger assumptions to obtain the classical results of general equilibrium theory and welfare economics, i.e., the existence theorem for an equilibrium and the theorems relating equilibrium allocations and Pareto optimal allocations (the so-called first and second welfare theorems).[3] The independence condition will forbid inter-personal comparisons of preferences. But Arrow explicitly introduces this condition to exclude scoring rules, more precisely to exclude Borda's rule. However, there is a slight misunderstanding in Arrow's original treatment of the condition. He considers an example with three voters, Messrs. j, k and l, and four candidates, a, b, c and d. The profile is such that for Ms. j and Mr. k the ranking is $a \succ b \succ c \succ d$, and for Ms. l, $c \succ d \succ a \succ b$. So a is chosen. If now b is deleted, what remains for Messrs. j and k is $a \succ c \succ d$ and for Ms. l, $c \succ d \succ a$. Then there is a tie between a and c. The slight misunderstanding refers to the fact that it is not Arrow's independence of irrelevant alternatives that is violated, but some independence of irrelevant alternatives condition whose origin is to be found in Nash's Bargaining theory {see Nash (1950)}. In Arrow's example, a is uniquely chosen in a set of four alternatives, but is not uniquely chosen in a subset of three. One can, of course, find even more dramatic examples where an alternative is uniquely chosen in the larger set but is not chosen at all in the smaller set although it still belongs to this smaller set.

Theoreticians have been rightly fascinated by Arrow's theorem and they first tried escape routes based on the weakening of the social rationality imbedded in the transitivity of $\succeq_S$. For instance, if the transitivity of $\succeq_S$ is replaced by its quasi-transitivity, i.e., by the transitivity of $\succ_S$, then a version of Arrow's theorem applied to **Q**-valued aggregation function is not true. As a matter of fact, the Pareto extension function is a counter-example to a theorem which would be similar to Arrow's theorem except that **P**-valuedness would be replaced by **Q**-valuedness. The Pareto extension function is an aggregation function for which for all x and $y \in X$, $x \succ_S y \Leftrightarrow$ for all individuals $i \in N$, $x \succ_i y$, and $y \succeq_S x$ otherwise. This function clearly satisfies conditions I, P and D⁻, and generates a quasi-transitive $\succeq_S$. However, if non-dictatorship is replaced by a no-vetoer condition, the result is restored.

---

3   See Arrow and Debreu (1954) and Arrow (1951a).

4   A French economist of the late 19th and early 20th century.

Definition 8

A *vetoer* is an individual $i \in N$ such that for all $x, y \in X$ and all $\pi \in \Pi'$, $x \succ_i y \Rightarrow x \succeq_s y$ where $\succeq_s = f(\pi)$.

Definition 9 (Condition V⁻, no-vetoer.) There is no vetoer.

Theorem 2

{Gibbard (1969).} *If $n \geq 2$ and $\#X \geq 3$, there is no **Q**-valued aggregation function satisfying U, P, I and V⁻.*

There is more in the original Gibbard's paper, since Gibbard shows that if f is a **Q**-valued aggregation function satisfying U, I and P, there exists an oligarchy, i.e., a group of individuals having full power if they act unanimously and whose members are all vetoers. For $n = 2$, majority rule gives a quasi-transitive social preference, but, in this case, each of the two individuals is a vetoer.

Other impossibility theorems were developed {see, for instance, for a rapid and partial presentation, Salles (2006)}. But, the independence condition was never questioned.

For a rather 'diagonal' defence of the independence condition, one can however refer to another very important result of social choice theory: the Gibbard-Satterthwaite theorem - a theorem conjectured by Dummett and Farquharson {see Gibbard (1973), Satterthwaite, Dummett and Farquharson, Dummett (1984) and Taylor}. A social choice function associates a unique alternative to a profile of individual preferences. Such a function is manipulable if, for a given profile, it can be advantageous for an individual to misrepresent her preferences. If, for instance, the given profile is a profile of sincere preferences whose value by the function is, say, a, then, by lying, i.e., by revealing a non-sincere ranking, an individual who sincerely prefers b to a can make the social choice be b. When applied to groups of voters, politicians (at least in France) generally speak of useful (i.e., tactical) voting: 'do not vote for your most preferred candidates since by doing so the result will be worse for you than if you vote for, say, your 2nd or 3rd or ... ranked candidate.' Famous examples of elections where voters forgot to vote usefully are the 2002 French presidential elections or the 2000 American presidential elections. If such a social choice function is surjective[5] and non manipulable, then, given a profile, one can construct a social (?) preference on the set of alternatives. This construction is thus a social welfare function. Very interestingly, this social welfare function satisfies Arrow's condition of independence of irrelevant alternatives (incidentally, this construction may be used to prove the Gibbard-Satterthwaite theorem, but there are other proofs).

In the next section, we will show that, if condition U is abandoned, then majority rule (which obviously satisfies the independence condition) is a social welfare function.

---

5   A mathematical condition which is rather innocuous: it asserts that for each option or candidate, there is a profile for which the function selects this option or candidate.

MAJORITY RULE AND BLACK'S ANALYSIS

As mentioned previously, the rebirth of social choice theory in the 1940s is due to the works of Arrow and Black. The main result of Black's writings in this regard concerns the majority rule and the existence of a transitive social preference generated by this rule when the individual preferences are appropriately restricted.

Black's original approach was geometrical. Suppose that the individuals have ordinal utility functions over a closed interval $[a, b]$ of the real line $\mathbf{R}$. Individual i utility function u_i represents her preference $\succeq_i$ in the sense that $u_i(x) \geq u_i(y) \Leftrightarrow x \succeq_i y$. That the function u_i be ordinal means that only the order properties of real numbers ($\geq$) are to be taken into account {it is then impossible, for instance, to distinguish between $u_i(x) = 4 \geq u_i(y) = 3$ and $u_i(x) = 864 \geq u_i(y) = 1$}. The single-peakedness condition is then defined in the following way. For each individual i, the utility function u_i has a unique maximum for the value $M_i \in [a, b]$, and for all x, y such that $a \leq x < y \leq M_i$, $u_i(x) < u_i(y)$ and for all x, y such that $M_i \leq x < y \leq b$, $u_i(x) > u_i(y)$. This means that u_i is strictly increasing on $[a, M_i]$ and strictly decreasing on $[M_i, b]$. Of course, it is possible that $M_i = a$ or $M_i = b$. Majority rule requires that $x \succ_S y \Leftrightarrow \#\{i : u_i(x) > u_i(y)\} > \#\{i : u_i(y) > u_i(x)\}$, and $y \succeq_S x$ otherwise. To simplify, assume that the M_i's are distinct and that the number of individuals is odd. Then there exists a unique Condorcet winner and this Condorcet winner is M_i^{med} such that $\#\{i : M_i < M_i^{\text{med}}\} = \#\{i : M_i > M_i^{\text{med}}\}$. This is the famous median voter theorem. Furthermore, the social preference generated by the majority rule, $\succeq_S$, is transitive. Of course, Black proposed developments dealing with the restrictive aforementioned assumptions. Arrow provided a discrete version of Black's analysis that could be stated in his set-theoretic framework. What follows is essentially a modified (but equivalent) version of Arrow's presentation.

Definition 10

The *majority rule* is an aggregation function for which for all $x, y \in X$ and all profile $\pi \in \Pi'$, $x \succ_S y \Leftrightarrow \#\{i : x \succ_i y\} > \#\{i : y \succ_i x\}$, and $y \succeq_S x$ otherwise.

Suppose there are three individuals Messrs. j, k and l with the following preferences on three alternatives, a, b and c: $a \succ_j b \succ_j c$, $b \succ_k c \succ_k a$ and $c \succ_l a \succ_l b$. This means that Ms. j prefers a to b, b to c and a to c, etc.. It is obvious that majority rule generates $a \succ_S b$, $b \succ_S c$ and $c \succ_S a$. This is the Condorcet paradox. It indicates that the majority rule is not a social welfare function if Condition U is satisfied (all the other conditions introduced in Section 1 are obviously satisfied).

Definition 11

Let $\{a, b, c\} \subseteq X$. A set of complete preorders $\succeq$ over X satisfies the condition of *single-peakedness over $\{a, b, c\}$* if either $a \sim b$ and $b \sim c$ or there is one of the three alternatives, say b, such that $b \succ a$ or $b \succ c$.

Let **BL** denote the set of complete preorders over X such that the condition of single-peakedness is satisfied for all $\{x, y, z\} \subseteq X$.

Theorem 3

{Black (1948).} *If* $\mathbf{P'} = \mathbf{BL}$ *and if, for any* $\{x, y, z\} \subseteq X$, *the number of individuals for which* $\neg(x \sim_i y$ *and* $y \sim_i z)$ *is odd, the majority rule is a social welfare function.*

This only means that the social preference is transitive.[6] With three alternatives, there are 13 complete preorders and 8 single-peaked complete preorders. Single-peakedness essentially means that among the three alternatives there is one which is never (strictly) the worst. There is an interesting and intuitively meaningful geometrical representation. If the three alternatives a, b and c are on a line with b between a and c, we have the following possibilities:

TABLE 5.A — BLACK'S SINGLE-PEAKEDNESS CONDITION OVER $\{a, b, c\}$

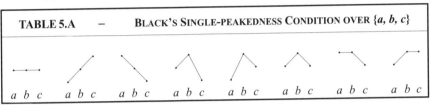

When the alternatives a, b and/or c are at the same horizontal level, this means that there is an indifference between them, and when one of the alternatives $x \in \{a, b, c\}$ is vertically above $y \in \{a, b, c\}$, this means $x \succ y$. Now a, b and c are linearly ordered, a being on the left, b in the center and c on the right. It is then very easy to interpret the admissible (single-peaked) preferences from a political viewpoint, for instance when a, b and c are candidates to an election.

If the condition of single-peakedness is acceptable and meaningful, then for many people there is no obvious reason why we should not use majority rule as it can appear as a solution to the Condorcet paradox and to the impossibility aspect of Arrow's theorem. But, of course, this does not solve the problem mentioned in the examples given by Michael Dummett in the foreword and by myself in the previous section. However, there are still many people including major economists with a deep knowledge of social choice theory who remain convinced supporters of the independence condition, the majority rule and the notion of Condorcet winner. Recently, two highly regarded economists, Partha Dasgupta and Eric Maskin (2004), made a plea in favour of these concepts. Interestingly, they considered another restriction as meaningful in the context of the 2002 French presidential election. The appropriate condition is due to Ward (1964). It says that for three alternatives there is one that every individual uniquely prefers to the other two, or that she ranks uniquely last. If this is true for all three-alternative subsets, then we are in the same situation as with single-peakedness: the social preference generated by majority rule will be transitive and we will have a Condorcet winner. Dasgupta and Maskin applied Ward's possibility result to the three main candidates to this 2002 French presidential election: Jacques Chirac, Lionel Jospin

---

6 Incidentally, we can avoid this condition of oddity if we only require that the asymmetric component of $\succeq_s$, $\succ_s$, be transitive. See Sen (1970) and Sen and Pattanaik (1969).

and Jean-Marie Le Pen. They postulated that in the voters' rankings, either Jean-Marie Le Pen was ranked 1st or was ranked 3rd. It is true that the results of the run-off exemplified that a quasi-unanimity of those who ranked Jospin 1st ranked Chirac 2nd and Le Pen 3rd. However, it was impossible to say anything about those who ranked Chirac 1st. I would conjecture that a non-negligible proportion of these voters ranked Le Pen 2nd and Jospin only 3rd. To be honest, I believe that, in a run-off between Jospin and Le Pen, Jospin would have got 65-70% of the votes, to be compared with the 80% obtained by Chirac. Incidentally, to have a Condorcet winner and/or a transitive social preference, it seems rather obvious that it is not necessary for all the voters to have preferences satisfying the single-peakedness condition or Ward's condition, but just a sufficient proportion of these voters. To the best of my knowledge, we do not know what is this sufficient proportion. All I can say is that it should be greater than $2/3$, as it is quite easy to prove that with exactly $2/3$, one can get a cycle. The Condorcet paradox was obtained above with three rankings. When we have two rankings among these three, these two rankings satisfy the single-peakedness condition or Ward's condition.

I believe that all my readers will now understand why Arrow's independence condition, the Condorcet winner property and majority rule (and more generally pairwise voting) were so important and successful. I will briefly conclude by mentioning when and how things began to change.

SCORING RULES AND BORDA

The first paper adopting a modern scientific approach to Borda's rule is probably Young's paper.[7] This provides a characterisation of Borda's rule, i.e., it gives a set of properties that uniquely define Borda's rule. Then, with an original approach, Dummett's book (1984) presents a theoretical partial overview of some of the main results of social choice theory (Impossibility *à la* Arrow and *à la* Gibbard-Satterthwaite), and describes and analyses various voting procedures, including Borda's rule. Without being too technical, Dummett (1997) further develops the descriptions of voting procedures, prominently including Borda's rule. Saari in a series of books and papers provides a deep mathematical analysis of scoring rules in general, and Borda's rule in particular {see, for instance, Saari (1995, 2001)}. He also compares scoring methods to pairwise methods in (2000, 2000a). A final remark: although Michael Dummett and Donald Saari are obvious supporters of Borda's rule, at least in some situations, they have both made crucial contributions to pairwise voting {see Dummett and Farquharson, and Saari (1997, 2006)}.

---

7   1974, pp 43-52. Young also wrote a more general paper on scoring rules, {see Young (1975)}.

Chapter 6

Assessing Borda's Rule and Its Modifications
Hannu Nurmi

Abstract

The BC is a positional voting procedure fairly often applied in non-political choice settings. It has a usual mixture of good and bad theoretical properties. It is monotonic and consistent and excludes the election of an eventual Condorcet loser. It, however, does not necessarily choose the Condorcet winner when one exists. Its strategic properties have also been found unattractive. Some modifications to it have therefore been proposed, notably Nanson's method. We also compare the BC with two of its recent modifications, the MBC and the QBS. It turns out that, although similar in spirit to BC, MBC and QBS do not share one of the former's main justifications: the exclusion of an eventual Condorcet loser. It is also shown that QBS tends to lead to more majoritarian outcomes than BC. We also touch upon the matrix vote which enables the voter to express his/her views on both candidates and positions simultaneously.

INTRODUCTION

The history of the BC is well-known. Introduced by Chevalier Jean-Charles de Borda to the Royal French Academy of Sciences in 1770 as a replacement of the then (and still now) widely used plurality voting, it met with a modicum of success in terms of practical application (in the French Academy of Sciences), but was soon largely forgotten to be rescued from oblivion about a hundred years later by E J Nanson and C L Dodgson.[1] It was not until Black's *magnum opus* (1958) in the end of the 1950's that BC was brought to a comparative context with other social choice rules. It is fair to say that the going has been all but smooth for BC. The main criticism levelled against it today echoes the attack of Marquis de Condorcet and is based on a binary intuition of winning {see Risse for a recent criticism and Saari (2006) for its rebuttal}.

In the following we shall first present some social choice criteria invoked in the debates on BC and see how the rule fares in terms of those criteria. We also evaluate an early modfication of BC, Nanson's method. We then focus on another - strategic - set of performance criteria and assess BC in the light of these. Thereafter, we discuss a couple of recent competitors of BC versus plurality voting as well as the modifications of BC itself: the MBC of Chapter 1 and the QBS of Chapter 2.

---

[1] McLean and Urken give a thorough account of the history of BC arguing *inter alia* that the BC was actually invented several hundred years before Borda by Ramon Lull. Borda was, however, undeniably the first to discuss the method in any systematic and comparative detail. Hence, the nomenclature seems wholly appropriate.

Borda Count: the Basic Properties

The BC is a point voting system where each voter provides a ranking. Each alternative is positioned in one and only one rank by each voter. In technical terms this means that each voter's vote expresses a complete and transitive preference order over the decision alternatives. Borda proposed that the lowest rank would be given a points, the next to lowest $a + b$ points, the next one $a + 2b$ points, and so on. In the preceding chapters, the values $a = 1$ and $b = 1$ have been applied. However, any other assignment of positive numbers will yield the same outcomes. The points given by each voter to an alternative are then summed up. This sum is called the Borda score of the alternative. The Borda winner is the alternative with the largest Borda score and the Borda ranking is the ordering of the alternatives consistent with their Borda scores, the larger the score, the higher the rank.

The main message of Borda's memoir presented to the French Academy was to show that plurality voting - i.e. one person, one preference system - may lead to quite unacceptable outcomes. To wit, it may happen that the plurality winner would be regarded worse than any other alternative by a majority of voters in pairwise contests. A slightly simplified version of Borda's example is presented in Table 6.A.

TABLE 6.A	4 voters	3 voters	2 voters
	A	*B*	*C*
BC VERSUS	*B*	*C*	*B*
PLURALITY VOTING	*C*	*A*	*A*

The table expresses the preferences of voters in the customary way. E.g., 4 voters rank *A* before *B* and *B* before *C*. Assuming that these preferences are revealed in the ballots cast, we observe that *A* would win the plurality contest by 4 votes against *B*'s 3 and *C*'s 2 votes. And yet, *A* would be defeated by both *B* and *C* in pairwise majority comparisons; *B* would win *A* with 5 votes against 4 and *C* would also win *A* by the same margin. Hence, the case for arguing that *A* expresses the will of the collective body is very weak, indeed. In modern terminology alternatives that are defeated by all others by a majority in pairwise contests are called Condorcet losers. It is clear that Borda wanted to avoid such alternatives being chosen. This was the main point of his criticism against plurality voting. One of the primary virtues of his proposal, BC, is to exclude the possibility of the choice of an eventual Condorcet loser.

Of the other theoretical properties of BC perhaps the best-known is the possibility that it may not elect a Condorcet winner, i.e. an alternative that in pairwise contests would defeat all others in pairwise comparisons. In Table 6.A, *B* is the Condorcet winner since it beats *A* with 5 votes against 4 and *C* with 7 votes to 2. In this example, BC happens to elect the Condorcet winner. Modifying the example slightly so as to get Table 6.B we see, however, that BC may not end up with the Condorcet winner ranked first. *A* is clearly the Condorcet winner, but *B* gets the highest Borda score.

TABLE 6.B	4 voters	2 voters	1 voter
	A	B	C
BC Versus	B	C	B
Condorcet Winner	C	A	A

In Table 6.B, the discrepancy between the winning criterion named after Condorcet and BC is particularly marked since *A* is the strong Condorcet winner, i.e. is top-ranked by more than 50% of the voters.

The critics of BC have pointed to the discrepancy between the BC outcome and the Condorcet winner as the main flaw of BC. Some - e.g. Riker (1982) - have also called attention to the "instability" of BC rankings under modifications - expansions or subtractions - of the alternative set (Fishburn 1974; Hill 1988). The following example illustrates (Nurmi 1998, p 126).

In Table 6.C, the Borda ranking is ***CBA***. Suppose, however, that ***B***, for some reason, is not available. Deleting ***B*** and recomputing the Borda scores for the remaining alternatives yields the Borda ranking ***AC***. This is a reversal of the ranking over these three alternatives in the original setting. Thus, among *A* and *C*, *C* is the winner if ***B*** is present, but ***A*** is the winner if ***B*** is absent. Hence, the Borda winner in the set X is not necessarily the Borda winner in all proper subsets of X containing it. In fact, Fishburn's result states that the Borda winner in a set X of alternatives is not necessarily the Borda winner in any proper subset of X except one. In other words, if an alternative is the Borda winner in a set consisting of 8 candidates, it has to be the Borda winner in no more than one out of the 127 coalitions it is a member of.

TABLE 6.C	2 voters	2 voters	2 voters	1 voter
	C	A	B	C
BC and Deleted	B	C	A	B
Alternatives	A	B	C	A

Early Remedy?

About a hundred years after the publication of Borda's memoir, E J Nanson (1883) published a systematic comparison of a variety of voting systems. In contrast to his predecessors in the theory of voting, Nanson was well aware of the major developments in his field. In particular, he knew that the Condorcet winner is not necessarily elected by BC. He set out to devise a modification of BC that did not have this flaw. Nanson's proposal - today called Nanson's method - is based on the observation that despite the fact that the Condorcet winner does not necessarily receive the highest Borda score, there is a connection between the Condorcet winner and the Borda scores. To wit, the Condorcet winner never gets the lowest Borda score. In fact, it can be shown that the Condorcet winner always gets a strictly higher than average Borda score.

These observations led Nanson to suggest that BC be used as an elimination device so that at each stage of the process, those alternatives with at most the average Borda score are eliminated. After the elimination, new Borda scores are computed for the remaining alternatives disregarding the eliminated ones. The process is repeated until we are left with a unique winner or a tie between some alternatives. The elimination criterion guarantees that if there is a Condorcet winner, it will not be eliminated. Thus, it will be elected by Nanson's method.

Nanson was, thus, able to secure the satisfaction of both Condorcet criteria - viz. that an eventual Condorcet winner be elected and that the eventual Condorcet loser not be chosen - by a method that is very much in the spirit of BC. However, the cost of securing the former criterion is high: Nanson's method is non-monotonic. In other words, additional support may turn a winning candidate into a losing one. This is illustrated by Table 6.D.

TABLE 6.D	5 voters	9 voters	5 voters	9 voters	13 voters	2 voters
	B	*B*	*A*	*A*	*C*	*A*
NANSON'S	*A*	*D*	*C*	*B*	*A*	*C*
METHOD IS	*C*	*C*	*B*	*D*	*D*	*D*
NON-MONOTONIC	*D*	*A*	*D*	*C*	*B*	*B*

Here *A* becomes the Nanson winner after first *D* and both *B* and *C* are eliminated. Suppose now that the left-most group of 5 voters changes its mind in *A*'s favour so that its ranking is *ABCD*. In the new profile, Nanson's method results in *C*. Thus, the winner *A*'s additional support renders it non-winner. This shows that Nanson's method is non-monotonic. The price of Condorcet consistency, that is, choosing a Condorcet winner when one exists, thus seems to be the loss of monotonicity. This price is perhaps too high. Hence the question mark in the section heading.

Incomplete Ballots: Borda's Forte Lost

When the number of candidates or policy alternatives considered is large, it is unreasonable to expect the voters to rank each and every one of them. Yet, BC in its basic form requires this. So, what to do if a person simply ranks a couple of his/her most preferred options, but leaves the rest blank? It would seem reasonable to allow this type of behaviour. Hence, the most voter-hostile way of proceeding - which is to disqualify such ballots - seems indefensible. After all, the voter has clearly expressed his/her ranking over a few alternatives. Moreover, it is plausible to assume that he/she has also provided a ranking between these alternatives, on the one hand, and those not ranked, on the other. He/she obviously prefers each ranked alternative to each not ranked one. But how to assign points to alternatives in this setting?

Several ways of proceeding can be envisioned:

i) Assume that incomplete ballots indicate a tie between all alternatives that have not been ranked and compute the Borda scores accordingly. For example, if there are 5 alternatives A, B, C, D and E and a voter ranks A before B leaving other alternatives unranked, we assign A 5, B 4 and C, D and E, the average score, i.e. 2 points, each. This would give each voter the same number of points to be distributed regardless of whether he/she ranks all the alternatives.

ii) Assume that all unranked alternatives are, in fact, ranked last, i.e. given zero points by the voter casting an incomplete ballot, and the ranked ones are given Borda scores as if all alternatives were ranked. In the above 5-alternative example, A would be given 5, B 4 and C, D and E 0 points each. This would allow the voter to make a disproportionately large difference between his/her favourites and the unranked alternatives. In fact, this would encourage strategic behaviour since by casting an incomplete ballot, a voter may increase the score difference between his/her favourites and the other alternatives from the difference he/she would be able to make by casting a complete ballot.

iii) MBC. This system, elaborated in the preceding chapters, reduces the Borda point of the 1st ranked alternative by 1 for every unranked alternative. In the preceding example, A would receive 2 and B 1 points, while C, D and E get 0 points each. Thus, the strategic incentives for preference "truncation" are smaller than in systems described above.

iv) QBS. This differs from the preceding one in introducing a new criterion for election of a candidate, viz. quota q. This is obtained by dividing the number of voters by the number of vacancies to be filled plus one. Any candidate who is ranked 1st by at least q voters is elected. In constituencies sending 3/4 representatives, also any pair of candidates which has been ranked 1st or 2nd by at least $2q$ voters is elected. Analogously, in constituencies sending at least 5 representatives, any triplet of candidates ranked 1st, 2nd or 3rd by at least $3q$ voters is elected.

The main motivation of these modifications is to handle incomplete ballots. They accomplish this in a very different manner, though. The first, i), assigns each voter - regardless of whether his/her ballot is complete - the same total of points, while ii), iii) and iv) do not. The second, ii), is particularly vulnerable to strategic manoeuvering since by truncating his/her ballot, the voter can increase the total point difference between his/her favourites and the rest of the alternatives more than would be possible under BC. To a lesser extent this holds for i) as well. MBC and QBS give less incentives for preference truncation since the point differences between ranked candidates remain the same as in BC and - furthermore - the maximum score is smaller than in BC.

Incomplete ballots are likely to be encountered in elections with large number of candidates. It turns out, however, that neither MBC nor QBS guarantees the exclusion of an eventual Condorcet loser. The following example illustrates this.

In Table 6.E, A is the Condorcet loser since it is defeated by all other alternatives in pairwise comparisons with 5 votes to 4. Alternative B gets the highest Borda score.

Suppose that the three rightmost groups consisting of 3, 1 and 1 voters, respectively, cast an incomplete ballot indicating only their 1st preference, while the leftmost group indicates its entire ranking. Under these circumstances, the MBC elects *A*, the Condorcet loser. Assume that four representatives are elected. Then also QBS includes the Condorcet loser *A*, since it, along with *B*, exceeds the quota 2. Thus QBS elects the Condorcet loser.

TABLE 6.E	4 voters	3 voters	1 voter	1 voter
	A	*B*	*C*	*E*
	B	*E*	*D*	*C*
MBC AND QBS MAY ELECT A CONDORCET LOSER	*C*	*D*	*B*	*D*
	D	*C*	*E*	*B*
	E	*F*	*G*	*F*
	F	*G*	*F*	*G*
	G	*A*	*A*	*A*

It can be shown that modifications i) and ii) in the above list can also end up with a Condorcet loser. Thus, all BC modifications of this section result in the choice of the Condorcet loser. The price for accommodating incomplete ballots with the above techniques may seem high.

How Robust Are the Condorcet Winners?

The fact that BC may not elect the Condorcet winner is often deemed its main flaw. The importance of the Condorcet winning criterion is visible in those incompatibility theorems where this criterion is shown to be incompatible with this or that desirable property of the choice rule. For example, there is a theorem showing the incompatibility between the Condorcet winning criterion and invulnerability to the no-show paradox {Moulin, (1988)}. Another one relates the Condorcet criterion with manipulability of choice functions {Gärdenfors, (1976)}. Clearly, the significance of these and other related results is the greater, the more compelling is the Condorcet winning criterion. Yet, an argument can be built to the effect that the criterion is not all that compelling. Let us look at Fishburn's (1973) example (Table 6.F).

TABLE 6.F	1 voter	1 voter	1 voter	1 voter	1 voter
	D	*E*	*C*	*D*	*E*
IMPLAUSIBILITY	*E*	*A*	*D*	*E*	*B*
OF THE	*A*	*C*	*E*	*B*	*A*
CONDORCET WINNER	*B*	*B*	*A*	*C*	*D*
	C	*D*	*B*	*A*	*C*

Here D is the Condorcet winner, but one could make a strong case for electing E. To wit, E is ranked 1st by as many voters as D, E is ranked 2nd by more voters than D and E is ranked 3rd by more voters than D. Moreover, E has no lower ranks in any voter's preference, while D is ranked once 4th and once last. Surely, E would seem more plausible choice than the Condorcet winner D. Now, why is that? The reason is simply that we know the entire preference rankings of all voters and in the light of those rankings E seems to be ranked higher on the average than D. There is a technical word - coined by Fishburn (1982) - for this type of superiority: positional dominance. An alternative A positionally dominates alternative B if A has at least as many 1st ranks as B, as many 1st or 2nd ranks as B, etc. until the penultimate rank. We see that positional dominance may contradict pairwise majority voting.

The case for the Condorcet winning criterion becomes even more contestable once we see that Condorcet winners are surprisingly unstable under modifications of preference profiles through adding or subtracting groups of voters. Saari (1995) shows that a group of voters whose preferences over alternatives form an instance of the Condorcet paradox, when added to an existing preference profile, may "destroy" a Condorcet winner. And yet, the Condorcet paradox is a completely symmetrical setting where an equal number of voters rank each of the three alternatives 1st, 2nd and 3rd. To illustrate, consider the following setting (Table 6.G) (Nurmi, 2002, pp 124-126).

TABLE 6.G	5 voters	3 voters
	A	B
BC AND (STRONG)	B	C
CONDORCET WINNER	C	A

TABLE 6.H	3 voters	3 voters	3 voters
	A	B	C
THE CONDORCET PARADOX	C	A	B
	B	C	A

Table 6.G exhibits a dramatic instance of the discrepancy between the Condorcet and Borda winners. A is the Condorcet winner, indeed, a strong one in the sense of being ranked 1st by a majority of voters. B, on the other hand, is the Borda winner.

Consider now an instance of the Condorcet paradox shown in Table 6.H. Unless one treats voters or alternatives in some discriminating fashion, there is no way of telling which of the three alternatives should be elected. The setting is a perfect tie. So, we have two settings: Table 6.G where the choice is clear, on the one hand, and Table 6.H where no alternative should be preferred to the others, on the other. Now, adding the voters of Table 6.H to the profile of Table 6.G should, intuitively, leave the winner of the latter profile intact. And it does, if one applies BC. However, if one resorts to any Condorcet extension method - i.e. a method that always results in the choice of the Condorcet winner when one exists - the outcome changes from A to B, the new Condorcet winner. So, adding a group of voters whose preferences form a tie, changes the outcome of Condorcet extension methods.

Saari also shows that nearly all positional voting procedures - e.g. plurality voting and anti-plurality voting - are sensitive to adding or subtracting voting groups of equal size but with diametrically opposed preferences such as ABC and CBA. Of positional procedures only BC is invulnerable to these kinds of changes. To illustrate, add 3 voters with preference CAB and 3 voters with opposing preference BAC to the Table 6.G profile where A is the plurality winner. It turns out that in the resulting profile, B emerges as the plurality winner.

Quite a strong case can thus be made for BC as it is the only procedure that leaves the winners intact after adding Condorcet paradox groups or groups with preferences that "cancel out" each other.

Ways Out of Majority Tyranny

One of the perennial problems of constitutional design is to avoid permanent majorities from exploiting any minorities without slipping into the rule of minority. The standard way of handling the problems of majority tyranny - or more neutrally expressed, majority decisiveness - is to impose high majority thresholds for proposals to pass in the collective decision making body. The extreme case is, of course, the rule of unanimity which *ipso facto* guarantees that no one objects to the decisions passed by the body. This rule has an unpleasant feature, though: any voter can veto any proposal. Hence, the rule has a very strong *status quo* bias.

In the other end of the majority rule spectrum is the simple majority principle which states that if a proposal is backed by strictly more than 50% of the voters, it will pass. Hence, any majority can dictate the decision outcomes. Baharad and Nitzan (2002) prove an interesting result relating the majority threshold to the type of point voting system. Point voting systems are methods based on individual preference rankings where $p(1)....p(k)$ are the points assigned to alternatives ranked $1^{st}, ... k^{th}$. In plurality voting $p(1) = 1$ and $p(2) = ... = p(k) = 0$, while in BC $p(1) = k, ... p(k) = 1$. Baharad and Nitzan's result states that when the voters vote sincerely and with majority threshold α; $(0 < \alpha < 1)$, the condition

$$\alpha(p(k) - p(k-1)) < (1 - \alpha)(p(k) - p(1))$$

implies that the point voting system is immune to majority decisiveness. Since in BC this expression reduces to

$$k > \frac{1}{1 - \alpha}$$

even a modest number of alternatives is sufficient to rule out tyranny of even large majorities. For example, 4 alternatives guarantee immunity to decisiveness of up to $3/4$

majority. This result pertains to sincere voting. When the voters can coordinate their voting strategies, BC guarantees immunity to all α-majority rules when $\alpha \geq {}^2/_3$ (Baharad and Nitzan 2002). Thus BC provides a fairly strong protection against majority tyranny.

What happens when we institute a quota in accordance with QBS? In contrast to what one would expect, the effect of the quota is to lower the threshold for majority decisiveness. To wit, by setting the quota at $n/(e+1)$, where n is the number of voters and e the number of elected candidates, one often enables smaller majorities to be decisive than would be the case if BC were applied. Stated in another way: in QBS one needs the coordination of larger groups to gain representation than in BC. Thus, QBS is less minority empowering than BC. Consider the example of Table 6.I.

TABLE 6.I	7 voters	7 voters	3 voters	3 voters
	A	*B*	*C*	*C*
	D	*C*	*D*	*D*
QBS AND BC	*C*	*D*	*B*	*A*
	B	*A*	*A*	*B*

Assuming that two representatives are to be elected, BC ends up with *C* and *D*. On the other hand, since the quota is 7, *A* and *B* are elected under QBS. The outcome of QBS remains the same if we assume that the two leftmost voter groups reveal only their 1st preferences. It seems, then, that QBS is considerably more majoritarian in spirit than BC.

A Word on Consistency

One of the virtues of BC is consistency (Young 1974). In social choice theory this concept is defined as follows. Suppose that two distinct groups of voters - say, two municipalities that together form a constituency - are electing a representative body from the same set of candidates using the same voting procedure. Suppose, moreover, that these groups end up with at least a partially overlapping set of representatives. Now, the procedure used by both groups is said to be consistent, if under these circumstances the procedure, when applied to the ballots of both groups simultaneously, always exactly results in the overlapping set of winners.

In single-winner elections consistency means that if candidate *B* wins in both municipalities, he/she always wins also in the constituency as a whole. Despite its intuitive plausibility, consistency is not a common property among voting systems (see, e.g. Nurmi 1987, pp 92-107). However, BC is consistent; QBS, on the other hand, is not. The example of Table 6.J illustrates.

The single-member constituency consists of East and West, the former with 9 and the latter with 10 voters. Applying QBS, *A* exceeds the quota in East and is elected,

	East			West		
TABLE 6.J	5	3	1	4	3	3
	A	*B*	*C*	*A*	*B*	*C*
QBS IS INCONSISTENT	*B*	*C*	*B*	*B*	*C*	*A*
	C	*A*	*A*	*C*	*A*	*B*

while in West it wins because it has the highest Borda score. Combining the ballots of East andWest, we observe that no candidate exceeds the quota and hence the winner is determined by the Borda scores. Now, it turns out that ***B*** wins. Hence, QBS is inconsistent.

Comments on the Matrix Vote

The matrix vote enables the voters to indicate their preference simultaneously over candidates and positions. More precisely the voter is able to indicate his/her preference over "states of affairs" where each state is a combination of a candidate and the office. One state of affairs could be, e.g. "candidate ***J*** in position ***A***". This, of course, tells something different of voter preferences than the assignment of Borda points to candidates (or, for that matter, to positions). Namely, for each position or office the voter can only reveal his/her favourite candidate precisely as in plurality voting. What distinguishes the matrix vote from plurality voting is that the voters also reveal their priorities regarding the positions. In other words, the matrix vote is a mixture of plurality and BC. The fact that for each position only one candidate is singled out by the voter is reminiscent of plurality voting, while the weights assigned to positions stem remind us of BC. Thus, the voters may rank the positions, but not the candidates to each position (except in the limited sense of indicating their 1st preference).

The matrix vote outcomes are determined on the basis of the MBC scores. For example in Table 3.W, (p 72), the first position to be filled is that of minister of ***B*** since the row corresponding to that ministerial post has the largest entry in the whole Table. The next posts are filled applying the same principle. Invoking the just mentioned interpretation of the scores, it can be said that the state of affairs where candidate ***Q*** becomes the minister of ***B*** has the largest collective preference among single ministerial post allocations.

This seems a plausible way to determine the composition of the cabinet. At least it provides the voters an incentive to think not only about their favourite candidates, but also about which tasks those candidates would be best suited to. On closer inspection, though, Table 3.W reveals something of an anomaly, viz. Mr. ***O*** becomes the minister of ***D*** and, yet, not a single voter has given him a single point for that ministerial portfolio. What we have here is a variation of the paradox of multiple elections discussed by Brams *et al*. (1997, 1998). When a ballot is taken separately on several policy issues, the (majority) winning combination of policies may be one that was supported by no voter. Here the portfolio allocation over candidates is one that is supported by not a single voter.[2]

The matrix vote combines preferential information of candidates with that of positions. The end result may, thus, grossly deviate from a position-by-position BC. In other words, if the voters were allowed to indicate their preference rankings over candidates for each position separately, the portfolio allocation could be very different from the one resulting from the matrix vote. This is not surprising since differences between BC and plurality voting are due to the fact that the former utilizes the preference information to a far larger extent than the latter. The matrix vote has one advantage over the position-wise BC, viz. it is relatively easy to implement and, moreover, it enables the voter to signal his/her priorities regarding offices to be filled.

Conclusion

The discrepancy between BC and the requirement that the Condorcet winner be elected whenever one exists is well known from the early days of the social choice theory. Nanson's method sets out to remove this discrepancy by eliminating alternatives and repeating BC, while simultaneously making sure that the eventual Condorcet winner is not eliminated on the way. The price of achieving compatibility is, however, high: Nanson's method is non-monotonic. More recent variations of BC - MBC and QBS - aim at allowing for incomplete ballots which are bound to become increasingly common in large sets of candidates. It turns out that while both of the modifications are monotonic, they may include a Condorcet loser in their choice sets. It is also possible that while in general successful in protecting minority opinions, QBS sometimes also leads to a more majoritarian outcome than BC. The matrix vote empowers the voter to express his/her opinion about both candidates and the offices to be filled.

---

2   An obvious, but perhaps impracticable way out of the paradox of multiple elections is to allow the voters to rank all allocations of individuals to ministerial posts and elect the allocation with the largest BC score. The impracticability stems from the enormous number of voting alternatives facing each voter.

Chapter 7

Human Rights and Voting Procedures in Plural Societies
Christine Bell

ELECTIONS

The right to vote in periodic elections stands at the heart of the international legal system. It is provided in all the main human rights conventions: the Universal Declaration of Human Rights (article 21),[1] International Covenant on Civil and Political Rights (article 25), the European Convention for the Protection of Human Rights (Protocol 1, article 3), and the Charter of the Organization of American States (article 23); (the African (Banjul) Charter on Human and Peoples' Rights does not explicitly have a right to vote, but article 13 guarantees the right to participate in government either directly or through freely chosen representatives). Yet the right says very little on its own about other matters that clearly go to making the right substantive in the sense of linking the outcome of elections with voter choice. The right says nothing about how much choice should the voter have – is one party enough; or what steps need to be taken to make the election fair? Other aspects of the international legal system, and in particular the UN's electoral support mechanisms, have addressed these matters.

Yet at a deeper level the totality of civil and political rights seem designed to institute the mechanisms and procedures now known as 'liberal democracy' as a vehicle for on-going conflict resolution. The right to elections, when coupled with the freedom of association, freedom of the press, the right to a fair trial, protection of the right to life, would seem to ensure that the right to periodic elections is capable of delivering some connection between the governors and the governed.

In many conflict situations, particularly those of ethnic conflict, the structures of liberal democracy have, however, been judged insufficient in diffusing conflict. The concept of periodic elections does not seem to deliver much to a minority in a situation of ethnic politics where the voters' preferences seem to be ethnically aligned rather than policy aligned. Here, the normal notion that those who lose in periodic elections must seek to persuade the electorate to vote for them next time, through policy promotion, simply does not seem to apply.

Self-determination

These situations if unaddressed, can lead to escalating conflict and secessionist claims. Here another human rights norm comes into play, and that is the right to self-

---

[1] The wording of this article is in the footnote on p 141.

determination.[2] However, the difficulty with this norm is that it is unclear to whom the right is attached, and what the remedy is. The right attaches to 'peoples', but 'peoples' are somehow different from 'minorities', and it appears not to include 'indigenous peoples'. Even when the right does apply, it appears to promise a choice of government, but the affirmation of territorial integrity means that secession seems prohibited, leaving open the question of what peoples are then entitled to by way of a remedy for their right.

Increasingly, the answer has been that peoples are entitled to representative forms of government. Where these cannot be delivered by periodic elections, then innovations such as autonomous regimes for minorities, or power-sharing between the majority and minority have been suggested. This concept has been labelled 'internal self-determination', in contrast to a concept of 'external self-determination' whereby colonised states had won their independence.

DECISION-MAKING

The ideas set out in this book take a different approach. Peter Emerson reframes the central problem of decision-making, not as one of finding the right 'mix' of ethnic groups to make the decision, but of finding a mode of decision-making which would prioritise consensus-building mechanisms over the 'winner-takes-all' dynamic of majoritarian voting. From this perspective, power-sharing and autonomous regimes replicate the basic structure of decision-making, i.e., they just aim to weigh the interests of minorities to the point at which they count. In doing this, they often stand charged with reinforcing the very labels of ethnicity which the international architects of such solutions seek to enable the society to transcend. The main alternative to power-sharing solutions are more 'integrative' ones, which aim to shape voter preferences at an earlier stage so as to force opposing groups into coalition. These stand charged with doing little to reassure minorities that they will be able to see the impact of their electoral choices. These two options - Lijphart's 'consociationalism' and Horowitz's 'integrationism' - appear to be the main theories.

Emerson's proposals aim to change not the structures which pre-determine voter preferences and choices, but the structures of decision-making itself - whether those of voters or those of their elected representatives. The attempt is not to eliminate the minority, by giving the minority some of the majority's power, but to eliminate the competition between majority and minority by creating a decision-making structure which enables them to compromise rather than compete. In place of majority and minority vetoes as the incentive to compromise, we get the incentive that it is the proposal which receives the most 'consensus' support, rather than the one which pips all others to the post, which will win. His proposal is a grand one in that it claims relevance not just to ethnic conflict, but to the whole business of government decision-making wherever it occurs. It aims to turn the notion of politics as confrontation, and elections as establishing winners and losers, on its head.

---

2   *Article 1.1, The International Covenant on Civil and Political Rights,* is quoted on p 142.

Why has the international community worked with autonomy and power-sharing, rather than ideas such as these? The short answer is that they work with what they know, what is tried and tested. Even if the results of the tests have not been encouraging, these options have the advantage of being 'the devil you know' as opposed to 'the devil you don't'. This not only means that international mediators know what they are selling, but wary minority groups can see what it is they are being sold in terms of numbers of elected politicians, numbers of ministries, the specific issues on which a veto will apply, and the precise mechanism for triggering the veto. All-inclusive voting is extremely threatening to all these certainties. The most extreme and powerful groups stand to lose control over their political agendas.

Many of the critiques of the MBC are practical – that it is too complicated, that people do not and cannot understand it. But examples do exist. In Northern Ireland, for example, there was an unattributed attempt to work with Emerson's ideas prior to the signing of the Belfast Agreement. A group of academics setting out positions in the talks across a spectrum and polling the Northern Ireland electorate on their opinions, and then working out which positions on very divided issues had the most chance of success. These positions came very close to the agreement's provisions, which they may well have influenced.

Human Rights Questions

How are we to evaluate this in human rights terms? What follows are some preliminary questions:

Are the MBC, QBS and matrix vote consistent with democratic rights? There could be an argument that political choice is violated by not allowing the majority to rule. Yet, as we have seen, human rights law itself says relatively little about how the results of an election can maintain any relationship between voter policy preferences and the policies of those they elect.

At some level it depends on what the rationale is. If elections are a good in themselves, then this argument might fly. But if elections are only a route to creating a connection of accountability – then arguably the MBC creates a much greater connection between voter and politician, because it links a greater number of people to supporting the decision. It arguably provides a more nuanced account of the voters' preferences, honouring some element of those preferences rather than all or none.

Is the MBC a progressive way to further realise the right to elections? This book makes the case that it is. Reservations which remain for me, concern less the point of principle, and more the practicalities of the implementation of the MBC. In particular, the consensors who frame the choice would seem to me to have a lot of control over how the choice is made. A badly designed MBC would dictate a choice. I have filled in too many multiple choice social surveys where the terms 'strongly agree' or 'disagree' do not accurately convey my opinions, and where the options I would like to see exhibited have not been sketched out at all.

On the other hand, it is entirely conceivable that political discourse changes in response to addressing these questions. It is difficult to predict exactly how. In a country of disciplined tactical voters, another concern is whether the MBC can be manipulated by the inclusion of extreme choices, or by vastly increasing the spectrum of choices. If there are too many choices then does the consensus become such a minimalist common denominator that it reflects little consensus at all? The role of the consensors is discussed on pp 17-8, while the issue of the irrelevant alternative is addressed on pp 90-1.

Finally, in situations such as peace agreements, there is a difficulty of how one puts together packages of agreements? People will accept sets of compromises depending on what is agreed elsewhere, and testing this in a series of options seems difficult. While Emerson seems to recommend testing each option, there is the additional question of whether in a complex legislative package, each option can be treated discretely. The referendum only offers a once off 'yes' or 'no', but has the advantage (and the disadvantage) of being able to at least accept or reject a package.

GOVERNANCE

Ultimately the MBC is about creating a connection between the governors and the governed, but also about creating a point of connection between the competing views and political opinions of the governed as between themselves. It is about creating a form of self-determination in which the question is not 'which self' gets to determine the future, but rather how the 'self' can be constantly re-defined through the attempt to reach agreement with the 'other', whether that other is conceived of in political, racial, or gendered, or any other terms. By promoting the compromise position, rather than the majoritarian one, it aims to build a body politic 'self' defined around the compromise. Self-determination as a right to all-inclusive voting procedures would constitute a right to have 'some' determination - some say, rather than a chance to affirm or veto.

What about the politics of persuasion, and the idea that the politician should persuade the voter? This would still exist. It is just that the range of choices would reflect the full range of the debate.

Chapter 8

Inclusive Decision-making in Mediation and Politics
Phil Kearney and Aileen Tierney

Introduction

This chapter explores how the inclusive decision-making and voting techniques described in Part I of this book might be integrated into the domains of alternative dispute resolution and politics.

INCLUSIVE DECISION-MAKING IN MEDIATION

Conflict is a natural process which occurs wherever differences are encountered. Some methodological approaches attempt to manage or reduce incidences of conflict, but Pearce and Littlejohn postulate that "suppressing moral conflict can be just as difficult as fighting it out". They state "(w)hen important moral differences are left unexpressed, points of view and perspectives on the world go unheard, and the interests of entire groups become marginalised in the process".[1] Consensus-based conflict resolution is about ensuring that the perspectives of many are presented in a way that allows for a plurality of options.

While conflict can be problematic, it does not have to be negative or destructive. The difficulty is not that the conflict exists *per se*, but that many do not have the skills required to work with it creatively. Indeed, conflict can be an opportunity for change and transformation. Pearce and Littlejohn suggest that "the ability of people from different social worlds to manage their differences is one of the most important issues of our time".[2] Moral conflicts such as whether abortion (p 130) should be legal, how the environment should be protected, how justice should be served, etc., can be very difficult to manage, they argue.

Becker *et al* share similar concerns about the potential of many protagonists to become fixed in polarised, win-or-lose positions, with the resultant loss of some of the compromise alternatives. They say, "each side considers its own position to be so vital and that of the adversary to be so dangerous, that neither seems mindful of the costs of the battle. Allegiance to one side or the other often requires individuals to set aside feelings and beliefs that do not fit easily with the official positions and statements associated with their 'side'. [Meanwhile], those who join neither side are devalued as uncaring or muddle-headed. The whole system suffers as valid concerns on both sides are belittled and important values are denigrated. Passion, energy, and material resources are depleted in fruitless and redundant battles. Participants in the battle, as well as many bystanders to it, are left frustrated, turned off, or sometimes despairing."[3 - opp.]

---

1   Pearce, W B, & Littlejohn, S W, p 6.   2   *Ibid.*

Conflict can appear at any level in society, such as in a relationship, a group, or an organisation. A systemic view would assume that all parties to a conflict along with wider contextual factors contribute to the generation and maintenance of the conflict to varying extents. In any attempt to resolve the conflict, it is therefore necessary to explore these multiple levels and constructions. For example, a conflict in a group or family could be considered in terms of the history of the group, the positions of those involved, and the beliefs and interpretations that each person holds about the causes and potential resolutions.

By the time those concerned seek help with conflict resolution, the scenario will usually be characterised by attributions of blame and counter accusations. In fact, people in conflict frequently present their dilemmas in non-contextual frameworks polarising good and evil, while simultaneously holding expectations of mediators to make judgements about the righteousness of their respective positionings.

Although there may be differing perceptions and expectations of the role of the mediation process, it continues to play a vital role in society. Indeed, Deborah Kolb describes the alternative dispute resolution movement as a worldwide confederation of people united by their belief that it is both possible and necessary to "bring a different kind of process to the problems of overcrowded and unsympathetic courts; to changing, conflict-ridden communities; and to the stalemates that accompany long and contentious struggles over public policy and international affairs".[4]

Mediation

Mediation is less about judgements and more about opening up possibilities where new conversations and new constructions can take place, i.e. creating possibilities in the 'in between'. In the same way, consensus politics is a shift away from binary decision-making to an exploration of a range of possible options.

The process of couple mediation involves interactions on a small scale which are not unlike those associated with larger societal conflict. Mediators are often trained to consider conflicting interests and not necessarily conflicting views of reality; nevertheless, mediation could also be seen as a co-constructed conversation with each contribution to the process arising out of a personally held set of beliefs. The meanings of what is said alter as the conversation moves from one disputant to another. John Shotter suggests that in our meetings with others, we cannot simply be ourselves.[5] We become ourselves through dialogue with others. Each kind of utterance is filled with various reactions to other utterances of the given exchange.[6]

---

3   *Fostering Dialogue on Abortion: A Report from the Public Dialogue Project*, Working Paper, Becker, C, Chasin, L, Chasin, R, Herzig, M, & Roth, S, 1992, p 1.

4   *When Talk Works: Profiles of Mediators*, Kolb, D M, (ed.), Jossey-Bass, 1994, p 2.

5   Shotter, J, p 94.

6   *Speech Genres and other Late Essays*, Bakhtin, M, (C Emerson and M Holquist, trans.), Austin, University of Texas Press, 1986, p 91.

According to Shotter, in order to open up new possibilities in our relationships with others, we need others to require us to make responses to them that bring forth ways of engaging that had not previously been available to us. By hearing and responding to each other differently and generating novel responses in ourselves and others, new relationship possibilities are created.[7]

Pearce and Littlejohn consider that what is at issue is not that the differences are so great that they cannot be bridged, but whether the participants, holding opposing viewpoints, choose to develop and exercise a wide range of ways of relating to each other.[8]

As Shotter suggests,[9] the gaps, the silences, the moments in dialogue where one person pauses sufficiently to orient themselves to respond both to the other's expressions and other influences in their talk, is the bridging of the divide. It is in these moments, he continues, that meanings unique to the exchange can occur. In this regard, the need for dialogue to hear the views of others and to generate new possible options in the decision-making process, creates the possibility of calling forth different responses in ourselves. Mediation encourages dialogue and therefore attention to the views of others.

Pearce and Littlejohn go on to suggest that while free speech may guarantee that people can say what they want, it may not necessarily ensure that all viewpoints will be heard. They feel society does not do a good job in helping people communicate creatively about their differences. The procedures involved in an MBC, in contrast, allow for the expression of multiple viewpoints, and thereby provides some redress to this position. Mediations are episodes of communication, as too are the discussions that take place to generate multiple options in the MBC decision-making process.[10]

Consensus in the Mediation Context

There are considerable possibilities for the application of consensus methods to any conflict, or indeed to any situations in which views have become polarised, resulting in a narrow range of apparent potential solutions.

With an ideological shift away from binary distinctions, i.e. for-or-against positionings, and through the subsequent dialogue that takes place in the generation of multiple options, a system which values greater diversity can emerge. Mediation seeks to find the best possible compromise for all parties, and consensus voting can also facilitate such an outcome. Indeed, some of the underlying values and ideals that inform both mediation practice and consensus voting include the following: granting a voice to all parties, avoiding binary distinctions that marginalize ideas into extremes, exploring the possibilities of the grey areas, and generating alternative ideas.

---

7 and 9 Shotter, J, p 94 and p 131.

8 and 10 Pearce, W B, & Littlejohn, S W, p 7 and p 9.

Both mediation and consensus voting, then, create contexts where less competitive, less fragmented relationships might be possible. This constitutes a quantum shift enabling participants not to hold 'a position' in relation to one set of ideas over another, but rather to embrace the multiplicity and complexity of all ideas and positions simultaneously. Consensus decision-making offers this possibility in its generation of multiple options and the mutual agreement to reach either a verbal or votal consensus on a compromise that may be the best option of the moment and one which most closely approximates to the collective will and wisdom.

Issues for Consideration in the Generation of Multiple Options

There are some areas that require reflection in the generation of options, and these include:

a) the need to attend to the contextual framework within which the conflict is occurring, and

b) the consideration of process ideas: i) how we talk and decide together, ii) the rules about who and what can be spoken about, and iii) some further elaboration of the discursive phase for generating multiple options within the consensus decision-making approach.

If taken as a decision-making tool and/or applied to mediation contexts in its own right, the MBC is stand-alone and arguably greatly evolved from anything majoritarian mechanisms have to offer; furthermore, it more closely resembles true democratic principles. As a tool for the resolution of conflict in the mediation context, it might be further enhanced by the development of the debate phase, thereby further enabling those in conflict to move beyond the belief in a singular truth and to live with a multiplicity of ideas.

At a pragmatic level, therefore, the consensus approach might draw more substantially from both systemic and social constructionist ideas and practices. These include the ways in which parties co-create meanings and their roles in any decision-making system. Further attention should be paid both to the subjugation of certain options and to mechanisms to elicit silenced voices and possibilities.

The ideas of Ludwig Wittgenstein inform us that the ways that we enter into conversations are often predetermined. There are pre-existing rules of engagement about how we speak, i.e., a grammar of communication. This impacts on what is possible in any given moment in our conversations together. In addition to this, the issue of power and hierarchy in relationships also needs consideration, i.e., who can speak, who is silenced and who is listened to.[11] Without attending to power relationships and the contexts within which dialogue takes place, the generation of options phase could become a superficial exercise in attempting to include all voices. The role of the option proposer(s) in relation to their own values, beliefs and biases; and the context

---

11 *Philosophical Investigations,* Wittgenstein, L, Basil Blackwell, 1953.

of hierarchy and power, all need to be considered. For example, where the threat of violence and oppression exists in relation to freedom of expression, mediation and/or consensus voting may not be applicable.[12]

Language is seen as constitutive by many practitioners whose epistemological framework is based in social constructionism. They place an emphasis on the 'person in conversation' within which opportunities for change are perceived to exist. Change is a dialogical process, and clarifying meanings occurs in conversation. Victoria Chen suggests that "the coordinated management of meaning [CMM] shares the vision of a truly democratic society in which promoting equality should go beyond mere theoretical exposition".[13] She does not elaborate her understanding of democracy but does expound the relative value of hearing all voices. Consensus politics is about providing opportunities to hear the multiplicity of voices.

Expanding the Dialogue

The process of generating options to reach either a verbal or votal consensus could learn much from the process of generating options in therapy conversations. Consideration should be given, not only to those options that are the most significant, but also to those that might have been silenced. In like manner, therapy could learn much from consensus decision-making in how to reach compromise and come to mutual agreements.

Systemic practitioners in their shift from linear causality highlight the ways in which meaning is co-created. Their use of particular types of questioning provides a context in which all those in conversation become more sensitised to the multiple descriptions that prevail in people's constructions of their own experiences. This type of questioning opens up possibilities for conflict resolution and decision-making based on compromise. Indeed, it encourages participants to move away from positions of strongly held 'truths' to an understanding of the myriad of positions and options for construing and being.

The need to attend to the context within which a conflict occurs is not included in the methodology outlined for the MBC in Chapter 1. In every other respect the MBC decision-making methodology complies with recognised democratic principles. If the skills and systemic orientation of professional mediators can be combined with the applications of social choice theory as described in this text we may then see the evolution of a pragmatic form of democracy which both resolves conflicts and pre-empts them.

---

12 Any majoritarian voting procedure, of course, would be even more inappropriate.

13 *The Possibility of Critical Dialogue in the Theory of CMM in Human Systems*, Victoria Chen, *The Journal of Systemic Consultation and Management,* Pearce W. B. & Kearney, J. (eds.), Leeds Family Therapy and Research Centre and Kensington Consultation Centre, Vol 15, issues 1-3, 2004, p 188.

INCLUSIVE DECISION-MAKING IN POLITICS

What might be the prerequisites for the application of consensus-based decision-making as detailed in Part I of this book to contexts of conflict and alternative forms of dispute resolution? A brief reference to some recent uses of the referendum as a method for decision-making or consolidating of mediated agreements may be illustrative.

The UN-sponsored mediation process in Cyprus provides a useful example. Over a five year period (1999 - 2004) different approaches to conflict resolution were employed and various formulas were arrived at to bring the divisions and conflict between the two communities to some mutually acceptable resolution. Kofi Annan, the Secretary General gave his name to a series of Agreements which were carefully negotiated.

At the end of the process, the (10,000 page!) agreement was put to the electorates of both parts of the island in simultaneous referendums: the accord was rejected by one side and accepted by the other (the results are on p 37n). As in any consociational ballot, joint acceptance was a prerequisite for implementation.

L N Nilssen, a political science student at the University of Lund, gives a most informative analysis of this mediation process.[14] He does not, however, pass comment on the use of referendums as the means of establishing the level of support in the two communities. As always, this (consociational but nevertheless) majoritarian methodology is taken as the *sine qua non* of large-scale decision-making.

Another recent example is the Italian constitutional referendum[15] where a single yes-or-no process was proposed to determine issues of great import and complexity – including increasing the powers of the prime minister, greater regional autonomy, etc.. The defeat of the referendum was taken as a victory for the recently elected prime minister, Romano Prodi, but other than that what could be said about the Italian people's views on the many issues involved? Absolutely nothing. The limitations of the method used were so evident that it received some critique in the international press but nowhere was there a suggestion of an alternative methodology or even a desire expressed that such an alternative should be found.

These comments are not intended to diminish the efforts of negotiators, politicians and combatants who have struggled in numerous scenarios to bring conflict to an end or to find an agreed outcome. It is intended as a critique of the severe constraints built in to the principles and practices on which these agreements - and the preceding negotiations - are based. It remains something of a mystery as to what keeps intelligent people wedded to such deficient majoritarian decision-making procedures.

---

14 *The Complexity of Mediation: an Assessment of UN Good Offices Mission in Cyprus, 1999 – 2004*, Nilssen, Lar Niklas, unpublished dissertation, 2005, University of Lund.

15 This revision envisaged changes to 55 of the 139 articles of the Italian constitution. *Inter alia*, the lower house of parliament would be responsible for national interests like foreign policy, defence and immigration, and the upper house would take on federal law. The vote on 25.6.2006 was lost by 62% to 39% on a 54% turnout. From http://c2d.unige.ch/ which is *the* web-site of referendums, based in the *Université de Généve*.

If the discussions are predicated on majoritarian principles, if the win-or-lose/victory-or-defeat metaphors remain as the subtext to the negotiations, then the outcomes will enshrine those principles too. The process is thus front-loaded in a way which massively constrains the scope of the conversation. All parties then proceed on a basis of mistrust and seek maximum advantage. It is inherent in the structure of the 'exchange' – if it may be called such.

Peter Emerson's alternative, the MBC, starts from a different place or perspective – one which acknowledges the others' right to existence and to have opinions, and it builds into the process a methodology which honours that starting point and facilitates its expression.

What has been a source of intrigue for those of us involved in developing new methods through the work of the de Borda Institute has been the consistent lack of interest in new models of decision-making amongst three key interest groups - practicing politicians, political scientists and political commentators. On a few rare occasions when the ideas were discussed in the abstract, there has been considerable interest shown by a number of senior politicians. Alas, once they were steered towards possible applications, the constraints of *realpolitik* asserted themselves.

Brian Lenihan, TD, the chairman of the Irish Government's Committee on the Constitution, was generous in the time he gave to discussing a submission made by the de Borda Institute to that body. However, when it came to a presentation to that committee on the thorny problem of resolving the Irish people's position on abortion, the de Borda delegation was received in a very different fashion.

The Government Green Paper on the subject[16] had outlined seven possible ways to proceed, including a variety of different legislative formulae. This lent itself to a multi-option decision-making method and we were eager to encourage a move in this direction. The response we received, however, was dismissive in the extreme. It included Liz McManus TD, who spoke of her responsibility to choose on behalf of the people, and who took great exception to the idea that the people themselves should decide what options would figure in a decision-making process. She felt this would usurp her moral responsibility as a public representative.[17]

On another occasion a group of academics hosted a seminar in University College Dublin to look at the merits of multi-option decision-making. Amongst those attending was the former *Taoiseach* (prime minister), Dr. Garret FitzGerald. Although he

---

16 *Green Paper on Abortion,* The Stationery Office, Dublin, (undated).

17 "As a politician I would have to maybe explain a little bit of what a politician does. You're presuming that what we are doing is trying to see - whatever the people want, we will deliver but of course that cuts out of the equation the idea that one has convictions oneself.

"I'm not a facilitator without... a viewpoint... I think that... your perspective is rather different to the perspective of somebody who is having to make decisions."

The All-Party Oireachtas *Committee on the Constitution, Fifth Progress Report,* 2000, p A214. The public hearing took place on 17.5.2000.

acknowledged some merit in the methodology under discussion, he felt that it was ultimately too risky in that the people, if given such power, might opt for an 'unacceptable' outcome. He cited capital punishment as an illustration.[18]

It would appear, then, that the people may not be trusted to discern correctly. But when they choose their representatives, apparently they do make wise choices. There is a conundrum here in the basis on which representative democracy stands and operates, and it requires further attention.

Concurrently and ironically in the Irish context, a key element in the economic success of the country of the past fifteen years has been the process of Social Partnership - a coalition of all the key players in the economic and social policy spheres, who have hammered out a series of increasingly complex agreements on taxation, pay increases and some provisions for disadvantaged sectors. This has contributed hugely to social cohesion, stability and economic growth. This is a consensus-based, extra-parliamentary process which the legislators endorse but to which they are somewhat marginal.

One of the initiators was the present prime minister, Bertie Ahern, who is regarded as a master at negotiation with a special talent for bringing an assortment of players together into a team. What he might do if he was drawing on the full resources available – i.e., in a government selected on the Emersonian principles outlined in the preceding chapters – is worth reflecting upon. Similarly it is worth thinking about how Social Partnership agreements might be enhanced and expedited if MBC decision-making was employed. The latest accord required more than a year of negotiation.

It might almost be said that in order to progress the key issues which would otherwise have been endlessly mired in political party squabbling, the very constraints of the adversarial parliamentary system have themselves brought about the creative solution of Social Partnership.

The power implicit in the winner-takes-all ethos of the majority vote is a difficult one to abandon. It has created a blood sport industry which combines media, pollsters, pundits and people in a circus just as gladiatorial as the arena of two thousand years ago. The complexity of modern society requires processes more subtle and inclusive and more capable of reflecting diversity in those situations where debate alone is inconclusive. The majority vote has the subtlety of *la guillotine*. In this book, in contrast, we are moving from the notion that 'democracy works on the basis of a decision by the majority'[19] to the discernment of the collective mind.

Most decisions happen spontaneously – some unconsciously, some by diktat, many through concession or consensus or from habit. Those circumstances where a formal method is required are rare, but important – e.g., deciding certain issues of public

---

18 The seminar did not conclude with an official report. Nevertheless, Dr. FitzGerald's *Reflections on the Irish State* portrays an author who, while he supports PR in elections, still advocates majority votes in decision-making. Irish Academic Press, 2003.

19 *Report of the Constitution Review Group,* Government of Ireland, 1996, p 398.

policy and electing people to serve in public office. To date we have reverted to divisive and dichotomous methods of voting in many of these instances. To be fair, it must be acknowledged that many countries have adopted various more sophisticated and proportional electoral systems, and these are often vast improvements on the cruder systems such as FPP. However, the distinction between elections and all the other types of decision-making is not widely recognised. It is possible to have a better electoral system embedded within an otherwise entirely majoritarian system of government, even though the latter can then negate the benefits of the more inclusive electoral system.

Other contributors to this book address the technicalities of social choice and do not examine the psychosocial web of the personal and political in which that decision-making takes place. In society at large, that web is defined more by metaphors of combat and feudal domination than by participation, collaboration and social partnership. Metaphors which reflect the complexity of modern society such as an interactive network or a mosaic of multiple perspectives would more closely fit with the multiculturalism and pluralism which is now to be found in most societies. Dichotomising is increasingly not just a blunt instrument but a vehicle for destruction and conflict.

It is most important that the alternative voting procedures proposed in this book are not seen as a drift towards some lowest common denominator in an effort to avoid conflict or distinctions. The methodologies are about fortifying the individual's right to have a voice and participate, they are predicated on robust debate as the prerequisite to any decision-making process, and they provide methods to resolve intractable difficulties when debate proves insufficient. The voting procedures are not proposed as a panacea or as a substitute for political passion either intra- or extra-parliamentary.

Furthermore, the methodologies are not yet tested to anything like a satisfactory degree. That, perhaps, is the most important message of this particular contribution and the request underlying all of Emerson's work to date. It is asked only that all three voting procedures – MBC, QBS and the matrix vote – be given some rigorous trials in a variety of settings – political and otherwise – so that flaws may be identified and the strengths, if any, be brought forth and refined into formulas for use in ways that enhance public discourse, conflict resolution and good governance.

By definition, mediation involves the generation of multiple options in the search for resolution of the issues – be it marital breakdown at the micro level, or conflict between communities or states on the scale writ large. The process requires reviewing the options, negotiating them and then selecting from amongst them. In some of the more contentious scenarios, the methodologies presented in this book could prevent breakdown and achieve otherwise impossible outcomes.

In the political domain, where reverting to the majority vote as the preferred vehicle for decision-making is woven into the fabric of our polity, the benefits of an open, inclusive and pluralistic debate are often undone by that decision-making method. Accordingly, a combination of systemic mediation and inclusive voting would greatly increase the resilience, accountability and pluralism of our democracy.

PART III

CONCLUSION

Chapter 9

The *Realpolitik* of Consensus Voting
Peter Emerson with Assistance from Elizabeth Meehan

NOTHING CAN STOP A MOVEMENT WHOSE TIME HAS COME

As has been evident throughout human history, those who are in power invariably endeavour to maintain the system from which they are the obvious beneficiaries. The kings and queens tried hard to retain their monarchies. Religious leaders have often followed parallel objectives. And in similar vein, most of today's premiers and presidents work to retain the *status quo* in their respective jurisdictions through such mechanisms as:

+ the easily manipulated decision-making process of the simple (though sometimes weighted) majority vote;

+ the often similarly simplistic and manipulable electoral systems, the worst of which are FPP and closed-list PR;

+ a majoritarian form of governance, and the most undemocratic but nevertheless widely accepted practice of political patronage by which an oligarchy of the senior members of the ruling party - elected dictators, to use Lord Hailsham's phrase[1] - decides who is, and who is not, to be in government.

These three democratic structures are all based on confrontational, win-or-lose processes, and their widespread use is in large part due to the adversarial ways of western civilisation. Other societies have sometimes used more consensual systems, if but at a local level. However, despite the insistence of early democratic theorists that majoritarian decision-making was legitimate only if it attended to the interests of minorities, the perceived wisdom in many countries takes it for granted a) that the basis of democracy is majority rule, and b) that such majority rule is effected by majority governments and majority votes in parliaments.

This is all a great advance on minority rule, of course. But it tends to ignore those all-inclusive structures which could form the basis of an even more democratic polity. So for the time being, public opinion tends to tolerate majoritarianism, at least in societies not caught up in inter-communal violence. Nevertheless, decreasing levels of participation in elections and referendums, combined with an undiminished level of political activity in pressure groups and street demonstrations, suggest this consensus is beginning to change. When it does, then may the politicians also change, but probably not before.

---

1   *The Dilemma of Democracy*, Quintin Hogg, Collins, 1978. The author makes frequent reference to this term throughout.

INFLUENCES FOR CHANGE

There are many influences which may help to lead public opinion to expect a more inclusive political structure.

a) The obvious inadequacies of majority rule in any post-conflict society.

b) Mediation and conflict resolution work, which dismisses the *closed* in favour of the more open question.

c) International observation of democratisation processes, for this relates to the globalisation of certain minimum standards.

d) The role of the media, which could be so productive; it sometimes discusses electoral systems, yet seldom if ever questions decision-making and the basic concept of majority rule.

e) The growth of interest in academic commentary, matching that of concerned citizens, in more participative or dialogical forms of democracy. This has been taken up by governments alarmed by falling electoral turn-outs, in the promotion of partnership-based decision-making in, for example, social policy delivery and community planning.

f) The *modus operandi* of society at large, where more and more committees come to decisions without resort to majority voting.

g) Advances in computer science, which have been seized upon by those who are interested in participatory democracy and which make multi-option preference voting so easy to use.

The Inadequacies of Majority Rule

As noted earlier (p 11), the practice or prospect of majority rule and/or the (suggested) use of a majority vote referendum has been part of the problem in numerous conflicts around the world. We mentioned Darfur, Northern Ireland, Rwanda, Sri Lanka and Yugoslavia. We could add Abhazia, Indonesia, Kashmir, Nagorno-Karabakh, Quebec and Western Sahara, because here too referendums have been proposed if not used, and seldom have they facilitated a resolution of the respective dispute. Indeed, in many instances, the very use of a majority vote has only exacerbated the problem.

Furthermore, in lands of great complexity such as the Russian Federation, any resort to such a simplistic tool could be unhelpful if not actually dangerous. This is because the very idea that any one group of people can concoct a border - of which both history and geography are always replete - might only prompt others to do the same, so making a Balkan-style clash inevitable. The phrase used to describe this phenomenon is "*matrioshka* nationalism", named after those famous Russian dolls which always hold another smaller one inside.[2]

---

2   *The Shaman's Coat, A Native History of Siberia*, Anna Reid, Phoenix, 2002, p 136.

Majority rule is also inadequate in international fora. Some organisations, like the UN Security Council or EU, use a form of weighted or qualified majority voting. They also sometimes act similarly to the committees mentioned in para f) opposite. In the EU, for example, the famous 'veto' is usually not what it sounds: a "no" vote that can trump the majority. When the veto is said to have occurred, it is not usually the result of a vote. Rather, it is the upshot of discussion leading to a decision not to act when it is clear from that discussion that at least one member state feels that such a core interest is at stake that agreement to proceed would be impossible.

On many occasions, however, those concerned dismiss any votal – even non-majoritarian – approach and rely instead on a purely verbal methodology (as often in the case of the EU 'veto'). Admittedly, this can be protracted and difficult, which may explain why agreements are often thrashed out in all-night sessions.

No resort is ever made to multi-option preference voting: it would be interesting to know why this is so. The most likely conclusion, as Christine Bell suggests (p 122), is that it has never even been considered. They prefer 'the devil' they know.

So let us return to post-conflict scenarios, where politicians from both or all sides come together to try and create some form of peace agreement. In such a setting, creating a degree of trust is crucial. To get former opponents if not indeed erstwhile enemies actually to trust each other is obviously very difficult, but it is even more difficult if a voting procedure is involved.

This is because, for all their talk of democracy and its ideals, many politicians, even at the best of times, do not like resorting to a vote. In fact, most of them allow a vote to take place only when they are already pretty sure of the outcome. We saw this in the UN Security Council on Iraq: when Bush and Blair knew they would get overwhelming support (sic) for resolution 1441, it was indeed put to the vote. In March 2003, however, when they knew they would not get such support, they just did not have the vote at all... but went to war anyway.

Another case in point refers to the conflict in Northern Ireland and the supposedly momentous decision taken by *Sinn Féin* at their 1998 *Ard Fheis* (Annual Conference) when they chose to let their members sit in the new NI Assembly, i.e., to recognise the partition of Ireland. To claim that the *Ard Fheis* took that decision, as if all the ground work had not already been done, would be a little disingenuous. To think that the leadership would have risked such a vote, without knowing full well that it would be successful, would be at best naïve; though this is not to say that the ground should not be prepared through dialogue with colleagues in any decision-making organisation.

A third instance relates to the use of party whips. In many cases, a government with a large majority knows that it can get pretty well anything through a parliamentary vote, but in those cases of doubt, it just cracks the whip – often with consequences for the careers of those party members who disobey. Here too, therefore, the vote is not the real decision-making process; that is all done in (what are no longer) the smoke-filled rooms and corridors of power.

Here, then, is the biggest obstacle to the introduction of a more consensual democracy: the element of trust. To submit a resolution for ratification - for that, rather than decision-making, is the best description of what does or does not happen in a majority vote - may sometimes be a little risky. But to allow the process to be more truly democratic a) by letting every participating party submit its own and debate all draft resolutions, and b) by allowing all concerned to take a multi-option preference vote, would often mean that the political leader was no longer in (almost) total control. The outcome of any two-option majority vote is usually predictable, and therefore the process is controllable. A multi-optional voting procedure, in which the outcome depends upon the preferences not only of their own supporters but also of their erstwhile opponents, would be far less manageable!

Similarly, when it comes to the appointment of a power-sharing executive, party leaders like to maintain a 'hands-on' grip of proceedings. The arrangements agreed in 1998 for the NI peace process had the effect of allowing the 'big' parties first to exclude the smaller ones from holding ministerial office. The former then devised a formula based on a d'Hondt analysis of the number of seats they held, by which each of these 'big four' parties would receive a share of the ministerial offices (p 81). At each appointment, the four party leaders retained total control of their share of the remaining stages. Nothing was left to chance. In other words, nothing was put to a vote.

The conclusion is sad, but the prospect of the politicians themselves adopting parliamentary voting procedures in which the outcomes would be quite unpredictable are slim. The best hope, therefore, is to rely on what is happening elsewhere in society.

Mediation and Conflict Resolution

When their children had grown up and left the nest, an elderly couple decided to sell up and choose somewhere smaller for their retirement. So they took it in turns to have a look at the property pages and, ah, she found the perfect place: a wee cottage with a pretty little garden, nice and quiet, not far from the village shop, perfect; and he found the perfect place: a wee cottage with a good garage, nice and quiet, within walking distance of the pub, perfect. And her 1st preference was not his 1st preference! They therefore got out the property pages again, and eventually realised that her 3rd preference was the same as his 4th preference. So they chose that, the option with their highest average preference rating... and as far as I know, they are still together.

Mediation can be effected both verbally and/or votally, and this applies to disputes and conflicts involving just two people or to those relating to two or more societies measured in millions. Either way, the mediation process must allow all concerned to participate in all stages of that process, so maybe it has been unwise to confine any peace talks to political leaders only. Obviously, they cannot be left out; no agreement excluding the protagonists of conflict could ever stick. As often as not, however, they are the very people who have broken the peace in the first place, and the ordinary citizens, weary of war, often have no way of expressing their albeit fearful desire for change. An obvious example concerns Radovan Karadžić, later to be indicted as a war criminal, who took part in negotiations on the future of Bosnia.[3] Similarly in Northern Ireland, the politicians had a virtual monopoly of the peace process, though some of the smaller and newer parties at the Talks – those whose voices in the end were restricted – did spring from the community.

As a general rule, however, elected representatives have a rather inadequate understanding of social choice theory and conflict resolution work. It must also be stated that some mediators have a somewhat shallow understanding of how consensus voting can be another tool by which reconciliation can be effected. As Phil Kearney and Aileen Tierney point out, pp 126-7, the potential for multi-option voting in mediation work is considerable.

When consensus voting does come to be used in mediation work, not so much at the family level perhaps, but certainly in industrial or political disputes, there will be a greater chance that such procedures may then filter into our political way of life.

International Work

Since the end of the Cold War, international organisations have also undertaken a lot of mediation work, especially in the Balkans and the Caucasus. And related to these conflicts, recent years have witnessed a rapid growth in the field of international election observation, starting with South Africa in 1994 and Bosnia two years later. This is seen as a very necessary part of the respective peace and/or democratisation process, and election observation missions are now a regular feature in countries of the former Soviet Union, for example.

There has been at least one superb consequence: the OSCE (Organisation for Security and Co-operation in Europe) has now been able to observe elections in quite a few western countries as well. In Nov. 2003, for instance, it came to observe the regional NI elections for the first time.[4] Unfortunately, however, the OSCE does not (yet) pass judgement on the choice of electoral system itself, not least because international organisations are the product of agreements between national governments, which do not want any interference in their own internal affairs.[5]

---

3   The International Conference on the Former Yugoslavia, which started work in September 1992, held 'negotiations among the ethnonationalist leaders of the three "warring factions"'. *Balkan Tragedy,* Susan Woodward, The Brookings Institute, 1995, p 303.

4   Only three persons came. Furthermore, they were not allowed into any polling stations, but only into the count. See OSCE/ODIHR Assessment Report of 19.12.2003.

5   The UN, for instance, was set up by three old men meeting in Yalta, and all three had an empire to protect. Accordingly, democracy notwithstanding, they made sure that their powers in the UN were greater than those of most other leaders: hence the concept of the permanent members of the UN Security Council and their veto powers.

Many other international bodies are also far from democratic. In the IMF, for example, decisions are taken by an 85% weighted majority... but the US has 17% of the vote, and the other members of G8 hold a further 30%. The effect, therefore, is that Washington can veto anything at all! *The Age of Consent*, George Monbiot, Flamingo, 2003, p 16.

One day, however, it is almost inevitable that the OSCE *will* express an opinion. This is partly because in some post-conflict settings - Bosnia in 1996 and Kosovo in 2001 - the OSCE itself chose the methodology. On both occasions, it chose PR; sadly, it opted for single preference varieties of PR-list, so the two elections were little more than sectarian head-counts. The point, however, remains: electoral systems are increasingly coming under international scrutiny in conflict resolution work.[6] The principle of proportionality has already been accepted; soon, perhaps, the notion that electoral systems should also be preferential may also be adopted.

The OSCE also observes referendums. Just as it does not comment on countries' electoral systems, so too it usually refrains from criticism of the two-option referendum. This silence, however, is also due to the predominance in western political circles of the belief in majority rule. It is an *idée fixe*: for many, the majority vote is beyond question, and the many include some of those working in the OSCE. So international support for multi-option preference voting is currently extremely limited.

The Media

Throughout the ages, societies have held beliefs and practices which only later generations decided were erroneous - theories or should we say myths like the divine right of kings. For the moment at least, there are very few in the popular media who are prepared to think that the perceived wisdom on majority rule is perhaps mistaken.

In countries such as the United Kingdom, it is thought that the public shares the politicians' view that because non-majoritarian electoral systems generally result in coalition governments, they therefore bring about an unwelcome instability; Italy is often pointed to as an example to be avoided. On deciding particular issues as opposed to choosing the party(ies) in government, it is also partly due to a widespread dislike of mathematics. When it comes to the pools or horse racing, many people are more than willing to crunch a few numbers together. Among many political journalists, however, there appears to be an assumption that a decision-making process, as long as it has involved either some sort of a vote (and/or a verbal agreement), is *ergo* democratic. They seldom question the respective voting procedure.

We do not understand why this is so. It is perfectly clear why many politicians would not want to contemplate the introduction of multi-option preference voting. But why the media should be so reluctant to even consider other methodologies is, to us at least, unclear. Instead, via various votes and polls which they themselves conduct, those responsible in the western media help to perpetuate the myth that majority voting is perfectly acceptable. Someday soon, we hope, this will all change.

---

6 The OSCE/ODIHR also observed the US elections of 2.11.2004. In its report dated 31.3.2005, it stated that "it is difficult for third party presidential candidates to appear on the ballot in all 50 states" (Section D), so maybe the days of FPP are indeed numbered.

Academia

The reticence of the media may be compared to the similar reluctance of some academics to address the deficiencies of majoritarian voting procedures. Many though not all political scientists, for example, share the concern noted above that a non-majoritarian system of electing a government may carry more costs than benefits. And as Maurice Salles points out on p 107, many leading economists still place their trust in majority rule. It is all quite extraordinary!

There are of course a few who do question this almost universal faith in the majority vote. Many of these work in 'think tanks' or in campaigning organizations such as Charter 88. One who has remained in the academy is Arend Lijphart who, as he says himself, initially believed in majority rule. Later, however, he became a firm advocate of consociationalism;[7] indeed, in many ways, he provided the inspiration for the Belfast Agreement. Proof positive, if such were needed, that the intellectual can and does influence government, when governments are in need of ideas.

In other fields, there are again the few. Many of the world's literary giants, for example, have opposed majoritarianism, not least Lev Tolstoy.[8] Others too should let their voices be heard, as should those in different professions. Psychiatrists, for example, should surely question the political and, dare we say, dangerous habit of reducing so many complex questions to choices of two supposedly diametric opposites, just as psychotherapists like Phil Kearney and Aileen Tierney do, p 130.

A further profession concerned with this question of majority voting is that of the constitutional lawyer. Since the end of WWII, there have been numerous developments in human rights legislation. At first, the 'principle' of non-interference was given rather too much prominence (for example, in the case of South Africa) but as Christine Bell points out in Chapter 7, the faint beginnings of a coherent set of democratic rights are now taking shape. This has become particularly noticeable as a new form of intervention has begun to emerge; the setting up of international administrations in so-called 'failed states'.

At the moment, however, most international agreements on human rights are painfully weak on democratic rights.[9] In an age of increasing internationalism, this is bound to

---

7 See for example his foreword in *Defining Democracy*, Emerson (2002).

8 "... the power of the majority over the minority... fails to secure a just rule". *The Meaning of the Russian Revolution,* Lev Nikolayevich Tolstoy, 1906, Section IV.

9 According to Art 21 of the 1948 United Nations Declaration of Human Rights:
   i) *Everyone has the right to take part in the government of his country, directly or through freely elected representatives.*
   ii) *The will of the people shall be the basis of the authority of government; this shall be expressed in periodic and genuine elections which shall be held by secret vote or by equivalent free voting procedures.*
   That is it! It talks only of elections. There is nothing about decision-making, and nothing on the structures of government.

improve, and maybe the clamour for change will first be heard in former conflict zones. The NI Human Rights Commission (NIHRC), for example, now accepts the fact that the NI electoral system should be proportional.[10] It does not yet propose that it should also be preferential; nor does it yet discuss different voting procedures for decision-making... but in time it will.

Like so many others, lawyers are prepared to consider electoral systems, but they are very reluctant to consider decision-making processes. Hence they seldom question majority voting, even when it is inherent in a subject which is often under their closest scrutiny: the right of self-determination.[11]

A classic example was the Arbitration Commission on Yugoslavia, chaired by Robert Badinter, for it suggested that any people wishing to exercise this right should hold a referendum. The implication, as always, was a majority vote. Granted, with regard to Bosnia, it added the proviso that such a vote "would be valid only if respectable numbers from all three communities... approved." But that proviso was ignored.[12] On the day of the vote, the barricades went up in Sarajevo, and within weeks Bosnia was at war.[13] The need, then, for international human rights charters to lay down minimum standards for decision-making cannot be over-emphasised.

Society at Large

Maybe the academic and the journalist will study decision-making in greater depth, when society at large has itself taken further steps in this direction. There are many committees and NGOs which reject the two-option majority vote in their own internal decision-making and choose instead a *modus operandi* based on what is usually a verbal consensus.

In politics, business and courts of law, however, many decisions are still taken by majority vote. Sometimes, of course, questions do have a binary nature: a prime example is 'guilty or not guilty?' But the idea that one individual should control the fortunes of a company just because he or she is rich enough to own 51% of its share capital is surely a little out-dated... and not a little undemocratic!

---

10 *The Proposed Bill of Rights for Northern Ireland Act 2004, Section 2 (1)*, published by the NIHRC, 2004.

11 "All peoples have the right of self-determination. By virtue of that right they freely determine their political status and freely pursue their economic, social and cultural development. ..." *Article 1.1, The International Covenant on Civil and Political Rights.* The UN General Assembly adopted this Covenant in 1996, and it came into force ten years later. At no point does the Covenant discuss the methodology by which a people - (whatever that is!) - may "freely determine" their status - cf. Christine Bell, pp 120-1 - and its only reference to decision-making concerns the workings of its Human Rights Committee, which it says shall take decisions by majority vote (*Article 39*).

12 *Balkan Tragedy,* Susan Woodward, Brookings Institute, 1995, p 280.

13 *The Fall of Yugoslavia*, Misha Glenny, Penguin, 1992, p 163.

As noted on p 86, many sporting organisations use fairly sophisticated decision-making procedures. Another institution, the Eurovision Song Contest, uses a BC variation, (admittedly in a telephone poll form of voting, which tends to allow for some pretty serious manipulation of the equivalent of the voters' register). Slowly but surely, therefore, more and more members of society are rejecting the majority vote.

At the same time, of course, more and more people are rejecting politics, or rather, party politics. Street demonstrations against the war in Iraq, for instance, and continued participation in what are often single-issue campaign groups, have shown that many citizens are no less concerned about the issues of the day than were their forebears. Their faith in party politics, however, is diminished, and this is all the more apparent in countries which use overly simple electoral systems: the US and UK the most obvious examples.

It is also worth pointing out that nearly all social surveys are *not* conducted on the basis of umpteen majority votes. Now is it not remarkable that the methodology used by the politician to ascertain the will of the people is not the same as that used by the social scientist? The consequences of course can be serious: throughout the troubles in Northern Ireland, numerous surveys suggested there was widespread if not overwhelming support for integrated education, mixed housing, power-sharing and so forth; yet the democratic process never managed to implement these measures. A similar pattern was evident in 1991 in Bosnia.[14]

This is not to say that social surveys are analysed according to (M)BC and/or Condorcet counts. Instead, in many cases, the interviewee is asked to rate his/her opinions in maybe five different ways: approve strongly, approve weekly, regard indifferently, oppose weekly and oppose strongly. It would obviously be unwise to base a social choice function on such answers; instead, such analyses often just indicate to what degree society approves of various options, without trying to suggest which one is the most popular overall.

One particular social survey deserves a special mention. With financial assistance from the British and Swedish governments, the Rwandan National Unity and Reconciliation Commission (NURC) initiated a nation-wide social survey on the '*gacacas*' - a system of village courts by which the Rwandan government hopes to overcome the legacy of the genocide. The report was conducted by one who was neutral to the conflict - a European - and he duly presented his findings to a large audience in Kigali. Towards the end of the discussion which followed, a member of the audience pointed out that, "asking yes-or-no questions is very unAfrican".[15] Perhaps we should add that it is also unscientific.

---

14 *The Death of Yugoslavia*, Laura Silber and Allan Little, Penguin, 1995, p 231.

15 The report, *Participation in Gacaca and National Reconciliation,* was published by the NURC in January 2003. It was discussed in some detail at a press conference on March 6th 2003 in the *Hôtel Mille Collines*, at which the first-named author of this chapter was present.

Computers

In other walks of life, western civilisation has made some superb advances, not least in computer science. As a result, what was impractical just a few years ago - a multi-option preference vote in parliament, or even such a vote in a national poll - is now perfectly possible. At the moment, two-option voting in the House of Commons is a very time-consuming process, involving as it does the members filing through two doors, one marked 'aye' and the other 'nay'. It could so easily be computerised, and one day, we are sure it will be.

Moves abroad are already afoot. In Russia's first post-*perestroika* democracy of 1989, the Supreme Soviet did use electronic voting. Unfortunately, however, as mooted on p 2, while the technology might have been sophisticated, the voting procedure remained the very opposite: the simple majority vote.

The procedure for appointing the Russian government was even more long-winded. Parliament was able to veto any ministerial appointment... and this it did with aplomb. On each occasion, the PM had to go back to his drawing board and start again, with no guarantee and little hope that any subsequent recommendation would then be accepted. The entire business took an age!

In Iraq, as is well known, the process of forming a post-Saddam Hussein government has been even more problematic: it lasted for months! With a matrix vote, both in Russia and Iraq, the whole operation could have been done in a couple of days at the most. Indeed, if the voting procedures had been computerised, albeit with the necessary safeguards of audit trails and so forth - a few hours would have been sufficient.

Some day soon, most elected chambers will have computers. Parliaments will then be able to use any voting system. And if they *may* use multi-option preference voting, then one day they surely will. In other words, the advent of computers means that the introduction of multi-option preference voting may perhaps, eventually, be inevitable. In addition, electronic voting could also be used in national polls.[16]

It is also the case that many governments have introduced the use of computer technology in public consultation, though this has a long way to go before becoming a truly interactive medium rather than one in which governments either inform people or allow them to carry out simple chores, such as filling in on-line forms in order to secure a service.[17]

---

16 *Inter alia,* the democratic process is one in which people come together to make decisions on their collective governance. Electronic voting could easily be a part of this process, but it should still be necessary for most citizens to go to vote - albeit on the computer - in a polling station.

17 *Modernising Government and the e-government Revolution: Technologies of Government and Technologies of Democracy,* John Morrison, in *Public Law in a Multi-Layered Constitution,* P. Leyland and N. Bamforth (eds.), Oxford: Hart Publishing, 2003, pp 157-188.

The Politician, the Mediator and the Mathematician

In his essay in Chapter 5, Maurice Salles describes the *contretemps* which there has been for over 200 years between the advocates of the Condorcet count and those who prefer an (M)BC. It is similar in a way to an earlier scientific argument on the nature of light: some said it was a wave form of energy, for how else could it defract; and others said, no no, it is particulate, for only particles can travel across millions of miles of empty space. Today we realise that the photon has both wave and particle properties. So both sides were right.

As the reader now knows, we feel that both the MBC and Condorcet are very good voting procedures. Many social choice economists agree; some of them, however, tend to consider countless theoretical arguments, usually based on the assumption that alternatives are mutually exclusive. But whenever a plurality of options is involved, it cannot be assumed that this is so. Indeed, even when only two options are involved, this may be a false assumption, (pp 2 and 17). Instead of thinking about options, therefore, they often choose to consider a different hypothesis, an election involving a plurality of candidates. Even in elections, however, mutual exclusivity may be unreal: one cannot say that Bush and Kerry were two complete opposites, for example, just as Stalin and Trotsky had much in common.

A multi-disciplinary approach is therefore necessary. The constitutional lawyer should meet with the political scientist, the psychoanalyst and the social choice economist, who should all accept that there are many different types of decision-making, some more democratic than others.

Secondly, in places like Kosova, it may be necessary to devise an electoral system which definitely does not comply with what might otherwise be obvious social choice standards.

And finally, we turn to the matrix vote. The possible rôle of this potential catalyst of power-sharing must not be underestimated, and it really should be 'on the table' in many negotiations. Indeed, it may be part of the solution, not only in post-conflict societies, but also when the question concerns the formation of a government as in Germany after the 2005 elections, or as in the UK whenever a prime minister is (over)due to resign.

Conclusions

The world will not survive if we continue to fight wars, not least because our fragile ecosystem cannot sustain the wanton destruction of oil spills off the Lebanese coast, for example, or of burning oil wells in the deserts of Iraq. Even less, of course, could it recover from a nuclear holocaust. It is not only from a belief in the sanctity of all life, therefore, that humankind must strive to prevent wars and in so doing to overcome the causes of war.

Furthermore, if we as a species are going to be able to tackle the huge problems confronting this planet - problems of deforestation, global warming and climate change, in an era of decreasing finite resources of water and oil - it must be obvious to everyone that we can only do this by a form of co-operation.

There are no greater arguments. Both the prevention of wars and the long-term survival of the planet depend, in part, on our ability to come to collective decisions and therefore on our ability to find a verbal and/or votal consensus.

The change to a more consensual polity will happen, one day; and must happen, if we are to see that day. But the change to this all-inclusive democratic structure will not happen via a majority vote; as implied on p 6, consensus will come when it already exists.

There are signs that such a consensus is already on its way. Some of these have been noted above. The roots of consensus might differ according to different interests; belief in fairness amongst some, pragmatism amongst others. This pragmatism of the politicians means that they are not wedded to majoritarian decision-making.[18] The Scottish Constitutional Convention and the Consultative Steering Group on the Parliament subscribed to a belief in the sovereignty of the people; hence their recommendations for the design of the electoral system and parliamentary procedures. Hence too, when electoral fortunes are at stake, it becomes possible for them to accept the need for different electoral systems in the devolved administrations from that still used for General Elections. And, as noted, concerns about their diminishing legitimacy and, indeed, their capacity to be the sole deliverers of policies, have compelled the politicians to promote, in the UK and elsewhere, consultative decision-making at the local level. It is to be hoped that their conversion will become sufficiently embedded not to disappear at the first whiff of a hint that the old ways might, once again, be more convenient.

---

18 The 'social partnership' exercise in Ireland, pp 131-2, is a case in point. Another Irish example of consensus politics was the Dublin Forum for Peace and Reconciliation.

PART IV

APPENDICES

Appendix I

A Comparison of Different Voting Procedures

DECISION-MAKING

In advocating one particular voting procedure, it is well to compare the relative accuracy of a number of different ones. It is also worth remembering that all of them are regarded as democratic... despite the fact that, in many instances, some of them produce quite different outcomes!

These different methodologies include the following.

TABLE App I.A		DECISION-MAKING PROCESSES
Majority voting	simple	where the winner needs just 50% + 1: this is used in most national parliaments and many referendums;
	weighted	where a 66% or 75% majority is required: it is used on certain important matters, such as changes to the South African constitution.
	qualified	where a specific formula is used, as in the EU, so that larger countries have more clout than smaller ones.
	special	(or consociational) where a form of weighted majority voting is used in which a majority in two or more constituencies is required simultaneously. It is used in some plural societies, in Belgium and Northern Ireland, for example.
Plurality voting		may be used when there are more than two options; it is used fairly extensively in referendums, for example in Finland.
Two-round voting		is also used in referendums, as in New Zealand; in addition, it is catered for though rarely used in the Norwegian parliament.
Serial voting		is used in the Swedish and Finnish parliaments.
Approval voting		has been used, albeit as an electoral system, in the UN.
The alternative or single transferable vote, AV or STV		is used as an electoral system, in Australia; in the USA, it is known as instant runoff voting or IRV.
Condorcet count		despite its accuracy, it is not used in any jurisdiction for the purposes of governance.
BC		is used as an electoral system in Nauru and Kiribati.
MBC		a BC which caters for partial voting.

In Table App I.B below, the x-axis shows the degree of choice involved in these various voting systems. Obviously, two-option voting gives the voter very little choice, whereas, at least in theory, multi-option voting can give the voter a much bigger selection. The y-axis indicates the degree to which the voters' preferences are taken into account. In majority voting, because the voter may express a 1st preference only, the counting procedure can take account of only these 1st preferences. The counting procedures in the other systems, however, can consider some or even all of the voters' other preferences.

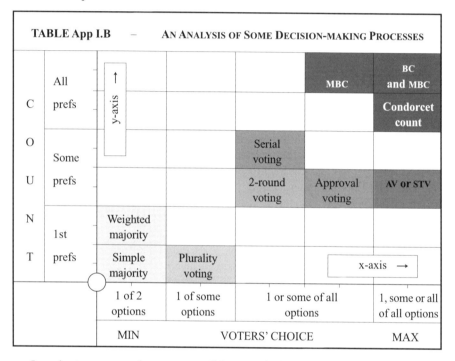

In order to compare the accuracy of these methodologies, consider a group of 10 people, Messrs *J* to *S*, voting on five options: *A, B, C, D* and *E*; and let us assume their preferences (prefs) are as follows:

TABLE App I.C						A VOTERS' PROFILE			
	Ms. *J*	Mr. *K*	Ms. *L*	Mr. *M*	Ms. *N*	Mr. *O*	Ms. *P*	Mr. *Q*	Ms. *R*	Mr. *S*
1st pref	*A*	*A*	*A*	*A*	*B*	*B*	*C*	*E*	*E*	*E*
2nd pref	*B*	*D*	*B*	*D*	*C*	*C*	*D*	*B*	*D*	*D*
3rd pref	*C*	*B*	*D*	*E*	*D*	*D*	*B*	*D*	*C*	*C*
4th pref	*D*	*C*	*C*	*C*	*E*	*E*	*E*	*C*	*B*	*B*
5th pref	*E*	*E*	*E*	*B*	*A*	*A*	*A*	*A*	*A*	*A*

A close examination of this voters' profile will suggest to the reader which option best represents the ten voters' consensus. But now let us see what the various voting procedures do.

Majority/Plurality Voting

In majority/plurality voting, only the 1st preferences cast are taken into account.

TABLE App I.D				—		A MAJORITY/PLURALITY COUNT			
	Ms. *J*	Mr. *K*	Ms. *L*	Mr. *M*	Ms. *N*	Mr. *O*	Ms. *P*	Mr. *Q*	Ms. *R*	Mr. *S*
1st pref	*A*	*A*	*A*	*A*	*B*	*B*	*C*	*E*	*E*	*E*

The scores are $A = 4$, $B = 2$, $C = 1$, $D = 0$ and $E = 3$, so nothing gets a majority. In a plurality vote, the winner is *A*, because 4 people think it is the best. The fact that all the other 6 people think it is the worst option is, under this system, of no consequence.

Two-round Voting

In two-round voting, we take a second round majority vote between the two leading contenders from the first round plurality vote. Which means that the voting procedure takes into account the subsequent preferences only of those who gave their 1st preferences to options other than *A* or *E*, that is, of Messrs. *N*, *O* and *P*.

TABLE App I.E				—		A TWO-ROUND COUNT			
	Ms. *J*	Mr. *K*	Ms. *L*	Mr. *M*	Ms. *N*	Mr. *O*	Ms. *P*	Mr. *Q*	Ms. *R*	Mr. *S*
1st pref	*A*	*A*	*A*	*A*	*B*	*B*	*C*	*E*	*E*	*E*
2nd pref					*C*	*C*	*D*			
3rd pref					*D*	*D*	*B*			
4th pref					*E*	*E*	*E*			
5th pref					*A*	*A*	*A*			

So, by a score of 6 to 4, the winner is now *E*.

The Alternative Vote

The alternative (or single transferable) vote, AV or STV, is a little complex. At the first stage of the count, we examine the 1st preference totals only, as in a plurality vote. If no one option has a majority, we move to the second stage, which is to eliminate the option with the smallest total and transfer its vote(s) according to the 2nd preferences expressed by those who voted for that option. The process is repeated until one option does have a majority.

Therefore, for the first stage of the count, the scores are $A = 4$, $B = 2$, $C = 1$, $D = 0$ and $E = 3$, which means option D is now eliminated. In the second stage, we eliminate option C, whose voter, Ms. P, gave (a 2nd preference to D, which is already eliminated, and) a 3rd preference to B. Therefore, the scores are now: $A = 4$, $B = 3$, $C = 0$, $D = 0$ and $E = 3$, which is a draw for second place between B and E. So, in the third stage, either B or E is eliminated, and either all of B's votes are transferred to E, or *vice versa*. The winner is either E or B. (In real life, where the number of voters is usually more than 10, the chances of such a tie are minimal.)

Approval Voting

In approval voting, every preference cast is regarded as an approval; in which case all five options get the top score of 10! If, however, we consider just the first two preferences as approvals, then the outcome would be $A = 4$, $B = 5$, $C = 3$, $D = 5$ and $E = 3$, so B and D could be joint winners in this system.

TABLE App I.F					–		An Approval Vote Count		
	Ms. *J*	Mr. *K*	Ms. *L*	Mr. *M*	Ms. *N*	Mr. *O*	Ms. *P*	Mr. *Q*	Ms. *R*	Mr. *S*
1st pref	*A*	*A*	*A*	*A*	*B*	*B*	*C*	*E*	*E*	*E*
2nd pref	*B*	*D*	*B*	*D*	*C*	*C*	*D*	*B*	*D*	*D*

If instead we take the first three preferences, the scores would be $A = 4$, $B = 7$, $C = 6$, $D = 9$ and $E = 4$, which would mean that D would be the outright winner. It all depends on where the line is drawn.

Serial Voting

In serial voting, the options are arranged in order – left-wing to right-wing or whatever – before a series of majority votes is taken, starting with the two outsiders. If the order is indeed *A-B-C-D-E*, the first round is a majority vote between A and E; and, as in two-round voting, E wins that pairing, 6:4. Next comes a contest between E and B, which, as we see from the table below, B wins by the same score, 6:4.

TABLE App I.G					–		A Serial Vote Count		
	Ms. *J*	Mr. *K*	Ms. *L*	Mr. *M*	Ms. *N*	Mr. *O*	Ms. *P*	Mr. *Q*	Ms. *R*	Mr. *S*
1st pref	*A*	*A*	*A*	*A*	*B*	*B*	*C*	*E*	*E*	*E*
2nd pref	*B*	*D*	*B*	*D*	*C*	*C*	*D*	*B*	*D*	*D*
3rd pref	*C*	*B*	*D*	*E*	*D*	*D*	*B*	*D*	*C*	*C*
4th pref	*D*	*C*	*C*	*C*	*E*	*E*	*E*	*C*	*B*	*B*
5th pref	*E*	*E*	*E*	*B*	*A*	*A*	*A*	*A*	*A*	*A*

So it is now between ***B*** and ***D***. But, as we can see from the table below, this pairing is a draw, by 5 to 5. So the final is a pairing between either ***B*** and ***C*** or ***C*** and ***D***. Now ***B*** > ***C*** by 6:4, and ***D*** > ***C*** by 6:4, so the joint winners are once more ***B*** and ***D***.

TABLE App I.H					–		ANOTHER SERIAL VOTE COUNT			
	Ms. *J*	Mr. *K*	Ms. *L*	Mr. *M*	Ms. *N*	Mr. *O*	Ms. *P*	Mr. *Q*	Ms. *R*	Mr. *S*
1st pref	*A*	*A*	*A*	*A*	*B*	*B*	*C*	*E*	*E*	*E*
2nd pref	*B*	*D*	*B*	*D*	*C*	*C*	*D*	*B*	*D*	*D*
3rd pref	*C*	*B*	*D*	*E*	*D*	*D*	*B*	*D*	*C*	*C*
4th pref	*D*	*C*	*C*	*C*	*E*	*E*	*E*	*C*	*B*	*B*
5th pref	*E*	*E*	*E*	*B*	*A*	*A*	*A*	*A*	*A*	*A*

BC/MBC

In a BC/MBC of five options, points are awarded to the various preferences as follows: a 1st preference gets 5 points, a 2nd preference gets 4 points, a 3rd preference gets 3 pts, a 4th preference gets 2 pts, and a 5th preference gets 1 pt.

TABLE App I.I					–		A BC/MBC			
	Ms. *J*	Mr. *K*	Ms. *L*	Mr. *M*	Ms. *N*	Mr. *O*	Ms. *P*	Mr. *Q*	Ms. *R*	Mr. *S*
1st pref	*A* = 5	*A* = 5	*A* = 5	*A* = 5	*B* = 5	*B* = 5	*C* = 5	*E* = 5	*E* = 5	*E* = 5
2nd pref	*B* = 4	*D* = 4	*B* = 4	*D* = 4	*C* = 4	*C* = 4	*D* = 4	*B* = 4	*D* = 4	*D* = 4
3rd pref	*C* = 3	*B* = 3	*D* = 3	*E* = 3	*D* = 3	*D* = 3	*B* = 3	*D* = 3	*C* = 3	*C* = 3
4th pref	*D* = 2	*C* = 2	*C* = 2	*C* = 2	*E* = 2	*E* = 2	*E* = 2	*C* = 2	*B* = 2	*B* = 2
5th pref	*E* = 1	*E* = 1	*E* = 1	*B* = 1	*A* = 1	*A* = 1	*A* = 1	*A* = 1	*A* = 1	*A* = 1

In this instance, then, the scores are: *A* = 26, *B* = 33, *C* = 30, *D* = 34 and *E* = 27; so the winner is ***D***.

Condorcet

In a Condorcet count, as in a BC/MBC, all preferences cast are taken into account. A Condorcet count considers all possible pairings which, in this example, are these:

A v *B*,   *A* v *C*,   *A* v *D*,   *A* v *E*
           B v *C*,   *B* v *D*,   *B* v *E*,
                         C v *D*,   *C* v *E*,
                                       D v *E*.

We have already encountered some of the pairings. In two-round voting, $E > A$ by 6:4. In serial voting, $B = D$ by 5:5, and $B > C$ by 6:4. The full tally is as follows:

$A < B$ by 4:6	$A < C$ by 4:6	$A < D$ by 4:6	$A < E$ by 4:6
	$B > C$ by 6:4	$B = D$ by 5:5	$B > E$ by 6:4
		$C < D$ by 4:6	$C > E$ by 6:4
and			$D > E$ by 7:3.

This can also be represented in table form; the winning score in each pairing is shown in dark tint, while any draw is shown in a lighter shade. One win equals 1 point, and a draw = $1/2$. So A gets no pairings, B gets $3^{1}/_{2}$, C gets 2, D gets $3^{1}/_{2}$ and E just 1; and the overall result is a draw between B and D.

TABLE App I.J					–	A CONDORCET COUNT	
		A	B	C	D	E	WINS
A			4	4	4	4	0
B		6		6	5	6	$3^{1}/_{2}$
C		6	4		4	6	2
D		6	5	6		7	$3^{1}/_{2}$
E		6	4	4	3		1

A summary of all the above results is shown below. The winners (and joint winners) are shown in dark tint, while the options in second (or third) place are in a light tint.

TABLE App I.K	A COMPARISON OF DECISION-MAKING PROCESSES BASED ON FULL BALLOTS						
O p t i o n	VOTING PROCEDURE						
	Simple/ weighted majority vote	Plurality Vote	Two round voting	AV STV	approval voting (two prefs)	serial voting	BC and MBC	Condorcet
A	?	4	4	4	4		26	0
B	?	2		6	5	6	33	$3^{1}/_{2}$
C	?	1			3	4	30	2
D	?	0			5	6	34	$3^{1}/_{2}$
E	?	3	6	6	3		27	1

Admittedly, this is just one simple and hypothetical example. Nevertheless, it ties in with experience, and it all suggests the most accurate measures of collective opinion are the MBC and the Condorcet count.

Partial Voting

But what happens when some people choose to express only some of their preferences? Let us assume that, the *A* lobby - Messrs. *J, K, L* and *M* - cast only some preferences, as shown below. Will this help the prospects for their favourite, option *A*? Let us have a look.

One possible voters' profile is like this:

TABLE App I.L — A Voters' Profile with Partial Voting

	Ms. *J*	Mr. *K*	Ms. *L*	Mr. *M*	Ms. *N*	Mr. *O*	Ms. *P*	Mr. *Q*	Ms. *R*	Mr. *S*
1st pref	*A*	*A*	*A*	*A*	*B*	*B*	*C*	*E*	*E*	*E*
2nd pref	*B*	*D*	*B*		*C*	*C*	*D*	*B*	*D*	*D*
3rd pref	*C*	*B*			*D*	*D*	*B*	*D*	*C*	*C*
4th pref	*D*				*E*	*E*	*E*	*C*	*B*	*B*
5th pref					*A*	*A*	*A*	*A*	*A*	*A*

Based on the above information *only*, readers are again asked to draw their own conclusions as to what option *should* come out on top. And then we shall consider what actually happens under the various methodologies.

The 1st preferences are unchanged, so the outcome of a majority/plurality vote is also unchanged. The result of a two-round vote is the same as well: a victory for *E* over *A* by 6:4; and the outcome under AV also remains as it was.

Under approval voting, if as before we take just the first two preferences cast into account, the scores are $A = 4$, $B = 5$, $C = 3$, $D = 4$, and $E = 3$ so *B* is now the outright winner although, here too, it all depends on where you draw the line.

In serial voting, in the first round, *E* beats *A* by 6:4, as we have just seen. Then it is *B* versus *E*, which *B* wins by 6:3. The third round is *B* v *D*, which *B* wins 5:4. And finally, *B* v *C* is 6:3 to *B*.

Table App1.M overleaf shows both the BC and the MBC points. For those voters who submit full ballots - Messrs. *N* to *S* - the BC and MBC points are of course identical. For those who submit partial votes, however - Messrs. *J* to *M* - while the BC points remain unchanged and are untinted, the MBC points do change and are therefore in tint.

In a straight BC, the scores are now $A = 26$, $B = 32$, $C = 24$, $D = 27$ and $E = 21$, so B is the winner and D is the runner-up, whereas before, with full ballots, it was the other way round, D first and B second. Option A, meanwhile, which was fourth, is now third. In an MBC, however, with the points awarded in tint, the scores are $A = 16$, $B = 26$, $C = 23$, $D = 24$ and $E = 21$; in this instance, therefore, the outcome is another win for B, but option A, having been a close third, is now last!

TABLE App I.M					–		A BC/MBC on a Partial Vote			
	Ms. *J*	Mr. *K*	Ms. *L*	Mr. *M*	Ms. *N*	Mr. *O*	Ms. *P*	Mr. *Q*	Ms. *R*	Mr. *S*
1st pref	$A = 5$ $A = 4$	$A = 5$ $A = 3$	$A = 5$ $A = 2$	$A = 5$ $A = 1$	$B = 5$	$B = 5$	$C = 5$	$E = 5$	$E = 5$	$E = 5$
2nd pref	$B = 4$ $B = 3$	$D = 4$ $D = 2$	$B = 4$ $B = 1$		$C = 4$	$C = 4$	$D = 4$	$B = 4$	$D = 4$	$D = 4$
3rd pref	$C = 3$ $C = 2$	$B = 3$ $B = 1$			$D = 3$	$D = 3$	$B = 3$	$D = 3$	$C = 3$	$C = 3$
4th pref	$D = 2$ $D = 1$				$E = 2$	$E = 2$	$E = 2$	$C = 2$	$B = 2$	$B = 2$
5th pref					$A = 1$	$A = 1$	$A = 1$	$A = 1$	$A = 1$	$A = 1$

In a Condorcet count, the pairing *A:B* is a score of 4:6, because the first four, including Mr. *M*, all prefer *A* to *B*, and all the others prefer *B* to *A*. When it comes to the pairing *C:D*, however, we simply do not know the opinions of Ms. *L* and Mr. *M*; and the score on this pairing is 4:4. The full tally is as follows:

$A < B$ by 4:6 $A < C$ by 4:6 $A < D$ by 4:6 $A < E$ by 4:6
$B > C$ by 6:3 $B > D$ by 5:4 $B > E$ by 6:3
$C = D$ by 4:4 $C > E$ by 4:3
$D > E$ by 5:3.

The final score is $A = 0$, $B = 4$, $C = 2\frac{1}{2}$, $D = 2\frac{1}{2}$ and $E = 1$.

TABLE App I.N			–		A Condorcet Count on a Partial Vote		
	A	*B*	*C*	*D*	*E*		WINS
A		4	4	4	4		0
B	6		6	5	6		4
C	6	3		4	4		$2\frac{1}{2}$
D	6	4	4		5		$2\frac{1}{2}$
E	6	3	3	3			1

A comparison of these methodologies, for the partial vote profile, is as shown below, with the winners and joint winners in dark tint, and the options in second or joint second in light tint. (The 'Simple/weighted majority vote' column has been removed because, needless to say, it is again inconclusive.)

TABLE App I.P	A COMPARISON OF DECISION-MAKING PROCESSES BASED ON PARTIAL BALLOTS						
Option	VOTING PROCEDURE						
	Plurality Vote	Two round voting	AV STV	approval voting (2 prefs)	serial voting	BC	MBC	Condorcet
A	4	4	4	4		26	16	0
B	2		6	5	6	32	26	4
C	1			3	3	24	23	2½
D	0			4		27	24	2½
E	3	6	6	3		21	21	1

But now let us compare all the voting procedures, under both scenarios: with full and partial voting. Winners (and joint winners) are in dark tint, seconds and joint seconds (or thirds) are in the lighter shade, and all the outcomes under partial voting are shown on a background of striped columns.

TABLE App I.Q	A COMPARISON OF DECISION-MAKING PROCESSES BASED ON FULL AND PARTIAL BALLOTS												
Option	VOTING PROCEDURE												
	Plurality vote		Two round voting		AV, STV		approval voting (2 prefs)		serial voting		BC		MBC		Condorcet	
A	4	4	4	4	4	4	4	4			26	26	26	16	0	0
B	2	2			6	6	5	5	6	6	33	32	33	26	3½	4
C	1	1					3	3	4	3	30	24	30	23	2	2½
D	0	0					5	4	6		34	27	34	24	3½	2½
E	3	3	6	6	6	6	3	3			27	21	27	21	1	1

In the final analysis, then, the actions of Messrs. *J, K, L* and *M* in voting only partially, do help their cause, slightly, if the voting procedure is approval voting; hardly at all if it is serial voting or Condorcet, and quite a lot if it is a straight BC. Under the rules for an MBC, however, the tactic backfires completely, for instead of losing by just 1 point, option *A* is now behind by 5 points!

One inherent advantage of the MBC is that the voting procedure itself encourages the voter to express as many options as possible, i.e., to participate to the full in the democratic process, (p 31). And, when everyone states not only their 1st preferences, but also their 2nd and subsequent preferences, it is indeed possible to identify that which is the best collective compromise. And that, may I suggest, is what democracy is all about!

More Complex Decision-making

In comparing these various voting procedures, we have only been concerned with the winning option and maybe the runner-up. But what is the situation in regard to more complex multiple decisions - shopping lists, budget allocations, or orders of priority?

Well, some decision-making processes cannot facilitate such subtlety. Majority voting, approval voting, AV and serial voting are obviously no good. Plurality voting does give an indication of relative popularities, but is not generally considered to be an accurate measure thereof. Both BC/MBC and Condorcet, however, can be used in this way, and outcomes will always give the relative strengths of *all* options.

ELECTORAL SYSTEMS

In comparing electoral systems, exactly the same general arguments apply. The situation, however, is rather more complex. Firstly, there is the question of constituency boundaries, a factor of often crucial importance in any single-member constituency election such as FPP, and one which is relatively unimportant in a top-up system. Secondly, there is proportional representation, which means there are many more variations of voting procedures to be taken into consideration.

A detailed comparison has already been undertaken elsewhere,[1] so suffice here to say that the more accurate systems are inevitably those which a) allow the voters to express more than just their 1st preferences,[2] and b) take all preferences cast into consideration in the count.[3]

---

1   Emerson (1998).

2   The main PR systems which do so are PR-STV and QBS.

3   QBS.

The Matrix Vote

As already noted, the matrix vote is to the best of my knowledge, the only comprehensive voting procedure by which an electorate can choose a proportional group of representatives of different status. In these pages, we have described the QBS matrix vote. There is no reason why some other variations cannot be tried. Indeed, the first model was based on a PR-STV count.

Given, however, the inclusive nature of the matrix vote, it is only sensible to base the two elements of a matrix vote count on inclusive procedures: hence the first part, the election, is a QBS, while the second part, the selection, is based on an MBC.

Appendix II

The Average Preference Rating and the Consensus Coefficient

AVERAGE PREFERENCE RATING

The formula for calculating the average preference rating is as follows:

when P_A = the average preference rating for Option A,

S_A = the MBC score for Option A,

V = the valid vote, and

n = the number of options,

then P_A = $(n + 1) - S_A/V$

or, to put it another way:

$$P_A = \left\{ \frac{V \cdot (n+1) - S_A}{V} \right\}$$

In any multi-option ballot, the best possible average preference rating is always 1. In an n-option ballot, if all the ballots are full ones, the worst possible average preference rating is n. In just such an n-option ballot, the mean average preference rating is given by the formula:

$(n + 1)/2$

TABLE App II.A		AVERAGE PREFERENCE RATINGS						
	formula	Number of Options						
		3	4	5	6	7	8	9	10
Best average preference ratings	1	1	1	1	1	1	1	1	1
mean average preference ratings	$(n + 1)/2$	2	2.5	3	3.5	4	4.5	5	5.5
bad average preference ratings	n	3	4	5	6	7	8	9	10

As we can see, average preference ratings vary according to the number of options on the ballot paper. For a more general guide, it may therefore be easier to use a consensus coefficient.

CONSENSUS COEFFICIENT

Let C_A be the consensus coefficient of option A.

When some of the voters submit partial ballots, we can no longer rely on average preference ratings, (p 17), so we use points and consensus coefficients instead. In a vote on n options, the maximum number of points any one option can receive in an electorate of V voters (if they all submit a full ballot) is $V.n$; so if all V voters give option B their 1st preference, option B gets $V.n$ points. In the same situation, the minimum number of points is V; so if everyone gives option D, say, their last preference - i.e., just 1 point - then D gets a score of V points.

In both full and partial ballots, a consensus coefficient is defined as follows:

$$C_A = \frac{S_A}{V.n}$$

This consensus coefficient varies from 1 to zero. If every voter submits a full ballot, and if every voter gives option A a 1st preference, then:

$$C_A = 1$$

If, however, everyone submits a partial ballot, and if nobody gives option E, say, anything at all, then:

$$C_E = 0$$

Accordingly, in a 6-option ballot, for an electorate of 20 people, if all 20 voters give option A their 1st preference, then A gets an MBC score of 120 and a consensus coefficient of 1. If, however, while every voter still gives option A a 1st preference, only 11 of the voters submit a full ballot while the other 9 submit a partial ballot of only one preference:

$$S_A = 11 \times 6 + 9 \times 1$$
$$= 75$$

and so

$$C_A = \frac{75}{20 \times 6}$$
$$= 0.63$$

Option A is still the winner. But obviously, if several members of the electorate submit only partial ballots, the level of consensus in that electorate is rather low. As we shall see in Appendix III, this effect of partial voting can be considerable.

In any majoritarian democracy, as was the extreme case in Germany in the 1930s, there is the danger that ghastly decisions will be taken as a consequence of a low turnout. For any post-conflict society, therefore, or maybe for every jurisdiction, society might be well advised to lay down certain minima for any decision to be considered democratic, and these concern a) the quorum of participants in parliament or the turnout of the electorate in any plebiscite, and b) the consensus coefficient of the winning option.

Appendix III

Partial Voting

When M. de Borda first proposed the BC, he realised that, like most other voting procedures, it was open to abuse. If people vote sincerely, then the outcome will indeed represent the collective will. But if not, if they vote tactically, they could possibly manipulate an outcome which did *not* represent the consensus. And he concluded by saying, "My scheme is only intended for honest men (sic)."[1]

In a BC/MBC, she who votes for all six options exercises 6-5-4-3-2-1 points. With partial voting, however, there is a difference: in a BC, he who votes for only one option exercises 6-0-0-0-0-0 points whereas, as the reader now knows, in an MBC, he exercises only 1-0-0-0-0-0 points.[2]

As Hannu Nurmi points out, {p 113 - his alternative i)}, some wish to overcome this BC phenomenon by awarding a common number of points to all the unmarked preferences, so to leave the points totals unchanged. According to this formula, the person who votes for only one option thus exercises 6-3-3-3-3-3 points (which is still, of course, a total of 21 points). But I am loathe to do this for, as the next paragraph explains, such a procedure still encourages the voter to be intransigent, albeit to a lesser extent than is the case in a straight BC.

A principal advantage of the MBC {p 113 - alternative iii)} is that it encourages (but does not force) the voter to participate fully in the democratic process, (p 31). A BC {alternative ii) of p 113} actually works the other way: by giving his favourite option his 1st preference and giving nothing else to any other option, he who wants to promote only his own option can thus, in a BC, give it a 6-point advantage over all the other five. According to the {alternative i)} 6-3-3-3-3-3 formula, he would exercise 6 points for his favourite, and a score of 3 for the other five, which would still give his option a 3 point advantage.

With the MBC, however, no matter how many options for which the voter casts preferences, the advantage for his/her favourite over his/her 2nd choice is always 1

---

1 Black, 1958, p 182.

2 This does not render the system unfair - see pp 16-7. He who votes '*A*-0, *B*-0, *C*-1, *D*-0, *E*-0, *F*-0' gives *C* a 1 point advantage over all the other options, about all of which he says absolutely nothing, i.e., zero. She who votes '*A*-0, *B*-0, *C*-2, *D*-0, *E*-1, *F*-0' gives *C* a 2 point and *E* a 1 point advantage over the other options, and so on.

   In other words, those who abstain have no influence on the outcome; those who vote partially have a correspondingly partial influence; and those who vote fully have a full influence. It all remains very fair.

point. Therefore, if he wants his favourite to get the maximum MBC score of 6 points, it is to his advantage to state his other preferences.

A voter casting only his first 3 preferences out of a possible total of 6 would exercise the following points:

TABLE App III.A — THE BC, MBC, AND NAURU VARIATIONS

BC {alternative ii) of p 113}	6, 5, 4, 0, 0, 0
A Nauru Borda count	1, $1/2$, $1/3$, 0, 0, 0
A Borda count (with a common score for all unmarked preferences) {alternative i)}	6, 5, 4, 2, 2, 2
MBC {alternative iii)}	3, 2, 1, 0, 0, 0

Appendix IV

Further Analysis of the Matrix Vote

The total number of different ways of voting in the NI Assembly would be (106 x 10) x (105 x 9) x ... x (98 x 2) x (97) which comes to over 1.15×10^{20}. In *Dáil Éireann* (the Irish Parliament), where 166 members choose a cabinet of 16 ministers, every TD (= MP) would have a choice of over 1.5×10^{35} ways of voting. While in the British House of Commons, with 651 members choosing a cabinet of 21 portfolios, there would be a choice of over 1.3×10^{56} different cabinets! It is indeed called pluralism!

It might be pointed out that, in addition to the conclusions drawn in Chapter 3, a little more analysis could be undertaken. If we refer to Table 3.AH on p 80 again, we can draw some more conclusions.

TABLE 3.AH and App IV.A	The Matrix Votes Results Example 3C						
	ELECTED CANDIDATES						Relative Importance MBC post totals
Minister	*L*	*N*	*Q*	*S*	*J*	*U*	
PM	42						57
Min. of *D*		30					44
Min. of *A*						21	41
Min. of *B*			40				40
Min. of *C*					28		38
Min. of *E*				32			32
MBC scores	42	30	40	32	28	36	

The maximum points total which could have been given to the six successful candidates, if, of course, all 12 members of parliament had expressed a full vote of 6 preferences for only those six candidates, would be 12 x 21, the number of points awarded by each of the 12 voters. Accordingly, the total of all the MBC scores of all the elected candidates divided by 252 would give the overall level of consensus with which this executive has been elected.

Maybe, too, the straightness or otherwise of the diagonal (or not so diagonal) line which links the final sums of Tables (3.Y, 3.AD) and 3.AH (on pp 73, 76 and) above is also relevant, but we will leave these subtleties to the mathematician.

Glossary

NB Items marked in italics are described elsewhere in this glossary.

Absolute majority see *majority*.

AMS, (additional member system) is a partially proportional electoral system based on one single preference vote and two counts; the first count is under *FPP*, the second count is by *PR-list*; see also *MMP*.

Anti-plurality Instead of voters casting one vote (of one preference) for their most favoured option or candidate, as in *plurality voting* and *FPP*, they cast one vote for their least favoured. In plurality voting, the winner is that which gets the highest score; in anti-plurality voting, it is the other way round.

Approval voting is a voting mechanism which can be used in decision-making and/or a (non-PR) election. The voter votes for as many options/candidates as he/she wishes; each 'approval' has the same value, and the option/candidate with the most approvals wins.

Arrow See *impossibility theorem*.

AV, (alternative vote) is a preferential voting mechanism which can be used in decision-making and/or a (non-PR) election. The voters vote 1, 2, 3... for their $1^{st}/2^{nd}/3^{rd}$... preferences. In the count, if no option/candidate gets 50% + 1 of the *valid vote* of 1st preferences, the least popular option/candidate is eliminated and its votes are transferred according to its voters' 2nd preferences. The process continues until an option/candidate gets or exceeds 50% + 1. See also *PR-STV*.

Average preference rating When all concerned submit a full ballot, an option's/candidate's average preference rating is the average of all the preferences cast in its favour. If 50% of the voters give option ***B*** their 3rd preference, while the other 50% give ***B*** their 4th preference, then ***B*** gets an average preference rating of $3^{1}/_{2}$.

BC, Borda count The Borda count, a points or rankings system, is a preferential voting mechanism which can be used in decision-making and/or a non-PR election, though it is more suitable in the former mode; (for its application to *PR* electoral systems, see *QBS*).

Where there is a choice of *n*-options/candidates, the voters vote 1, 2, 3... for their $1^{st}/2^{nd}/3^{rd}$... preferences. A 1st preference gets *n* points, a 2nd preference gets *n-1* points, a 3rd preference gets *n-2* points, and so on... and the winner is the option/candidate with the most points. (The outcome is exactly the same, of course, if instead of the *n, n-1 ... 2, 1* formula, use is made of another formula: *n-1, n-2 ... 1, 0*.)

If all voters submit a full ballot, exactly the same outcome can also be determined by calculating each option's *average preference rating*... and the winner is the one with the best rating. See also *MBC* and *consensus coefficient*.

Binary decision-making	is where every decision is based on a two-option, for-or-against choice, or a series of such *majority votes*.
Citizens' initiative	is a mechanism whereby a minimum number of citizens can demand a *referendum* on a topic of their own choosing.
Coalition:	
majority	a coming together of some parliamentary parties to form a government which commands a simple *majority* in that parliament;
grand	a majority coalition involving the two biggest parties;
all-party	a power-sharing government involving all the main parliamentary parties.
Composite	A composite policy is an amalgam based on two or more compatible policies.
Condorcet	A Condorcet count or pairings vote is a preferential voting mechanism which can be used in decision-making and/or a (non-PR) election. The voters cast their $1^{st}/2^{nd}/3^{rd}$... preferences on (all) the options/candidates. In the count, pairs are examined separately and, in let us say a three-option contest, if B is more popular than A and if B is also more popular than C, then B shall be the Condorcet winner. See also *paradox of voting*.
Consensor	In *consensus* decision-making, the chair or facilitator is assisted by a team of independent and impartial consensors who recommend which voting mechanisms if any are to be used, and which options are to be included on any relevant ballot paper.
Consensus coefficient	If S_A is the MBC score of option A, if V is the valid vote, and if n is the number of options/candidates to be voted on, the consensus coefficient C_A is defined as $S_A/V.n$ In other words, the consensus coefficient is the MBC score divided by the maximum possible score; and it varies from good to bad, from 1 to zero.
Consensus:	
verbal	an agreement, usually taken after lengthy discussions in which all concerned have agreed to a compromise;
votal*	an agreement, usually taken when all the participants a) accept the principle of compromise and b) identify the most popular compromise via a suitable multi-option vote such as an MBC.
Consociationalism	a form of government where *majority votes* are taken by two or more electorates voting simultaneously, and where decisions are taken if the majorities of both or all electorates give their consent: both unionist and nationalist in Northern Ireland, both Fleming and Walloon in Belgium, or all three - Catholic, Moslem and Orthodox - in Bosnia.
Constituency	A non-PR electoral system is used in a single-seat constituency, a geographical area represented by just one elected representative. In a multi-member constituency, a *PR* (or even a non-PR) electoral system can be used to elect two or more representatives.

---

* This is a new meaning of the word 'votal'.

Constituency (cont.)	The word 'constituency' may also be used in a non-geographical sense, to describe a particular group of people who, *inter alia*, relate to one or more representative.
Cycle	see *paradox of voting*.
Democracy	in theory, rule by the people, 'demos'. It can be direct, as it was - for some of the people! - in ancient Greece; or it can be indirect, via a parliament of elected representatives.
consensual	rule by elected representatives of as many political parties as is feasible;
consociational	rule by an 'inter-ethnic' and/or 'cross-community' *majority coalition*;
majoritarian	rule by a group which has the support of a *majority*.
d'Hondt	see divisor system.
Dictatorship$^-$, D$^-$	or non-dictatorship. If a voting procedure complies with the condition D$^-$, it should not allow the strict preference order of just one individual to determine the similar strict social preference, i.e., a social preference independent of everybody else's preferences. See also *impossibility theorem*.
Divisor system	is a rule of thumb for allocating seats according to party strengths; (see also *quotas*). Every party's vote total is divided by a prescribed set of divisors to give a series of descending scores. Seats are awarded to the parties with the highest resulting scores. Different sets of divisors give marginally different results: |					
---	---	---	---	---	---
d'Hondt	1	2	3	4	....
Sainte Laguë	1	3	5	7	....
modified Sainte Laguë	1.4	3	5	7	....	
Droop	see *quota*.
Electorate	all those eligible to vote.
FPP, (first-past-the-post)	is a non-preferential non-PR electoral system where the voter casts one 'x' only. Elections under FPP with just two candidates are *majority votes;* those with three or more candidates are *plurality votes*.
Franchise	or suffrage: the right to vote in public elections.
Gibbard-Satterthwaite	This theorem states that any voting procedure involving three or more options/candidates is either *dictatorial* or manipulable.
Hare	see *quota*.
Impossibility theorem	Arrow's impossibility theorem states that a voting procedure which complies with the conditions D$^-$, I, P and U, i.e., non-*dictatorship*, *independence*, *pareto* and *universality* - and whose outcomes are transitive social preferences, i.e., rankings with possible ties, is impossible.
Independence, I	if a voting procedure whose outcomes are social preferences complies with the condition I, the outcome over every subset of two options/candidates must be based only on the voters' preferences over these respective two options/candidates. See also *impossibility theorem*.

Irrelevant alternative	An option, **B**, is said to be 'irrelevant' if all the voters prefer at least one other named option. In other words, if literally everyone thinks option **D**, say, is better than option **B**, then **B** may be regarded as irrelevant.
IRV, (instant runoff voting)	the American name for *AV*.
Kemeny's rule	This rule uses the concept of 'distance' between preferences to find a linear order, i.e., a ranking without ties, whose sum of distances to the agents' linear orders is minimised. When only one option/candidate has to be elected, it then takes the top alternative of that linear order. (If Ms. *j* has preferences **A, B, C,** and Mr. *k* has preferences **A, C, B,** then they both prefer **A** to **B** and **A** to **C**, and disagree only on **B** and **C**, so the 'distance' between *j* and *k* is 1. If, in contrast, Ms *l* has preferences **C, B, A**, then *j* and *l* disagree over **A** and **B**, over **A** and **C**, and over **B** and **C**, so the distance between *j* and *l* is 3.)
Level, consensus	see *consensus coefficient*.
Majoritarianism	the belief in and/or practice of *majority rule*.
Majority	(see also *coalition*);
absolute	50% or more,
consociational	see *consociationalism*,
qualified	this is used in the EU, where different countries have different numbers of votes and where the result depends on a certain weighting,
relative/simple	may be only the biggest minority,
weighted	$^{2}/_{3}^{rds}$ or some such other ratio greater than $^{1}/_{2}$.
Majority rule	is a form of *democracy* based on decision-making by *majority vote*.
Majority vote	Majority voting can be used in decision-making and/or a (non-PR) election if there are only two options/candidates. The option/candidate with the *majority* of the votes is the winner. See also *plurality* and *FPP*.
Matrix vote	is a *tabular* electoral system which is both proportional and preferential. An electorate can use a matrix vote to elect a fixed number of persons to form a team consisting of personnel in different positions or portfolios - as when a parliament elects a power-sharing government or the membership of an association elects an executive committee.
MBC, (modified Borda count)	is a preferential voting mechanism which can be used in decision-making and/or a (non-PR) election. It differs from the *BC* in that it always allows for partial voting, under the following rules: if someone casts preferences for all *n* options/candidates, points are awarded as in a BC: *n, n-1, ... 2, 1*; if, however, the voter votes for only *m* options/candidates, the points awarded are *m, m-1, ... 2, 1*. Accordingly, in a 5-option ballot, he who votes for only 1 option gives his favourite only 1 point; she who votes for 2 options gives her favourite option 2 points, and her 2nd choice 1 point; and so on; and he who votes for all 5 options gives his favourite the full 5 points, his 2nd choice 4 points, etc.. See also *consensus coefficient*.

MMP (multiple-member proportional)	is a non-preferential *PR* electoral system based on two single preference votes: the first count is of an *FPP* vote in a small constituency, while the second count is of a *PR-list* vote in a larger, regional or national constituency; see also *AMS*.
Modified Sainte Laguë	see *divisor system*.
Monotonicity	A voting procedure is said to be monotonic if, in all circumstances, an increase in an option's/candidate's popularity automatically leads to that option/candidate having a greater chance of success.
Multi-member	see *constituency*.
Nanson's method	Aware of the most glaring weaknesses of both a *BC* (*irrelevant alternative*) and a *Condorcet* count (the *paradox*), Nanson proposed a series of BC votes and in each count, all options below the average points score shall be eliminated, before a further BC vote is initiated. The eventual winner will be the *Condorcet* winner, if indeed one exists.
Pairings	see *Condorcet*.
Paradox of voting (also known as a cycle)	the situation which can occur in *binary* or *Condorcet* voting on more than two options/candidates, when there are more than two voters, with more than two opinions. When Ms. *J*, for example, has preferences *A-B-C*, Mr. *K* has *B-C-A*, and Ms. *L* has *C-A-B*, then if we take three *majority votes*, *A* is more popular than *B*, *B* more popular than *C*, and *C* more popular than *A*. This is the paradox. It can be written either as:

$$A > B, B > C \text{ and } C > A \quad \text{or as} \quad A > B > C > A > ...$$

The same sort of thing can happen in a sports league. If England beats Scotland, Scotland beats Wales, and Wales beats England, then no-one knows who are the champions.

Pareto, P	if a voting procedure complies with the condition P, then if everyone prefers option *A* to option *B*, the social preference *A* is said to be 'pareto superior' to *B*. See also *impossibility theorem*.
Partial vote	see *MBC*.
Patronage, party political	The term applies to those instances when a party leadership appoints persons to positions of power and/or prestige in return for 'loyalty' or other 'favours'.
Plebiscite	is usually a *referendum* on the topic of national sovereignty.
Plural society	one in which there are two or more ethnic or religious groups.
Plurality	the largest minority.
Plurality voting	Plurality voting can be used in decision-making and/or a (non-PR) election, if and when there are three or more (a *plurality* of) options/candidates. As in *majority voting*, the voter casts an 'x' for one option/candidate only. In the count, the option/candidate with the most votes wins, even if it does not receive an *absolute majority* of the votes but only the largest minority, a plurality. See majority vote and *FPP*, as well as *anti-plurality voting*.

Points system	see *BC/MBC*.
Positional voting	a vote involving a single preference only.
PR (proportional representation)	An electoral system which aims to ensure that party candidates (and sometimes independents) are elected in proportion to the number of votes gained by each party/candidate is said to be proportional. Electoral systems based on PR are used in multi-member *constituencies*.
Preference or preferential voting	A term used to describe those decision-making and electoral voting procedures in which the voter expresses a 1st preference and (maybe also) a 2nd and subsequent preferences.
Preference rating	see *average preference rating*.
Preferendum (Borda)	An *MBC*.
PR-list	In most PR-list elections, each party "lists" its candidates in its own order of priority, and voters cast 1 preference only. Seats are awarded to parties on the basis of a *divisor* or *quota* system. Accordingly, if party X wins n seats, then either the first n names from the top of the party X list (in a *closed* system) or the first n most popular candidates in party X (in an *open* system) are deemed elected.
PR-list, closed	a non-preferential electoral system in which voters vote for one party only.

PR-list, open	in the three main types of open non-preferential PR-list electoral systems, the electorate chooses:
	   i) either one party or one candidate of that party,
	   ii) one or more candidates of one party only,
	   iii) one or more candidates of one or more parties.

Profile, voters'	A voters' profile is their particular set of 1st and subsequent preferences cast. In other words, the profile reveals all the preferences cast, but not the voters' identities; the voters remain anonymous.
PR-STV (PR, single transferable vote)	is a preferential electoral system based on *AV*, though instead of the *quota* being set at 50% + 1, it is smaller - c. 33% + 1 in a 2-seater, 25% + 1 in a 3-seater, etc. - and transfers take place, not only from candidates eliminated, but also from those elected with a surplus over and above the quota. PR-STV *constituencies* usually have from 3 to 6 elected representatives.

QBS (quota Borda system)	is a preferential *PR* electoral system which is based on both a *quota* and an *MBC*. In a multi-member *constituency* electing four representatives, for example, in Part I of the count:
	  + any candidate gaining the quota is elected;
	  + any pair of candidates getting two quotas is elected;
	(any candidate who has just been elected is not counted in any further calculation); then, in Part II of the count:
	  + any pair of candidates gaining one quota is 'elected', the seat going to the particular candidate of that pair with the higher MBC score;
	  + similarly, any triplet gaining one quota gets one candidate elected;
	  + and if seats are still to be filled, they are awarded to those candidates with the highest MBC scores.

GLOSSARY

Qualified majority	see *majority*.
Quasi-chaotic	A voting procedure is said to be quasi-chaotic if the vacillation of just a few voters can cause a completely different outcome.
Quorum	is a minimum number or percentage required for a sitting to be valid.
Quota	is a specified number of votes which, if attained, ensures the election of the candidate concerned; the most common quotas are the Hare (which is defined as the *valid vote* divided by the number of seats), and the Droop (which divides the valid vote by the number of seats plus one). See also *divisor*.
Rankings	see *BC*.
Referendum	is usually a two-option *majority* but sometimes a multi-option *plurality* or *two-round* vote by which the electorate may 'decide' a matter of policy. See also *plebiscite* and *citizen's initiative*.
Sainte Laguë	see *divisor system*.
Serial voting	is a decision-making voting mechanism in which options are placed in order from, let us say, cheap-to-expensive or left-wing to right-wing; a *majority vote* is taken between the two extremes and the loser is eliminated; a second vote is taken between the winner and its new extreme opposite; and the process continues until there is just the one option remaining: the overall winner.
Sincere voting	In any voting procedure, a voter is said to vote sincerely when she votes for those options/candidates she considers to be the best, without taking any *tactical* considerations into account.
Single-peaked preferences	A voter's preferences are said to be single-peaked if, when the options are laid out on, say, a cheap-expensive or left-right axis, his 2nd and subsequent preferences lie in descending order to one side and/or the other of his 1st preference.
Special voting	the term used in Belgium for their form of *consociationalism*
STV (single transferable vote)	is another name for *AV*; see also *PR-STV*.
Suffrage	see *franchise*.
Tabular voting	A tabular voting procedure enables the voter to express her preferences according to two criteria simultaneously. The relevant ballot paper, a table, consists of two axes and, in a *matrix vote*, for example, while one axis may indicate ministerial positions, the other may relate to the candidates and the voter's order of preferences.
Tactical voting	In any voting procedure, a voter is said to vote tactically (as opposed to *sincerely*) when, instead of voting for his preferred option or candidate, he chooses the option or candidate that may result in what he judges in the circumstances to be his best possible outcome.
Threshold	The threshold of an electoral system is the minimum percentage of votes required for a candidate to be elected; this is usually the logical consequence

Threshold (cont.)	of the specific mathematics of the electoral system concerned, but there can also be a laid-down minimum of, say, 5% as in Germany.
Top-up	A top-up is the second part of an election count, applicable to some electoral systems like *AMS*, in which votes are counted in a different way and/or in a bigger *constituency*, to ensure a greater degree of overall proportionality.
Transitive order	If someone prefers option F to option C, and she prefers option C to option D, then if the preferences are transitive, she also prefers F to D.
Turnout	the number of people who, literally, turn out to vote; it is normally expressed as a percentage of the total *electorate*.
Two-round voting	is a voting mechanism which can be used in decision-making and/or a (non-PR) election. The first round is a *plurality vote*, while the second round is a *majority vote* between the two leading options/candidates from the first round.
Two-tier electoral systems	These consist of two parts, with one count (which may be *PR*) in small *constituencies*, and a second count or *top-up* (which must be PR) in larger regional or national constituencies.
Universality, U	if a voting procedure complies with the condition U, any individual can have a preference given by any possible ranking of the options/candidates. See *impossibility theorem*.
Valid vote	is the number of voters deemed to have handed in a proper, valid vote; this figure equals the *turnout* minus the invalid vote.
Veto	is the power to prevent legislation, as in a presidential veto, or to render a *majority vote* inoperable; in $^{2}/_{3}^{rds}$ *weighted majority* voting, a substantial minority of over 33% may, in effect, exercise a veto.
Votal	see *consensus*.
Voters' profile	see *profile*.
Weighted voting	see *majority*.
Whip	A party whip is an instruction from the leadership to its elected representatives to vote in a certain way. The term 'whip' may also apply to the party functionary who issues such orders. And those who fail to obey may, as a result, lose the party whip... and thus their careers!
Win-win decision	A win-win decision is one in which (nearly) everybody wins something but (almost) no-body wins everything. It is the opposite of a *zero-sum decision*.
Zero-sum decision	In a zero-sum decision, voters are in a win-or-lose situation: some win and win everything; the others lose everything.

List of Tables

No.	Table			Page
Chapter 1				
1.A	An MBC Ballot Paper			19
1.B-D	Three MBC Ballot Papers, Examples			20
1.E	An MBC Ballot Paper on the Size of the Executive			22
1.F-G	Single-peaked Curves			23
1.H	Probable All-party Coalitions			24
1.I	An MBC Ballot on the Size of the Executive			25
1.J-K	The Voters' Profile	Full Ballots	Example 1A	26-7
1.L	The Voters' Profile	Partial Ballots	Example 1B	28
1.M	A Condorcet Count			30
1.N	A Comparison of Different Voting Procedures			31
1.P-R	An MBC Ballot and Results on an Agenda		Example 1C	32-3
1.S-T	Ballot Papers for an MBC Election of a Sub-committee			34
1.U	Electing a Sub-committee, the Voters' Profile		Example 1D	36
Chapter 2				
2.A	A QBS Ballot Paper			42
2.B-F	QBS Vote, Examples			43-4
2.G-H	A QBS Profile and Count	Partial Ballots	Precursor I	46-7
2.I-J	A QBS Profile and Count	Partial Ballots	Precursor II	48-9
2.K-L	A QBS Profile and Count	Partial Ballots	Example 2A	50-1
2.M-N	A QBS Profile and Count	Full Ballots	Example 2B	52-3
2.P-Q	A QBS Profile and Count	Full Ballots	Example 2C	54-5
2.R	An Analysis of QBS Elections		2A, 2B & 2C	56
2.S-T	Electing a Sub-committee, Profile and Count		Example 2D	58-9
Chapter 3				
3.A	A QBS Matrix Vote Ballot Paper			63
3.B-F	Matrix Vote, Valid/Invalid Votes, Examples			64-5
3.G-M	Matrix Vote, a Very Hypothetical Case		Precursor	66-7
3.N	Matrix Vote Nominations			68
3.P-Y	Matrix Vote Ballots, Profile, Count & Results	Full Ballots	Example 3A	68-73
3.Z-AD	Matrix Vote, Ballots, Profile, Count & Results	Partial Ballots	Example 3B	74-6
3.AE-AH	Matrix Vote, Ballots, Profile, Count & Results	Full Ballots	Example 3C	77-79
3.AI	A Matrix Vote Analysis			80
Annex A	The Individual Votes	Full Ballots	Example 3A	82-3
Annex B	The Individual Votes	Partial Ballots	Example 3B	84-5

LIST OF TABLES

Chapter 4

4.A-C	The Irrelevant Alternative	90
4.D	A QBS Anomaly	93

Chapter 5

5.A	Black's Single-peakedness Condition over (a, b, c)	107

Chapter 6

6.A	BC Versus Plurality Voting	110
6.B	BC Versus Condorcet Winner	111
6.C	BC and Deleted Alternatives	111
6.D	Nanson's Method is Non-monotonic	112
6.E	MBC and QBS may elect a Condorcet Loser	114
6.F	Implausibility of the Condorcet Winner	114
6.G-H	BC and (strong) Condorcet winner, and the Condorcet Paradox	115
6.I	QBS and BC	117
6.J	QBS is Inconsistent	118

Appendix I

App I.A	Decision-making Processes	149
App I.B	An Analysis of Some Decision-making Processes	150
App I.C	A Voters' Profile Full Ballots	150
App I.D	A Majority/Plurality Count	151
App I.E	A Two-round Count	151
App I.F	An Approval Vote Count	152
App I.G-H	Two Serial Vote Counts	152-3
App I.I	A BC/MBC	153
App I.J	A Condorcet Count	154
App I.K	A Comparison of Decision-making Processes Full Ballots	154
App I.L	A Voters' Profile Partial Ballots	155
App I.M	A BC/MBC on a Partial Vote	156
App I.N	A Condorcet Count on a Partial Vote	156
App I.P	A Comparison of Decision-making Processes Partial Ballots	157
App I.Q	A Comparison of Decision-making Processes Full and Partial Ballots	157

Appendices II - IV

App II.A	Average Preference Ratings		160
App III.A	The BC, MBC and Nauru Variations		163
App IV.A	Matrix Vote Results	Example 3C	164

Biographical Notes

Professor Christine Bell

Christine Bell is Director of the Transitional Justice Institute and Professor of Public International Law at University of Ulster. She read law at Selwyn College, Cambridge, (1988) and gained an LL.M in Law from Harvard Law School (1990), supported by a Harkness Fellowship. In 1990 she qualified as a Barrister at law. She subsequently qualified as an Attorney-at-law in New York, practicing for a period at Debevoise & Plimpton, NY. From 1997-9 she was Director of the Centre for International and Comparative Human Rights Law, Queen's University of Belfast.

She was chairperson of Belfast-based Human Rights organization, the Committee on the Administration of Justice from 1995-7, and a founder member of the NIHRC established under the terms of the Belfast Agreement. In 1999 she was a member of the European Commission's Committee of Experts on Fundamental Rights. Her publications include *Peace Agreements and Human Rights* (OUP 2000) and a report published by the International Council on Human Rights *Policy entitled Negotiating Justice? Human Rights and Peace Agreements* (2006).

Phil Kearney

Phil Kearney is a founder member and currently Co-director of Clanwilliam Institute in Dublin, Ireland, a psychotherapy training and research centre. He completed a Masters in Family Therapy in Philadelphia in 1980 and a MSc in Trinity College Dublin in 1990. He has also worked in development work in Sudan and as co-ordinator of the Irish Green Party.

Professor Elizabeth Meehan, BA, DPhil, FRSA, NYAS, AcSS, MRIA.

Elizabeth Meehan is Professor Emerita in the School of Law (Institute of Governance) at Queen's University Belfast and Adjunct Professor in the School of Politics and International relations at University College Dublin. She graduated from Sussex University in 1976 with a degree in Politics and was awarded a DPhil by Oxford University in 1982. She has been employed or held visiting fellowships at Bath and Manchester Universities and Trinity College Dublin. Her research and publications cover citizenship (EU and UK), gender and politics (US, UK, EU and in the devolved administrations in the UK), devolution, and British-Irish Relations, particularly in the context of their common membership of the EU and their cooperation over Northern Ireland. She has served on boards and panels of the UK ESRC and is currently a Council Member of the Irish Research Council for the Humanities and Social Sciences. She is an elected Fellow, Academician or Member of the Royal Society of Arts, the New York Academy of Sciences, the Academy of Learned Societies in the Social Sciences and the Royal Irish Academy (and member of its Council).

Professor Hannu Nurmi

Hannu Nurmi was born on August 24th, 1944. He was Associate Professor of methodology of social sciences (University of Turku) 1976-1995, a Fulbright-Hays scholar (Johns Hopkins University) 1972-1973, British Academy Wolfson Fellow (University of Essex) 1978, Government of Finland/David and Nancy Speer Professor of Finnish Studies (University of Minnesota) 1998, and Dean of Faculty of Social Sciences (University of Turku) 1991-1996. His present position is Professor of Political Science (University of Turku) and Academy Professor (Academy of Finland).

His previous publications include *Comparing Voting Systems*, D. Reidel, 1987; *Rational Behaviour and the Design of Institutions,* Edward Elgar, 1998; *Voting Paradoxes and How to Deal with Them* and *Voting Procedures under Uncertainty* both from Springer-Verlag, 1999 and 2002. At the same time, he has published articles in *Electoral Studies, Social Choice and Welfare, Journal of Economics/Zeitschrift für Nationalökonomie, European Journal of Political Research, Political Studies, Scandinavian Political Studies, Group Decision and Negotiation, British Journal of Political Science, Journal of Theoretical Politics, Representation* and *Synthese.*

Professor Maurice Salles

Maurice Salles was born in a Lower Normandy village on 23 December 1943. He studied economics at the University of Caen (*Doctorat d'Etat* in 1974) and mathematics from books. He taught at Caen as an *"assistant"* and *"Chargé de cours"* before becoming professor at the University of Nantes in 1979. In 1982, he returned to Caen as professor of economics where he now remains.

His work is essentially in social choice and voting theory, including fuzzy social choice and cooperative games aspects of voting, with some incursions into individual decision theory and into the mathematical methods of economics. Salles was one of the founding editors of the journal *Social Choice and Welfare* in 1984 and has been the coordinating editor since. He is Secretary-Treasurer of *The Society for Social Choice and Welfare* (SCW) at the Institute for SCW and the *Maison de la Recherche en Sciences Humaines* (MRSH) in the University of Caen and Research Associate of CPNSS at LSE, the London School of Economics.

Aileen Tierney

Aileen Tierney is Co-director of Clanwilliam Institute in Dublin. She completed a Masters in Social Science in University College Dublin in 1993 and is currently involved in PhD research in the University of Tilburg, Netherlands. She was founder of a disability support group for parents and involved as Irish coordinator in an Inter-regional disability project between Wales and Ireland. She has recently been involved in development work in Chang Mai province in Northern Thailand.

Bibliography

NB Those marked by an asterisk* refer to the author's work; those which carry a • are from Maurice Salles' Chapter 5, those with an § relate to Hannu Nurmi's Chapter 6, and those unmarked are from Phil Kearney and Aileen Tierney in Chapter 8.

- • ARROW, KENNETH, 1950, *A Difficulty in the Concept of Social Welfare*, Journal of Political Economy (58), pp 328-346.
- *• - 1951 and 1963, *Social Choice and Individual Values*, Yale.
- • - 1951a, *An Extension of the Basic Theorems of Classical Welfare Economics*, J. Neyman (ed.), Proceedings of the Second Berkeley Symposium on Mathematical Statistics and Probability, University of California Press.
- • ARROW, KENNETH and DEBREU, G, 1954, *Existence of an Equilibrium for a Competitive Economy*, Econometrica (22), pp 265-290.
- § BAHARAD, E. and NITZAN, S., 2002, *Ameliorating Majority Decisiveness through Expression of Preference Intensity*, American Political Science Review 96, pp 745-754.
- * BAKER, KEITH MICHAEL, 1975, *Condorcet - From Natural Philosophy to Social Mathematics*, University of Chicago.
- • BANKS, J., DUGGAN, J., and M. LE BRETON, 2006, *Social Choice and Electoral Competition in the General Spatial Model*, Journal of Economic Theory (126), pp 194-234.
- • BLACK, DUNCAN, 1948, *On the Rationale of Group Decision Making*, Journal of Political Economy (56), pp 23-34.
- *• - 1958, *The Theory of Committees and Elections*, Cambridge.
- * *Belfast Agreement*, 1998, the Governments of the United Kingdom and of the Republic of Ireland.
- * BOGDANOR, VERNON, 1981, *The People and the Party System*, Cambridge.
- § BRAMS, S., KILGOUR, D. M. and ZWICKER, W., 1997, *Voting on Referenda: The Separability Problem and Possible Solutions*, Electoral Studies 16, pp 359-377.
- § - 1998, *The Paradox of Multiple Elections*, Social Choice and Welfare 15, pp 211-236.
- * BUTLER, DAVID and RANNEY, AUSTIN, 1994, *Referendums around the World*, AEI Press.
- • CONDORCET, J.A.-N. CARITAT DE, 1785, *Essai sur l'Application de l'Analyse à la Probabilité des Décisions Rendues à la Pluralité des Voix*, Imprimerie Royale.
- • DASGUPTA, P., and MASKIN, E., 2004, *The Fairest Vote of All*, Scientific American (290), March, pp 92-97.

BIBLIOGRAPHY

*   *Dayton Agreement* or, to give it its full title, *The General Framework Agreement for Peace in Bosnia and Herzegovina*, 1995, 'the parties', the Governments of Bosnia, Croatia and Yugoslavia.

*•   DUMMETT, MICHAEL, 1984, *Voting Procedures,* OUP.

*•   -   1997, *Principles of Electoral Reform,* OUP.

•   DUMMETT, MICHAEL and FARQUHARSON, ROBIN, 1961, *Stability in Voting*, Econometrica (29), pp 33-43.

*   EMERSON, P. J., *1978, That Sons May Bury Their Fathers, 'Samizdat'.*

*   -   1991, *Consensus Voting Systems, 'Samizdat'.*

*   -   1994, *The Politics of Consensus, 'Samizdat'.*

*   -   1998, *Beyond the Tyranny of the Majority,* The de Borda Institute.

*   -   2000, *From Belfast to the Balkans,* The de Borda Institute.

*   -   2002, *Defining Democracy*, The de Borda Institute.

*   FARQUHARSON, ROBIN, 1969, *Theory of Voting,* New Haven.

§   FISHBURN, P., 1973, *The Theory of Social Choice*, Princeton: Princeton University Press.

§   -   1974, *Voting Paradoxes,* American Political Science Review 68, pp 537-546.

§   -   1982, *Monotonicity Paradoxes in the Theory of Elections*, Discrete Applied Mathematics 4, pp 119-134.

§   GÄRDENFORS, P., 1976, *Manipulation of Social Choice Function,* Journal of Economic Theory 13, pp 217-228.

•   GIBBARD, A., 1969, *Social Choice and Arrow's Conditions,* unpublished paper.

•   -   1973, *Manipulation of Voting Schemes: A General Result*, Econometrica (41), pp 587-601.

•   GUILBAUD, G. TH., 1952, *Les Théories de l'Intérêt Général et le Problème Logique de l'Agrégation, Economie Appliquée* (5), pp 501-584.

§   HILL, I., 1988, *Some Aspects of Elections - to Fill One Seat or Many,* Journal of the Royal Statistical Association, Series A, 151, pp 243-275.

*   IDEA, 1997, *The International Handbook of Electoral System Design,* IDEA.

•   KEMENY, J.G., 1959, *Mathematics Without Numbers*, Daedalus (88), pp 577-591.

*   KHAZEN, EL FARID, 1991, *The Communal Pact of National Identities,* Centre for Lebanese Studies.

*   -   1998, *Prospects for Lebanon, Lebanon's First Postwar Parliamentary Elections.* Centre for Lebanese Studies.

*   LAKEMAN, ENID, 1974, *How Democracies Vote,* Faber and Faber.

* LIJPHART, AREND, 1977, *Democracy in Plural Societies*, Yale University Press.
* - 1994, *Electoral Systems and Party Systems*, OUP.
* - 1999, *Patterns of Democracy*, Yale University Press.
* MCLEAN, IAIN, 1987, *Public Choice, an Introduction*, Blackwell.
* - 1989, *Democracy and New Technology*, Polity Press.
*§ MCLEAN, IAIN and URKEN, ARNOLD B., 1995, *Classics of Social Choice*, eds., University of Michigan.
* MASCART, JEAN, 2000, *La Vie et les Travaux du Chevalier Jean-Charles de Borda*, 1919. Presses de l'Université de Paris-Sorbonne.
* MONJARDET, B., 2005, *Social Choice Theory and the Centre de Mathématique Sociale: Some Historical Notes*, Social Choice and Welfare (25), pp 433-456.
§ MOULIN, H., 1988, *Condorcet's Principle Implies the No Show Paradox*, Journal of Economic Theory 45, pp 53-64.
§ NANSON, E. J., 1883, *Methods of Election*, Transactions and Proceedings of the Royal Society of Victoria XIX, pp 197-240. (Reprinted in McLean and Urken).
* NASH, J.F. JR, 1950, *The Bargaining Problem*, Econometrica (18), pp 155-162.
* NURMI, HANNU, 1987, *Comparing Voting Systems*, Dordecht, Reidel.
§ - 1998, *Rational Behaviour and the Design of Institutions*, Cheltenham: Edward Elgar.
§ - 2002, *Voting Procedures under Uncertainty*, Berlin-Heidelberg-New York: Springer-Verlag.

PEARCE, W. B. and LITTLEJOHN, S. W., 1997, *Moral Conflict: when Social Worlds Collide*, California, Sage Publications.
* *Representation*, a quarterly journal published by The McDougall Trust in London.
* REILLY, BENJAMIN, 2001, *The Borda Count in the Real World*, Macmillan Brown Centre for Pacific Studies.
* - 2002, *Social Choice in the South Seas*, International Political Science Review, Vol. 23, No. 4, Oct.
* RHODES, P. J.,2003, *Ancient Democracy and Modern Ideology*, Duckworth.
*§ RIKER, W. H., 1982, *Liberalism and Populism*, W H Freeman and Co..
*§ RISSE, M., 2005, *Why the Count de Borda Cannot Beat the Marquis de Condorcet*, Social Choice and Welfare 25, pp 95-113.
* ROBBINS, L., 1935, *An Essay in the Nature and Significance of Economic Science*, Macmillan.

- *§ SAARI, DONALD G., 1995, *Basic Geometry of Voting,* Springer.
- • - 1997, *The Generic existence of a Core for q-Rules,* Economic Theory (9), pp 219-260.
- • - 2000, *Mathematical Structure of Voting Paradoxes 1: Pairwise vote,* Economic Theory (15), pp 1-53.
- • - 2000a, *Mathematical Structure of Voting Paradoxes 2: Positional Voting,* Economic Theory (15), pp 55-101.
- *• - 2001, *Chaotic Elections,* American Mathematical Society.
- * - 2001a, *Decisions and Elections,* Cambridge.
- §• - 2006, *Which Is Better: The Condorcet or Borda Winner?* Social Choice and Welfare, forthcoming.
- • - 2006a, *Hidden Mathematical Structures of Voting,* unpublished paper.
- • SALLES, M., 2006, *Limited Rights as Partial Veto and Sen's Impossibility Theorem,* unpublished paper.
- • SATTERTHWAITE, M.A., 1975, *Strategy-Proofness and Arrow's Conditions: Existence and Correspondence Theorems for Voting Procedures and Social Welfare Functions,* Journal of Economic Theory (10), pp 187-217.
- • SEN, A.K., 1970, *Collective Choice and Social Welfare,* Holden-Day.
- • - 1987, *On Ethics and Economics,* Blackwell.
- • SEN, A.K. and PATTANAIK, P.K., 1969, *Necessary and Sufficient Conditions for Rational Choice under Majority Decision,* Journal of Economic Theory (1), pp 178-202.
- * SHEERAN, MICHAEL J, 1983, *Beyond Majority Rule,* Regis College.
- SHOTTER, JOHN, 2004, *On the Edge of Social Constructionism: 'Withness'-thinking versus 'Aboutness'-thinking,* KCC Foundation Publications.
- * SIGMUND, PAUL E., 1963, *Nicholas of Cusa and Medieval Political Thought,* Harvard.
- • TAYLOR, A., 2005, *Social Choice and the Mathematics of Manipulation,* Cambridge University Press and Mathematical Association of America.
- • WARD, B., 1965, *Majority Voting and Alternative Forms of Public Enterprise,* The Public Economy of Urban Communities, J. Margolis (ed.), Johns Hopkins University Press.
- §• YOUNG, H. P., 1974, *An Axiomatization of Borda's Rule,* Journal of Economic Theory 9.
- • - 1975, *Social Choice Scoring Functions,* SIAM Journal of Applied Mathematics (28), pp 824-838.

Index

NB Proper names are in bold, and countries/regions are in small caps. Items marked * are described in the glossary, and authors with a + are mentioned in the bibliography.

A

ABHAZIA	92n, 136
Ahern, Bertie	131
AMS*, see electoral	
Annan, Kofi	37n
anti-plurality*, see decision	
approval voting*, see decision	
Arrow, Kenneth+	99-100, 103-4, 106, 108
see also impossibility theorem	
AUSTRALIA	149
AV*, see decision and electoral	
average preference rating*	1, 4, 12, 15, 17
	18, 20-1, 22, 25-7, 33, 88, 91, 160-1

B

Badinter, Robert	142
Baharad, E+	116-7
Bakhtin, M	125
BALKANS, see Yugoslavia	
Banks, J+	102
BC*, see decision and electoral	
Becker, C	124
Belfast Agreement+, see Northern Ireland	
BELGIUM	21n, 149, 166, 171
Bentham, Jeremy	103
binary process*	vii, 2, 6, 18, 86, 95
	99 et seq., 109, 125-6, 141, 142
Black, Duncan+	7n, 17n, 99-100
	106-7, 161n
Blair, Tony	2, 87-8, 137
Bogdanor, Vernon+	79n
Bolsheviks	10n
Borda, Jean Charles de	7-8, 99
	109, 110, 111, 162
BOSNIA	xii, 8n, 21n, 58, 69, 92n, 142, 166
Dayton Agreement+	37n, 81
electoral system	5, 140, 143
peace process	138-9
Brams, Steven+	118
Bukharin, Nicholas	11
Bush, George W	18n, 87-8, 137, 145
Butler, David+	88n

C

Carroll, Lewis, see **Dodgson**	
CAUCASUS	92n, 139
CD-Rom, *Decision-maker*	4, 6, 91
CDU (Germany)	24n
Charter 88	141
Chen, Victoria	128
Chernomyrdin, Viktor	11
Chirac, Jacques	37n, 107-8
citizens' initiative*	3, 87n
coalition, all-party*	2, 24 et seq., 61, 121
grand*	24n
majority*	24n, 140
composite*	17, 18, 26, 88
compromise	vii-viii, 1, 4-5, 15
	21, 26, 88, 121, 123, 125-6, 158
computers	2, 4, 8, 9, 57, 88, 136, 144
computer program, *Decision-maker*	4, 6, 91
Condorcet count*	
see decision-making	
Condorcet, Le Marquis de+	viii, 15n
	99, 109
Condorcet winner*	viii, 86, 90, 99
	102 et seq., 109 et seq.
confidence, vote of no, see constructive	
conflict resolution	1, 120, 124 et seq.
	136, 138-9, 140
consensors*	17-8, 20, 26, 89, 91, 122-3
consensus	4, 5-6, 7, 8, 15-7, 21, 22
	31, 33, 67, 81, 91-2, 97
	121-3, 124 et seq., 135, 138
	139, 146, 151, 161, 164
coefficient*	12, 17, 20n, 21, 22
	25-8, 31n, 36, 91, 160-1
sufficient	21, 92
verbal*	6, 7, 17, 21
	127-8, 138, 142, 146
votal*	6, 7, 8n, 17, 21, 22 et seq.
	26, 127-8, 138, 139, 146
consistency	109, 117-8
consociationalism* see decision	
constructive vote of no confidence	37
Coomeraswamy, Rudhika	11n
Copeland, A H	17n
CROATIA	37n, 92n
CSU (Germany)	24n
Cusanus, Nicholas	7
Cycle, see paradox	
CYPRUS	37n, 129

D

DARFUR, see Sudan
Dasgupta, Partha+ 107-8
Dayton Agreement,+ see Bosnia
de Borda Institute 130
debate, inclusive, procedures for 17-8
 91, 127-8
Debreu, G+ 104n
Decision-maker, CD-Rom, see computer
decision-making systems
    comparison 29-31, 56, 149 *et seq.*
    compound decisions 32-3
 88, 158
  anti-plurality* 116
  approval voting* 29-31, 86, 149 *et seq.*
  AV* 29-31, 86, 149 *et seq.*
  BC* 7-8, 16, 17n, 18n, 21, 29-31
 86, 88, 95, 99 *et seq.,* 109 *et seq.*
 142, 143, 144, 149 *et seq.,* 160-1, 162-3
  Condorcet count* viii, 17n, 29-31
 86, 91, 99 *et seq.*
 109 *et seq.,* 143, 144, 149 *et seq.*
  Condorcet + BC/MBC 17n, 31, 86
 91, 111, 144, 155, 158
  consociational* 8, 21, 29-31
 37n, 60, 129, 141, 149
  majority voting* vii, 1-4, 6, 7, 9, 11
 16n, 21n, 29-31, 33, 37
 86-7, 88, 89, 92, 94, 116-7
 131, 132, 135-8, 140-5, 149 *et seq.*
  MBC* 4, 6, 8-9, 10, 12, 15 *et seq.*
 41, 86-8, 90-1, 109, 122-3
 126-8, 130-2, 143-4, 160-1, 162-3
    analysis 113-4, 149 *et seq.*
    ballot paper 19-20, 22, 25, 32
    counting procedure 16-7, 20-1
    manipulation in 88-93, 122
  Nanson's method* 17n, 109, 111-2, 119
  plurality* viii, 29-31, 37, 86
 88, 109-10, 116, 149 *et seq.*
  qualified majority voting* 8, 137, 149
  serial voting* 29-31, 86, 149 *et seq.*
  special vote, see consociational*
  two-round vote* 29-31, 37
 86, 88, 149 *et seq.*
  weighted majority voting* 8, 10n
 29-31, 135, 137, 149 *et seq.*
democracy*, definition of vii, 3-4, 21
democracy, consensual* 6, 11, 128n
  consociational* 21n, 141
  majoritarian* 11, 135, 161
Desai, Lord Meghnad viin
Deutscher, Isaac 10n
d'Hondt divisor* 56, 80-1, 138
dictatorship, non-, D⁻ * 103
divisors*, see d'Hondt and Sainte Laguë
Dodgson, Rev 8, 9, 17n, 109
Doyle, William 21n
Droop quota* 44n, 56, 80n
Dummett, Sir Michael+ 8n, 9, 86n, 94n
 95, 99, 102, 105, 107-8
DUP (NI) 60n, 93

E

EAST TIMOR 37n
election observation missions 139-40
electoral systems, a comparison 56-7, 158
  AMS* 40n
  AV* 39, 94
  BC* 7, 34, 94, 112-9
    NAURU variation 38, 149, 161
  Condorcet count* 109 *et seq.*
  FPP* 3, 5n, 31n, 39, 60n
 88, 132, 135, 140n, 158
    LEBANON, variation 5, 60
  majority voting* 80, 81, 94
  matrix vote* 6, 9, 10, 12, 34n
 61 *et seq.,* 109, 122, 144, 145, 159
    analysis 79-80, 118-9
    ballot paper 62-5
    counting procedure 65, 82, 84
    manipulation in 95-7
  MBC* 12, 15n, 34-6, 40, 95
    ballot paper 19-20, 34
    counting procedure 16-7, 20-1
    in QBS 5, 40 *et seq.,* 92-5
    in the matrix vote 9, 63
 65 *et seq.,* 96, 159, 164
  MMP* 40n
  plurality, see also FPP 80, 118-9
  PR 5, 6, 56-7, 131n, 132, 140, 158
  PR-list* 5n, 56, 79, 80n, 140
    closed* 135
    open* 5n, 60
  PR-STV* 5n, 39n, 44n, 56-7, 58-60
 79, 80n, 94, 158n, 159
  QBS* 5-6, 8-9, 10, 12, 15n
 34, 39 *et seq.,* 109, 122, 132, 158n

electoral systems, QBS*, (cont.)
- analysis   56, 113-9
  - ballot paper   42-4
  - counting procedure   41, 44-45, 57
  - in the matrix vote   6, 63
      65 *et seq.*, 97, 159
  - manipulation in   92-5
  - with top-up   45, 60
  - top-up*   40, 45, 51n, 58, 60, 158
  - two-round*/two-tier*   39, 40
- electronic voting   2, 8, 91, 144
- EU   8n, 37n, 137, 149, 168

F

Farquharson, Robin+   4n, 102, 105, 108
FDP (Germany)   24n
FINLAND   149
Fishburn, P+   111, 114-5
FitzGerald, Garret Dr.   130-1
FRANCE   7, 37n, 87, 99, 104n, 105, 109
- electoral system   107-8

Fulbrook, Mary   10n

G

Gärdenfors, P+   114
gender   40, 41, 93, 123
GERMANY   10-1, 24n, 37, 40n
    87, 145, 161, 172
Gibbard, A+   105
Gibbard-Satterthwaite theorem*   105, 108
GIBRALTAR   37n
G8   139n
Glenny, Misha   142n
GP (Germany)   10n, 24n
    (NI)   58n
GREECE   167
GUAM   37
Guilbaud, G Th+   99

H

Hailsham, Lord   135
Hare quota*   56, 80n
Hill, I+   111
Hitler, Adolf   10, 87
Horowitz, Donald   121
Hughes, Colin A   88n
Human rights   120-3, 141-2
    see also UN Charter
Hussein, Saddam   144

I

IDEA+
IMF   139n
impossibility theorem*   99 *et seq.*
    see also Arrow
independence, I*   99, 101-2, 105, 107
INDONESIA   37n, 136
Interahamwe   11n
invalid vote, see valid
IRAQ   87, 137, 143-5
IRELAND   89, 130-1, 137, 146n
    Dáil Éireann   164
Irish News   8n
irrelevant alternative*   17n, 90-1
    93, 99, 104, 105, 123
IRV*, see also AV   149
ITALY   11, 129, 140

J

Jospin, Lionel   107-8

K

Kamenev, Leo   11
Karadžić, Radovan   138-9
KASHMIR   136
Kemeny, J G+   99
Kemeny's rule*   99
KENYA   10n, 11
Kerry, John   145
Khazen, el Farid+   5n, 60n, 81n
KIRIBATI   149
Kolb, D M   125
KOSOVA/O   11, 140, 145
KPD   10n

L

Lakeman, Enid+   80n
Le Pen, Jean-Marie   108
LEBANON   81, 145
    electoral system   5, 60
Left, The (Germany)   24n
Lenihan, Brian   130
Lenin, Vladimir Ilych   10n
Lijphart, Arend+   80n, 121, 141
Little, Allan   143n
Littlejohn, S W+   124, 126
Lull, Ramon   109n
LUXEMBOURG   60

M

Machakos Protocol	11
Mackerras, Malcolm	88n
McLean, Iain+	9n, 15n, 109n
McManus, Liz	130
majority rule*	vii, 4, 11, 99 *et seq.*
	116, 122, 135-8, 140-1
majority vote* see decision and electoral	
Mandela, Nelson	21n
manipulation	2, 6, 18n, 61
	86 *et seq.*, 123, 143, 162
Maskin, Eric+	107-8
matrix vote* see electoral	
MBC*, see decision and electoral	
media	136, 140
see also *Irish News* and *Oslobodjenje*	
median voter theorem	106
mediation	1, 7, 124 *et seq.*, 138-9
Mensheviks	10n
Milošević, Slobodan	37n
MMP*, see electoral	
Monbiot, George	139n
Monjardet, B+	99
monotonicity*	95, 109, 112, 119
Morrison, John	144n
Moulin, H+	114
Mugabe, Robert	2

N

NAGORNO-KARABAKH	92n, 136
Nanson, E J+	17n, 109, 111-2
Nanson's method*, see decision	
Napoleon, Bonaparte	7, 87
Nash, J F+	104
NAURU	38, 149, 162-3
New Ireland Group	8
NEW ZEALAND	37, 40n, 88, 149
NEWFOUNDLAND	37
NIHRC	142
NILSSEN, L N	129
Nitzan, S+	116-7
no confidence vote	37
NORTHERN IRELAND	8-9, 11, 69, 89, 143
Assembly	62, 137, 164
Belfast Agreement	21, 37n, 58n
	80-1, 122, 141
consociationalism*	21n, 60, 149, 166
DUP	60n, 93

electoral system	5, 58, 60n, 139, 141
peace process	9, 21, 146n
power-sharing	81, 143
referendum	2n, 92n, 136
SDLP	92n
Sinn Féin	8, 137
UUP	8
NORWAY	149
NURC (Rwanda)	143

O

ODIHR	139n, 140n
Osama Bin Laden	18n
OSCE	139-40
Oslobodjenje	11n

P

pairings, see Condorcet	
Paisley, Rev. Ian	60n, 89, 93
paradox of voting*	17n, 91, 99, 106
	114-6, 118
pareto, P*	102-4, 105
partial votes*	11, 16-7, 20, 28-31
	43-4, 46-51, 65, 74-6, 89, 91-2
	112-4, 149, 155-8, 160-1, 162-3
party funding	40
'party-preference'	40, 45
patronage*, party political	18, 135
Pattanaik, Prasanta+	107n
peace process	4-5, 60, 61
	81, 123, 137, 139
BOSNIA	138-9
NORTHERN IRELAND	9, 21, 139, 146n
SOUTH AFRICA	21, 139
Pearce, W B+	124, 126
plebiscites*, see also referendums	37
plurality vote*,	
see decision and electoral	
points system, see decisions, BC	
political parties	
Bolsheviks	10n
CDU/CSU (Germany)	24n
DUP (NI)	60n, 93
FDP (Germany)	24n
GP (Germany)	10n, 24n
(NI)	58n
KPD (Germany)	10n
Left (Germany)	24n
Mensheviks	10n

political parties (cont.)		referendum,* two-option	4n, 11, 37, 87
SDLP (NI)	92n		123, 129, 136, 139-40, 141, 142, 149
Sinn Féin (NI)	8, 137	in...	
Social Democratic Workers'		ABHAZIA	92n, 136
Party (Russia)	10n	BOSNIA	8n, 92n
SPD (Germany)	10n, 24n	CROATIA	37n, 92n
UUP (NI)	8	CYPRUS	37n, 129
positional dominance	115	DARFUR	136
power-sharing	2, 4, 6, 61, 73	EAST TIMOR	37n
	80-1, 121-2, 138, 143, 145	FRANCE	7, 37n
PR*, PR-list*, PR-STV* see electoral		GERMANY	37n, 87
preference voting*	vii-ix, 4, 9, 15 *et seq.*	GIBRALTAR	37n
	61, 88, 136, 137, 138, 140, 144	ITALY	11, 129
preferendum, see also MBC	8	KASHMIR	136
Prodi, Romano	129	KENYA	10n
proportionality	5, 34, 39-40	KOSOVA/O	11
	50-7, 58, 61, 81, 140, 142	NAGORNO-KARABAKH	92n, 136
Prunier, Gérard	11n	NORTHERN IRELAND	2n, 89
			92n, 136
Q		QUEBEC	136
QBS*, see electoral		SUDAN	11
qualified majority,* see decision		WESTERN SAHARA	136
quasi-chaotic*	94	YUGOSLAVIA	11, 37n, 136, 142
QUEBEC	136	**Reid, Anna**	136
questions, closed	1-2, 8, 11, 136	**Reilly, Benjamin+**	21n, 38n
open	1, 136	*Representation+*	viin, 88n
quorum*	161	**Riker, W H+**	111
quota*	40n, 94, 102, 113	**Risse, M+**	99, 109
gender	40	**Robbins, L+**	104
in QBS	5, 40n, 41, 42, 44-5	**Rousseau, Jean-Jacques**	21n
	46 *et seq.*, 93-4, 113, 117-8	RUSSIA	10n, 11, 17n, 87, 95, 136, 144
in Hare and/or Droop	44n, 56	RWANDA	11, 45, 136, 143
in matrix votes	65 *et seq.*		
		S	
R		**Saari, Donald+**	18n, 38, 99
Rambouillet, see Kosovo/a			108, 109, 115-6
rankings*	99 *et seq.*, 109 *et seq.*	Sainte Laguë*, divisor	56, 80n
see also decision, BC		**Satterthwaite, M A+**	105
Ranney, Austin+	88n	**Schulze, Markus**	94n, 95n
referendum*	3, 16n, 129n, 135, 136, 140	SCOTLAND	146
referendum,* multi-option	15, 16n, 37	SDLP (NI)	92n
	91, 96, 144, 149	self-determination	120-1, 123, 142
in...		**Semenov-tian-Shanski, A P**	17n
FINLAND	149	**Sen, A K+**	102, 104, 107n
GUAM	37	serial voting*, see decision	
NEWFOUNDLAND	37	**Shotter+**	125-6
NEW ZEALAND	37, 88, 149	**Sigmund, Paul E+**	7n
SINGAPORE	37	**Silber, Laura**	143n
SWEDEN	2n, 37	sincere voting*	6, 89, 97, 105, 162

SINGAPORE 37
single-peaked preferences* 22-3, 32
 89, 99, 106-8
Sinn Féin (NI) 8, 137
social choice theory xii, 6, 12, 99 *et seq.*
 109, 119, 139, 143, 144
Social Democratic Workers' Party
 (Russia) 10n
social survey 122, 143
SOUTH AFRICA 92n, 139, 141, 149
 peace process 21
SOVIET UNION, see also Russia 11, 139
SPD (Germany) 10n, 24n
special voting*, see decision
SRI LANKA 11, 136
Stalin, Joe 10n, 11, 145
straw poll 17
STV*, see AV and PR-STV
sub-committees, elections of 34-6, 58-9, 79
SUDAN 11, 136
SWEDEN 2n, 37, 143, 149
SWITZERLAND 2, 60
SYRIA 87

T

tactical voting* 6-7, 89-93
 105, 113, 123, 162
Taylor, A+ 105
Thatcher, Margaret 2
threshold*, decision-making 21, 116
 elections 5n, 39-40
Tideman, Nicolaus 95n
TIMOR 37n
Tolstoy, Lev Nikolayevich 141
top-up*, see electoral
transitive orders* 99 *et seq.*, 110
Trotsky, Leon 11, 145
two-round voting*, see decision and electoral
two-tier*, see electoral
TURKEY 37n

U

UK 80, 87, 140, 143, 145, 146
 electoral system 5n, 143
 House of Commons vii-viii, 144, 164
UKRAINE 80
UNITED NATIONS 129, 139n, 142n, 149
 Charter 7, 16, 17, 120, 141n
 Security Council 32, 87-8, 137, 139n

universality, U* 100-1, 105, 106
Urken, Arnold B+ 9n, 15n, 109n
US/USA 87, 139n
 electoral system 39n, 105
 140n, 143, 149
USSR, see Russia
utilitarianism 103
utility function 106
UUP (NI) 8

V

valid/invalid votes* 11, 20, 43-4, 64-5, 162
veto* 21n, 92, 116, 121-2
 123, 137, 139n, 144
votal consensus*, see consensus
vote of no confidence, see constructive
Voting Matters 94n

W

Walras, M E L 104
Ward, B+ 107-8
weighted majority voting*, see decision
Weimar Republic, see also Germany 37n
Weiner, Douglas 17n
WESTERN SAHARA 136
whip*, party 2, 4n, 18,
 19, 62, 87, 96, 137
will, collective 2-4, 7, 15, 17n
 22, 127, 141n, 143, 162
 of parliament/council 2-6, 15
win-or-lose, see zero-sum
win-win*, decision-making 1, 4
 elections 5, 39, 81
Wittgenstein, L 127
Woodward, Susan 139n, 142n

(X and) Y

Young, H P+ 99, 108, 117
YUGOSLAVIA 11, 17n, 37n, 81n
 92n, 136, 138-9, 142

Z

zero-sum,* 4, 5n, 81, 125, 129, 135
Zinoviev, Gregory 11